BEYOND THE HOME FRONT

Beyond the Home Front

Women's Autobiographical Writing of the Two World Wars

Edited by

Yvonne M. Klein

Professor of English
Dawson College
Westmount
Quebec
Canada

First published 1997 by
MACMILLAN PRESS LTD
Houndmills, Basingstoke, Hampshire RG21 6XS
and London
Companies and representatives
throughout the world

ISBN 0–333–66961–4 hardcover
ISBN 0–333–67016–7 paperback

A catalogue record for this book is available
from the British Library.

10 9   8   7   6   5   4   3   2   1
06 05 04 03 02 01 00 99 98 97

Printed in Great Britain by
J.W. Arrowsmith Ltd, Bristol

Contents

Contents

Acknowledgments

This anthology came about as I tried to provide readings for the students in my course 'Women and War.' Although an enormous number of auto-biographical accounts and autobiographically-based fiction by women about their war experiences has been published over the last eighty years, virtually none of it remains in print. What is available, though excellent, gives only a partial and narrowed view of the extent of the impact of war on women's consciousness in the twentieth century. I hope that the selections in this volume, drawn from both world wars and chosen for their inherent literary quality as much as their historical value, will suggest the range and interest of this body of work and encourage its recovery.

I should like to thank all those who helped and encouraged me in this undertaking, most particularly my students in various sections of my course 'Women and War,' and my friends and colleagues Jessie Taras, Ann Pearson, Judy Adamson, Dana Hearne and Karla Jay. I am grateful to my daughters Philippa and Marina for their support and encouragement. Most of all, however, my gratitude goes to those women who lived through the world wars of this century and to those who did not; it is to them that this book is respectfully dedicated.

A NOTE ON THE TEXTS

An effort has been made to present selections with little internal editing. Where this has proved impractical, elisions have been indicated by three asterisks. All ellipses and other punctuation are original, though obvious typographical errors have been silently corrected. The spelling conventions of the original texts, whether British, American, or Canadian, have been preserved. My comments are set in a different, sans serif, typeface.

PERMISSIONS

Grateful acknowledgement is made to the following for permission to reprint:

Aubrac, Lucie. *Outwitting the Gestapo*. Translated by Konrad Bieber with the assistance of Betsy Wing. © 1993 by the University of

Nebraska Press. Originally published as *Ils partiront dans l'ivresse* © Éditions du Seuil, 1984.

Bagnold, Enid. *A Diary Without Dates*. London: William Heinemann, 1919. Reprinted by permission of Reed Consumer Books Ltd.

Banghardt-Jöst, Cristal. 'In the Stocks'. *Surviving the Fire: Mother Courage and World War II*. Seattle: Open Hand Press, 1989. Edited and translated by Lilo Klug. Reprinted by permission of Open Hand Press.

Borden, Mary. *Journey down a Blind Alley*. New York, Harper, 1946. Reprinted by permission of HarperCollins Publishers Inc.

Brittain, Vera. *Testament of Youth*. London: Macmillan 1933; London: Virago, 1978. Reprinted with the permission of Paul Berry, her Literary Executor, Victor Gollancz, Ltd. London, and Virago Little, Brown.

Brittain, Vera. *England's Hour*. London: Macmillan, 1941 and Futura Macdonald & Co, 1981. Reprinted by the kind permission of Paul Berry, her Literary Executor and Victor Gollancz Ltd., London.

Craig, Grace Morris. *But This Is Our War*. Toronto: Univ of Toronto Press, 1981. © Univ of Toronto Press. Reprinted by permission of Univ of Toronto Press.

Dayus, Kathleen. *Where There's Life*. London: Virago, 1985. © 1985 Kathleen Dayus. Reprinted by permission of Little, Brown.

Farmborough, Florence. *A Nurse at the Russian Front: A Diary 1914–1918*. Constable, 1974. Reprinted with the kind permission of the estate of Florence Farmborough.

Haldane, Charlotte. *Truth Will Out*. London: Weidenfeld & Nicholson, 1949. Reprinted by the kind permission of RJM Burghes.

Hillesum, Etty. *An Interrupted Life: The Diaries of Etty Hillesum 1941–1943*. Edited by J.G. Gaarlandt. New York: Pantheon, 1984. Reprinted by the kind permission of Françoise Gaarlandt-Kist.

Isaacson, Judith Magyar. *Seed of Sarah: Memoirs of a Survivor*. Chicago: Univ of Illinois Press, 1990. © 1990 Judith M. Isaacson. Reprinted by permission of IMG-Julian Bach Literary Agency, Inc.

Jameson, Storm. *London Calling*. New York: Harper, 1942. © Renewed 1970 by Storm Jameson. Reprinted by permission of HarperCollins Publishers, Inc. and Peter Fraser Dunlop.

Keith, Agnes Newton. *Three Came Home*. Boston, Little, Brown & Co, 1947. © 1946 Agnes Newton Keith. © renewed. Reprinted by permission of Little, Brown & Co.

Kitagawa, Muriel. *This Is My Own: Letters to Wes & Other Writings on Japanese Canadians 1941–1948*. Edited by Roy Miki. Vancouver: TalonBooks, 1985. © Muriel Kitagawa. Reprinted by permission of TalonBooks, Vancouver, Canada.

Introduction

THE GREAT WAR

On 31 May 1915, a German airman leaned out of his Zeppelin over London and dropped a bomb that landed on Stoke Newington and killed Elsie Leggatt, aged three. Her sister, May, died a few days later and both little girls were among the first civilian air-raid casualties in London. More than a thousand Britons would share their fate before the war was over. One likes to imagine that the unnamed German aviator would not have loosed his bomb had he known on whom it would land, since he, like the other young men enlisted in every army of the time, presumably shared the conviction that women and children were innocents whose preservation and protection demanded any sacrifice a soldier might be called upon to make. Nevertheless, the deaths of these two children, whether random or intentional, remain a haunting portent of the direction warfare would take in the coming century, a century defined by war.

Few events of this century have been so mythologized as has the Great War. Disillusion, the lost generation, the slaughter of the innocents, the deaths of the best and the brightest, all have entered the common consciousness as the truth about that conflict. Along with this collective nostalgia for innocence lost exists another, more sinister, idea which the labors of scholars have been unable to dislodge from the popular memory – that on the whole, women benefitted from the war at the expense of men. The post-war revulsion against the image of the harpy picking at the bones of heroes fallen on the battlefield has been amply documented;[1] so too has been the relatively limited improvement in the social situation of women attributable to the war. Nevertheless, seventy-odd years after the Great War, my students tell me confidently every year that the war was a good thing for women: it got them the vote and jobs.

For the women who labored and feared through those four years, the war hardly seemed a boon. Some few, like some men, viewed the war as a great adventure, a chance to reject a 'world grown old and cold and weary' and find or invent a new heroic self. But for

---

[1] See Sandra M. Gilbert and Susan Gubar, *No Man's Land*, Vol. 2: *Sexchanges* (New Haven: Yale UP, 1989) Chapter 7.

most women, the war meant loneliness, exhaustion and loss, for which the chance to work filling shells or scrubbing hospital wards hardly compensated.

Writing in 1911, Charlotte Perkins Gilman in America and Olive Schreiner in South Africa each supposed that the increasing involvement of women in public political life would ultimately result in a world without war. Schreiner is perhaps a bit less essentialist in her reasoning than Gilman, for she does not attribute to women any higher ethics or morality, merely a concrete experience of childbirth that would forbid a light-hearted approach to slaughter. But the writer who proclaims: 'We take all labour for our province' could not complete her sentence with the qualification, 'except, of course, for war.' Instead, she concludes, 'It is our intention to enter into the domain of war and to labour there till in the course of generations we have extinguished it.'[2] What that labor was to involve remained, however, undefined.

Others of that particular generation of feminists were more definite. As early as 1908, Mabel Stobart came to the conclusion that until women could defend themselves, full social equality would elude them. She translated this insight not into a call for military or self-defense training for women, but into a demand that they be utilised as part of the national defense, doing 'women's work' of caring for the casualties of war. To this end, she organized an all-female ambulance unit, which saw its first service in that run-up to the Great War, the Balkan War of 1912–13.

If Stobart's logic seems less than impeccable, it is perhaps because her pacifism inhibited her from articulating the real advantage to women of her scheme – that the exigencies of war would afford them an opportunity to perform parallel, even identical, feats of courage and competence to those demanded of men of military age. It was, however, a conclusion that Emmeline Pankhurst and her daughter Christabel embraced with bloody-minded enthusiasm. It may well be that their ten-year guerilla warfare against the state made the transition to the rhetoric of armed warfare a natural one. Though it inflicted no actual casualties upon the authorities who were its object, it was a campaign waged with martial commitment and discipline. Significantly, in announcing a temporary end of 'the war of women

---

[2] *Women and Labour* (London: Virago, 1978) 178.

against men,' Mrs Pankhurst imagined women taking up their traditional, gendered roles in time of war: 'As of old, the women become the nurturing mothers of men, their sisters and uncomplaining helpmates.'[3]

Most of Mrs Pankhurst's followers, and many other women, were not prepared to settle for so conventional a part. Mrs Pankhurst herself was in the forefront of the struggle to open munitions work to women, and at wages equal to those of the men they would replace. The inevitable corollary to women's employment in previously reserved occupations was that the men they freed from the shop floor proceeded to the Front, with deadly consequences to themselves and others. To the degree that women could be said to benefit economically from war work it was possible to implicate them in the slaughterhouse that the Western Front rapidly became. The failure of the war-militant suffragettes to confront the moral ambiguities of their demand for women's participation, even conscription, in the war effort tainted the cause of women in general and in no small measure accounts for its post-war loss of moral authority.

The popular image of suffragettes grasping the main chance with bloody hands while their brothers and sweethearts died miserably in the mud of France had its foundation more in gender-antagonism than in actual fact, despite the excesses of the two Pankhursts and of hyper-patriots like Jessie Pope. A significant section even of the militant WSPU refused to follow Mrs Pankhurst into war-fever. Her second daughter, Sylvia, who, like Emmeline Pethwick-Lawrence earlier, had been ousted from the organization, was active in the cause of peace and labored throughout the war to protect munitions workers from exploitation and unsafe working conditions. Hannah Mitchell, an early organizer of the WSPU in Manchester, similarly opposed the war and rejoiced when her son announced his conscientious objection to military service. When Christabel toured the United States in 1915, her unconditional support of the war shocked the suffrage societies before whom she spoke, while they warmly greeted Emmeline Pethwick-Lawrence, who followed close on her heels, as she called for a women's peace party to end not merely the Great War, but all wars, in an appeal that had the support of Olive Schreiner.

Regardless of the strong feminist tradition of pacifism, a number of women, not all of them especially young, seized the opportunity

---

[3] Quoted in Midge Mackenzie, *Shoulder to Shoulder* (New York: Knopf, 1975) unpaged.

of the war to gain entry into activities that they previously barely dreamed of. Gertrude Stein's account of her and Alice's exploits with the Ford ambulance cheerfully admits that middle-aged women might appear absurd as they learned new skills on their own, though she also reveals a thoroughly non-ironic pleasure in learning them. Pacifist or not, Mabel Stobart spent an entire winter on horseback in the Balkans[4] as a commissioned major in a hospital column. Florence Farmborough, also on the Eastern Front, greeted news of the Women's Battalion of Death with enthusiasm and was sorely disappointed when the young Russian women failed to acquit themselves on the battlefield as well as she had hoped. Mrs Pankhurst was present at the blessing of their colors in Moscow on 4 July 1917 and described the event as 'the greatest thing in history since Joan of Arc.'[5] It was, however, the redoubtable Flora Sandes who went the furthest towards transforming herself happily into a soldier. Her memoir, published in 1916 when she was forty years old and a non-commissioned officer in the regular Serbian army, speaks in the accents of a naive eighteen-year-old subaltern, fresh from school and proud to be part of the world of men at last. The Baroness de T'Serclaes, that odd, lonely, and immensely brave woman who spent almost the entire war in her first-aid station on the front line in Belgium, might be speaking for all these women when she remarked, 'I cannot deny that though I hate the waste and destructiveness of war, I have been happiest and most effective in wartime.'[6]

Few of the young women of the war generation, however, had so simple or singular a response to the war or found a way free of conflict to align themselves with it. Furthermore, many of those young women closest to the experience of the war itself underwent a parallel, though not identical, transformation of consciousness to that of their male

---

[4] The Balkans, and Serbia in particular, was especially dear to the hearts of certain feminists. There was a tradition that permitted women who had followed their husbands to the front to take up their fallen husbands' arms if they so chose. In Albania, local custom allowed for 'dedicated virgins' to dress as men and fight for their families' honor when sons were lacking. These peculiarities allowed Mrs Pankhurst, who made support of Serbia part of her war-time agenda, to present the Balkan nations as somehow more open to the cause of women than western Europe. Certainly Serbian officials were more than happy to let strong-minded English and Scotswomen have their way, if it meant favorable publicity back in England and the possibility of increased military aid.

[5] *Illustrated London News*, 4 August 1917.

[6] *Flanders and Other Fields: The Memoirs of the Baroness de T'Serclaes, MM* (London: Harrap, 1964) 17.

counterparts, as horror subsumed rhetoric and loss, not gain, became the war's likeliest legacy. Vera Brittain's *Testament of Youth*, written in 1933 in the hope of inoculating the younger generation against the seductions of the new war she foresaw, describes the various way-stations a middle-class young woman of feminist convictions might pass through on the way to thorough exhaustion with the war.

When war broke out, Vera was preparing herself at Oxford to enter the world of men and to enter it on terms equal to her brother and male friends. She had won her place at the university by means of a dedicated application to repairing her educational deficiencies that bordered on the heroic. But the war threatened her dreams of an egalitarian career and a companionate marriage. Like most young men and many young women of the time, she sensed that the war would be a generational experience of an overwhelming sort, one that would mark off participants from non-participants, combatants from non-combatants, so that the two would forever after speak to one another across a gulf of non-comprehension.[7]

Early in the war, with her fiancé, Roland, freshly off to the Front and she herself training as a VAD, Vera feared losing Roland to the world of male war experience at least as much as she did losing him to an enemy shell, and perhaps a little more. After all, were he to die he could be perfected in memory (as indeed he was). If he survived, his resentment of those, including Vera, who had not served, to which he was already giving coded expression,[8] might well make any future equal relationship impossible. She was at once angry at him for entering so completely into a world that excluded her and angry that she could not be angry without guilt.

Anger of this kind might be criticized as selfish, but selfishness at least argues for the persistence of a self. By the middle of the war, Vera has suffered personal loss and an utter exhaustion of spirit. In this condition, her decision to marry a man she does not love as a kind of compensation for his wound makes sense to her, whereas her younger self greeted such a choice with derision. By the end of the war, she can no longer feel at all.

---

[7] See Paul Fussell, *The Great War and Modern Memory* (Oxford: Oxford UP, 1975) Chapter V, for a discussion of the role of euphemism and censorship in sheltering civilians from full comprehension of the nature of the carnage.

[8] A poem Roland sent her from the Front, 'Violets from Plug Street Wood,' represents the duality of his feelings towards her. On the one hand, the violets he sends her stand for 'Life and Hope and Love and You.' On the other, as he says, she did not see the mangled head of the dead soldier round which they grew: 'Sweetest, it were better so.'

Such emotional anesthesia might be seen as a function of 'survivor guilt,' that profound sense of unworthiness which may follow a catastrophe escaped. It is, however, as well the product of the extraordinary isolation in which Vera Brittain appears to have spent the war. We look in vain through the wartime sections of *Testament of Youth* for evidence of a sense of solidarity with other VADs comparable to the battlefront loyalty to their comrades that animated frontline soldiers when patriotism failed. Its absence is not simply peculiar to Brittain, however; a number of the women represented in this volume who worked in similar situations express much the same separation from and even antagonism towards other women in the hospitals. Enid Bagnold accuses the nursing sisters of condescension and indifference; Florence Farmborough finds the English nurses arrogant and brutal in their methods; there appear to be no other women at all in Mary Borden's ward. Cut off from whatever sustenance might be found in a sisterhood of shared experience, the nurses are left to themselves to numb the guilt they feel for surviving at all and for their inability to provide comfort commensurate with their patients' hideous suffering. A nurse, says Mary Borden, 'is blind so that she cannot see the torn parts of men she must handle. Blind, deaf, dead – she is strong, efficient ... a machine inhabited by a ghost of a woman – soulless, past redeeming.'[9] Her blindness echoes the literal blindness of her patient and is a retribution for her failure to remember him. A genuine wound seems easier to bear than this – Elizabeth Sergeant, an American journalist come late to the war and accidentally wounded by a grenade, is pleased to share the experience of her generation despite her physical pain.

A comparable sense of separation did not appear to afflict women on the shop floors of munitions factories, although it is certainly true that the classless 'mateyness' of war propaganda which united ladies and their maids on the production line was largely a journalistic fiction.[10] Women entering war factories may have been taking up work new to women but they were doing it in old institutions which were not about to change to accommodate inexperience. Factory hands had, over generations, worked out strategies of solidarity and survival that new employees learned at some cost to themselves. These strategies did not yield to either patriotism or guilt. Kathleen Dayus gets no sympathy as a fourteen-year-old school leaver when her zeal lowers

---

[9] *The Forbidden Zone*, 59.
[10] Gail Braybon, *Women Workers in the First World War* (London: Routledge, 1984) 162.

the piece-work rate; working-class Liz ignores Pamela's reminder to replace her cap, preferring the risk of being scalped to deference to the rules.

Women's subjective experience of the First World War in North America did not simply replicate that of British women. Although Canadian men answered the British call to arms as volunteers in 1914, Canada, far less industrialized than Britain, did not require the labor of proportionately as many women to replace them, especially as conscription was never actually imposed. In order to assure the passage of the Conscription Act, women were enfranchised in 1918 not for what they had done, but for who they were – the close relatives of servicemen. In Britain, the suffrage movement had split over support for the war, but all militant suffrage demonstrations were suspended for the duration. Such was not the case in the United States, where Alice Paul led the Women's Party into a persistent vigil before the White House demanding the vote. Informed that the only bills that could be considered in the present emergency were 'war measures,' the Women's Party maintained that suffrage legislation qualified as such on the grounds that democracy could not be fought for abroad while being denied at home.[11] Their demonstrations provoked the government into a series of attacks and arrests which kept the issue alive in the press throughout the war.

Their characteristically American demand that the rhetoric of democracy be honored in practise was also at the heart of Ida B. Wells-Barnett's Chicago protest of the legal lynching of black troops. Politically less radical, perhaps, but by no means less determined, the 'Y ladies,' Addie Hunton and Kathryn M. Johnson, fought hard to go to France not just to bring comfort to black servicemen, but also to bear witness to their valor and to support their claims for equal citizenship bought by their sacrifice.

The root experience of the war which unites women on both sides of the Atlantic and indeed, on both sides of the war, is that of loss. First, of course, was the loss of those one loved – the husbands, fathers, brothers, lovers who marched, sometimes incomprehensibly, like Edward Thomas, off to the mud of France and never came back. Their loss echoes through the century, still keenly felt seventy years later as Myfanwy Thomas remembers her dead father or Grace Morris

---

[11] Doris Stevens, *Jailed for Freedom* (New York: Boni & Liveright, 1920) 83.

Craig her fiancé, a delayed victim of the war who died on the eve of their wedding. Anna Eisenmenger experienced another sort of loss in addition to the deaths of her husband, son, and daughter-in-law – the loss of everything upon which her stability and happiness had depended. No longer the middle-aged, middle-class housewife, she has been transformed by necessity into a tough, law-breaking survivor, bewildered by what she has become.

The greatest loss of all, perhaps, was the promise of the century, the sunlit world of possibility that had beckoned the New Women before the war. The young soldiers lost their illusions on the battlefield, but their sisters no less lost theirs behind the lines. The loss was absolute: never again would it be possible to embrace the future altogether without irony. As Muriel Spark, who was born in 1917, suggests in her short story, 'The First Year of My Life,'[12] told from the point of view of an omniscient, unsmiling infant, even those barely born during the war swallowed disillusion with their mother's milk.

THE SECOND WORLD WAR

There are those who view World War II as merely the second act of a war which began in August 1914, and the twenty years that intervened between the two as an uneasy entr'acte. However valid this notion may be from certain perspectives, it is hardly accurate as far as women are concerned. In that intermission, military thinking about women underwent a profound revision. For the Allies, at least, the preservation of the sanctity of womanhood had been an expressed war aim, a means of drawing lines in the Great War. At its crudest, as in an American recruiting poster, the barbarian Hun, in an eerie foreshadowing of King Kong, lumbers onto the American shore clutching the pale and broken body of European womanhood. 'DESTROY THIS MAD BRUTE: ENLIST' is the call, in lurid orange. Yet well before the war was over, it had become clear that the bodies at the greatest risk in this conflict were male, not female. It might almost appear that the high commands of the major military powers agreed after the war that such would never again be the case. Certainly the mothers in 1939 who saw their children off to safe exile in the countryside with what stoicism they could muster or who themselves

---

[12] Muriel Spark, *The Collected Stories of Muriel Spark* (New York: Dutton, 1985).

later huddled in shelters under a relentless rain of bombs could be forgiven if they came to the conclusion that they had been conscripted to serve in the front lines. The respective casualty figures for the two wars tell the tale: civilian casualties in the First World War constituted about 20 percent of the toll; in Europe during the years 1939–45, civilian casualties outnumbered military deaths by a wide margin, perhaps as much as three to one.[13]

Something else changed in those twenty years. In the Great War, there were no real paradigms for appropriate women's activity. Once the call had, however reluctantly, gone out to women to play their part in the war effort, those who responded seized the opportunity to enlarge the tasks offered them in creative ways. The corollary of the isolation we observe in the war service of so many of these women was autonomy. In the case of the rich and well-connected, it could be almost absolute. Mary Borden sat alone in a field hospital that she had bought and paid for; when, twenty-five years later, she tried to replicate her earlier war work, she found she was neither rich enough nor free enough to manage it. No matter that the two wars would blend ineluctably in her mind: these were different times and her efforts, though tolerated because of her reputation and her husband's position, met with a kind of amused indifference tinged with embarrassment.

Regardless of the vast social change which would come about as a result of the Second World War, women's first-person accounts of their military or munitions service leave the impression of conflict with rigid structures that would yield only slightly and grudgingly to accommodate their needs. Absent is the exhilarating sense of new territories opened and explored that we find in certain of the narratives from the Great War. Just as Allied soldiers in the Second World War could not be disillusioned in the way their elder brothers and fathers had been by the realities of modern warfare, servicewomen and munitions workers appear to expect (and get) less in the way of liberation than the previous generation of women had imagined. From the beginning, they were recruited into war service 'for the duration,' especially in North America. As a Canadian recruiting film put it, women 'wear wings on their shoulders so that men might fly.'[14] Far fewer promises were made that war service would lead to

---

[13] Casualty figures are notoriously difficult to come by – these are based on a table appearing in James Ellis, *World War II: A Statistical Survey* (New York: Facts on File, 1993) 253–4. Civilian deaths include those who perished in the concentration camps.
[14] *Wings on Their Shoulders*, National Film Board of Canada, 1943.

broader social participation for women after the war. On the contrary, the call to women to engage in the war effort generally assumed that this work was as uncongenial to them as fighting was to the men in the services. Women's work was needed to shorten the war and to get back to normal as rapidly as possible. Perhaps because of this reduced anticipation, women writing about the Second World War appear more sharply conscious of the operation of class distinction and more resentful of it than most of the middle-class women who left behind reminiscences of their Great War service.[15] The overall impression left by accounts of life on the home front is of crushing boredom and grinding deprivation punctuated by moments of terror. Indeed, much the same could be said of frontline narratives from both wars: 'the home front,' that rhetorical construct of the Great War meant to sharpen the civilian sense of being part of the war effort, had become, like too many other rhetorical devices, a grim reality. Only the children, sturdily facing evacuation with their thumbs firmly up, could find adventure in the war.

As war became more total, distinctions between enemy and ally were harder to draw. Evidence of the failure of the Communist ideal so revolted Charlotte Haldane, touring the besieged Soviet Union as a member of the British Communist Party, that she subsequently left the Party. She at least could go home and take a moral stand. For Soviet women, left behind in starving Leningrad, the options were narrower. Elena Skrjabina must forgive her former maid, Marusha, for trading her sexual favors for food from the official warehouse and herself for accepting some of it and hoping for more. As Anna Eisenmenger had found twenty years earlier, extreme deprivation forced compromises on Skrjabina that her pre-war self would have found unimaginable.

Within the total war on the self that the concentration camp represented, there were rarely good choices. In the camps, women could either 'choose' to give their babies over to be killed or refuse and be gassed with them. At the very best, one could decide, as did a woman kapo at Auschwitz, in refusing to take any advantage of her position, that if she could give the other women nothing, at least she would take nothing away. 'I mustn't make them feel,' she said, 'that

---

[15] In this volume, Enid Bagnold is something of an exception to this generalization. This general obliviousness to the workings of class may simply be a function of the persistence of the arrogance of pre-war class attitudes.

I want to cut myself off from them.'[16] Likewise, in order to embrace a common fate, Etty Hillesum went 'voluntarily' to the Westerbork transit camp in Holland, where she intended to become the 'thinking heart' of the concentration camp and where she found herself caught in the moral complexities that beset any member of the Jewish organization of such a place. 'In what fatal mechanism,' she asks, 'have we become enmeshed?' There is no clear answer to her question.

Although camp conditions were designed to reduce the prisoners to atomized entities battling one another for physical subsistence, community and solidarity did survive. Charlotte Delbo nearly perishes from despair when she is separated from the others on a work gang; another prisoner, Lulu, restores her by giving her the gift of a moment's privacy in which to weep. Sylvia Salvesen uses the marginal protection afforded her by her social position to organize what medical aid she can for the other women in Ravensbrück and survives to testify at the trial of the camp matron and to forgive her.

Whether Matron Elizabeth Marshall felt the need to be forgiven is not established. Certainly a much more minor camp official, Frau Anna Fest, remembering her years as an SS guard at a camp like the one that held Judith Magyar Isaacson, appears to view herself as almost as much a victim as those she guarded. Taking refuge from guilt in naivete, she terms herself 'ein klein Doofi mit Plüschohren'[17] (a cloth-eared little dumbbell); she denies not what she did in the camps, but that she understood it. Thus she extends her sentimental sympathy both to her charges and to Ilse Koch, 'a woman after all.' The optimism of the feminists of the early part of the century regarding women's natural morality would be severely tried by the spectacle of Elizabeth Marshall, Ilse Koch, and even little Frau Fest.

Among much else, the camps involved an utter assault on the female identity of women inmates. As Isaacson remembers, the starved and shaven women initially had difficulty recognizing each other as women at all. In a letter she wrote to her American in-laws in her still imperfect English just after the war, she recalls the incident and generalizes it: 'Without hair even in womenclothes, everybody looked man. For two days, we couldn't get accostumed [sic] to it and we

---

[16] Tadeusz Borowski, *This Way to the Gas, Ladies and Gentlemen* (New York: Penguin, 1979).
[17] Alison Owings, *Frauen: German Women Recall the Third Reich* (New Brunswick: Rutgers UP) 329.

always told each other – please Mr or – hallo, my little boy.'[18] In a courageous attempt to snatch back a shred of self, Isaacson contrives a kerchief for her head and for a pleasant moment can dream of going to the Sorbonne. Her new singularity leads almost instantly to her being picked for what she fears will be rape – having tenuously recovered a feminine self, she also recovers a female vulnerability.

The fear of rape is omnipresent in war narratives, but actual descriptions of it are uncommon. As Isaacson herself points out, 'The Anne Franks who survived rape don't write their stories.'[19] It was not, for example, until well after her release from a Japanese internment camp that Agnes Keith could bring herself to talk about the sexual assault she had suffered and which nearly cost her life.

Keith's narrative suggests that the traditional middle-class heterosexual model of feminine behavior was poor preparation for life in a prison camp. The women with whom she was interned squabbled among themselves, betrayed one another, and were fiercely territorial in defending the sliver of accommodation allotted them and their children. Only the Roman Catholic nuns appear to exhibit a generosity of spirit, which Keith attributes to their religious faith and their familiarity with a life of deprivation. The reader, however, wonders if they do not behave better at least in part because of their experience in a female community and because they do not feel incomplete in the absence of men.

The enormity of the victimization implicit in the camps may occasionally overwhelm our awareness of the real, stubborn, and sometimes spectacularly successful battle against Nazism waged courageously in Europe by both men and women. Charlotte Delbo was sent to Auschwitz because of her activities in a Communist cell of the French Underground; Sylvia Salvesen to Ravensbrück for her opposition to the Nazi occupation of Norway; Lucie Aubrac only narrowly avoided a similar fate for herself and her husband by a daring and inventive stratagem that involved a brilliant manipulation of a German officer's conventional attitudes toward women. In a startling, and little-known, demonstration that appeals to patriarchal conviction could override Nazi ideology, the wives of Jewish men successfully demonstrated for a week in the streets of Berlin to secure the release of their husbands and families. It was to this resistance that Rita Kuhn owed her freedom.

---

[18] Isaacson, 151.
[19] Isaacson, 145.

After the war in Europe ended and the joy and release expressed by Gertrude Stein had faded, the survivors were left to assess those years as best they could. For those complicit in Nazi terror, the task was one more often avoided or ignored than undertaken. In Germany, the questions of the generation that came of age after the war sometimes prompted reflection. Christa Wolf looks into her daughter's clear eyes and tries to explain the complexities of her own childhood; she refuses to absolve herself on the grounds of youth, remembering with shame the moment she sat by the side of a field, chewing on meat denied to the Polish women forced laborers. Cristal Banghard-Jöst, born in 1949, pounds out a series of questions about a war-time event in her home town to which answers will never be forthcoming. A woman stood accused of having a sexual relationship with a Polish POW. She was forced to play her part in the central Second World War spectacle of female humiliation – her head was shaved, as were those of Frenchwomen after the war judged guilty of collaboration, as were the new inmates of the concentration camps. Guilty or innocent, victor or vanquished, the final insult offered these women is a crowing assault on their very gender.

Nor is reflection reserved only for the losing side. In a remarkable novel by Ella Leffland, *Rumors of Peace*,[20] the narrator, a little girl growing up in California during the war, grows past her fear and hatred of her Japanese neighbors to pause appalled and shaken at the news of the atom bombing of Hiroshima. That panic, coupled with greed and racism, created the internment camps in the United States and Canada like the one described by Muriel Kitagawa. It was in one such camp that the narrator of Joy Kogawa's *Obasan* learns of the death of her mother at Nagasaki years before. The hairless mother, the hairless dying child stand as mute and anguished witnesses to the progression towards total war that began so long ago in 1914. The assault on the distinction between civilian and soldier, the long, slow conscription of women and children into the front lines of a war where they must serve unarmed ends here, with an enemy soldier who has become a bald baby dying of leukemia four years after the war is over.

---

[20] I have not included a selection from this novel since it is not clearly autobiographical. Nevertheless it provides unparalleled insight into the impact of a war fought thousands of miles away on the consciousness of a sensitive child. Thus it reminds us that in time of total war, not every victim lives within the sound of gun or bomb.

THE GREAT WAR

MABEL ANNIE STOBART

(1862–1954)

In her autobiography *Miracles and Adventures* (1935), Mabel Stobart recounts the events of a remarkable life. Mother of two, widowed and remarried, she spent portions of her life in the African veldt and in British Columbia. In 1907, in the midst of a war scare in London she came to the conclusion that women were poorly prepared in the event of an invasion and would achieve the vote only if they could demonstrate their ability to aid in the national defense. To that end, she founded the Women's Sick and Wounded Convoy Corps, intended to serve near the field of battle as an emergency medical facility. It and Mrs Stobart saw their first service in the Balkan War in 1912 over the objections of the British Red Cross. She returned to the field in 1914, when she went to Belgium to set up a field hospital; caught in the German invasion, she narrowly escaped being shot as a spy. Nevertheless, she promptly returned to Belgium at the request of the Belgian Red Cross to establish a hospital wholly staffed by women. When this was successfully in place, Mabel Stobart went back to the Balkans once more, where she served as a commissioned major in charge of a hospital column during the three-month retreat on the Balkan Front. She was fifty-three at the time, spending eighteen hours a day on horseback in the mountains in winter. After her return from the Balkans, she wrote accounts of her adventures and engaged in an extensive series of lectures both in Britain and in the United States. In her later years, she became an ardent Spiritualist.

On my arrival in London in 1907, I found that people were living in daily fear of a German invasion. We have most of us forgotten that first scare, but it was very real then, and according to the *Daily Mail* we should scarcely have time to finish our breakfasts before the German armies would be fusillading our front doors. And also at this moment, the 'Votes for Women' agitation was sadly upsetting social equilibriums. I had been outside the range of suffrage politics and had never even heard it discussed (my husband was a masculinist), but I could not help being a feminist, for I knew from personal experience that women could do things of which tradition had supposed they were incapable. I viewed the situation from an angle of my own. My feeling was that if women desired to have a share in the government of the country, and this seemed a legitimate ambition, they ought to be capable of taking a share in the defence of their country.

I thought that in the present agitation women were putting the cart before the horse, and I made up my mind to try to provide proof of women's national worthiness, in the belief that reward of political enfranchisement would be the natural corollary. I want to lay stress on this point, for this was the secret motive power that initiated my War work. I don't remember speaking on any suffrage platforms, I contented myself with the secretly-held belief that in helping women to take a share in the national defence I was working none the less effectively for the goal of women's enfranchisement. And it is today some slight satisfaction to realize that, when all is said and done, it is the War work which women in all spheres of life performed so admirably that made it at last impossible for the vote to be further denied.

Yes – but what could women do in national defence? I certainly did not want them to fight, to take life. Nature asks us to create life, a responsibility we have accepted much too lightly. But one night I went to see a play then in vogue called *An Englishman's Home*.[1] That was, as I write, twenty-five years ago, but I remember, as though it were last night, the feelings with which I left the theatre. The play was crude, inartistic, melodramatic, and far-fetched, but it hit straight home. I have never before or since felt so humiliated as I felt that evening on leaving the theatre.

An Englishman's home was invaded by the enemy and the women could do nothing even to staunch the wounds of their men-folk. I forget the details. But I asked myself what could *I* have done? What could all these 'votes for women' claimants have done? What was there we could do or should be allowed to do in case of foreign invasion? I found that, in schemes of national defence, no provision was made for the help of women. A great deal had been made of Florence Nightingale's victory, but its present-day results were small, and only, at the best, affected trained hospital nurses.

About this time, someone called her attention to the Women's First Aid Nursing Yeomanry, which was being organized along lines which Mabel Stobart found impractical, if romantic. She determined to found her own

---

[1] Written by Major Guy Du Maurier, DSO; it was staged in 1909.

service, the Women's Sick and Wounded Convoy Corps, which was intended to facilitate the movement of the wounded from the field hospitals to the base hospitals in the rear. After a three-year period of rigorous training, the Corps saw its first service in the Balkan War of 1912–13, in aid of the Bulgarian Army. The Corps was again to see service the following year.

* * *

I want here to record a curious fact. The subject of War occupies so many pages of this book that I may possibly be regarded as a belligerent character. But I have come across two newspaper cuttings which throw some light upon the opinions I then held and still maintain as to the evils of war.

I wrote a letter which appeared in the *Daily News*, dated August 5th, 1914. In this letter I referred to the grave decision to be declared that day, and, lamenting the barbarity and unimaginative folly of war, I suggested that the whole trouble was due to the double standards of morality which prevail. One standard for men and another for women: one for individuals and another for nations. Unfortunately the discrepancy between the standards of men and women has now, since the War, been reduced in the wrong direction, whilst that between individuals and nations remains as great as heretofore.

The other cutting refers to a meeting (at which I was one of the speakers), which took place on the evening of August 4th, 1914. In the *Daily News and Leader* of August 5th, the following account appears: The article is headed 'Women's protest against the War. Great Peace Rally in London. Representative Voice of Europe,' and goes on to say: 'Many distinguished women, each representing one or other of the largest women's organizations in this country and in Europe, spoke last night at the great meeting in the Kingsway Hall, which had been called four days before as a peace demonstration, but was in tone (so quickly have events moved) almost a last rally of peace forces and common sense.'

Every one of the speakers spoke from the text of part of the resolution passed unanimously, which read, 'Whatever its result the conflict will leave mankind the poorer, will set back civilization, and will be a powerful check to the amelioration of the conditions of the masses of the people on which the real welfare of nations depends.' Speakers present on the platform were Olive Schreiner, Mrs Fawcett, Mrs Despard, Mrs Pethick Lawrence, Mrs George Cadbury, Mrs Creighton, Mrs Barton, Miss Mary MacMillan, Madame Malmberg (the Finnish patriot), Madame Schwimmer (Hungarian Representative on the International Suffrage Alliance), Madame Thomaian, Switzerland, and many others.[2] I was one of the speakers.

The women's demonstration against war had been called at a moment when there was still a possibility that the great calamity might be averted, and it was a protest against the time honoured methods of force in the settlement of national disputes; a protest, passionate, sane, practical, of the civilized against the barbaric; of the spiritual against the material.

It was during the course of that evening that, at Westminster, the weighty question of the intervention of our country was decided in the affirmative. The news reached Kingsway Hall before we had dispersed. Lady Muir McKenzie, who was present at the meeting, came up to me as we left the platform and asked me what I should be doing in the matter. I replied that I should, of course, put into practice my belief that women should and could take an active part in National Defence.

It is true that our own country was not being immediately attacked, but a small and practically defenceless nation was being wrongfully attacked, and, as our statesmen well understood, the boundaries of this island are on the other side of the narrow strip of water which, before the days of aeroplanes, made Great Britain an island. Lady Muir McKenzie said that she would support any effort I might make, and we decided then and there to move in the direction of forming Women's Units to do women's work of relieving the suffering of sick and wounded, or of any other service that might be required.

The next day we took a room as office and headquarters in St James's Street, organized the Women's National Service League (with myself as Director and Lady Muir McKenzie as sub-Director), with the aim of providing a body of women qualified to give useful service at home or abroad. We formed both Foreign Service and Home Service

---

[2] Virtually a roll-call of the leading suffrage activists of the day. Olive Schreiner, the South African novelist, author of *Story of an African Farm*, was a highly regarded feminist theorist. Millicent Fawcett was the head of the National Union of Women's Suffrage Societies, a moderate suffrage group. Charlotte Despard, who had been associated with Emmeline Pankhurst and the Women's Social and Political Union (WSPU) had by this time split with the Pankhursts over questions of tactics and direction and founded another activist organization, The Women's Freedom League. Emmeline Pethick-Lawrence and her husband, Frederick, were strong supporters of the WSPU until forced out of the organization in 1912. In short, with the exception of the Pankhursts themselves, this meeting enlisted the support of both the moderate and activist wings of the suffrage movement.

Divisions. The former included women doctors, trained nurses, cooks, interpreters, and all workers essential for the independent working of a hospital of war. The Home Services Division were to offer their services for any work that was needed. * * *

Recruiting began at once, and the response both with regard to numbers and money was miraculous. Supported by Earl Grey, Sir Alfred Mond, Lady Cowdray (who gave us an X-ray apparatus), Lady St Davids, Clementine Waring, and other good friends, we collected, within a fortnight, £1200 for equipment. The Hampstead Garden Suburb[3] contributed £200, and many generous donors made the task an easy one. We soon recruited a fully-qualified staff of women doctors, nurses, orderlies, etc.

I again approached Sir Frederick Treves, Chairman of the Red Cross Society, but was again repulsed. He said that there was not work fitted for women in the sphere of war. I reminded him of the work of the Women's Convoy Corps in Bulgaria, but he said that was exceptional, and that I was an exceptional woman, etc. I then consulted my good friends and supporters Lord and Lady Esher, and the result was that through their sympathetic intervention I received an invitation from the Belgian Red Cross at Brussels to establish in that city a hospital for French and Belgian soldiers.

---

[3] A planned community. Mabel Stobart's residence in the Suburb was to prove instrumental in aiding her release when being held in Belgium by the Germans as a spy. A high-ranking German officer intervened to save her from being shot in part because he was an admirer of the planning reforms represented by the Hampstead Garden Suburb.

SYLVIA PANKHURST

(1882–1960)

With her mother, Emmeline, and sister, Christabel, Sylvia Pankhurst was one of the founders of the militant suffrage group, the WSPU. Her repudiation of her mother and sister's war-induced jingoism cemented the political and personal rift which had developed between them. Sylvia Pankhurst spent the war years in London's East End, among the city's poorest inhabitants, where the effects of the war-time exploitation of London's laboring classes was only too evident. *The Home Front* (1933) records her responses to what she experienced there.

Out of 27,241 women who had by this time registered for war service, only 2,332 had been given work. Propaganda was insistent to get women into the munition factories, and every sort of work ordinarily performed by men. The sections clamouring for the military conscription of men saw in the industrial service of women a means to their end. Feminists who were advocates of Conscription for men believed themselves adding to the importance of women by demanding that women also should be conscripts.

The reawakened W.S.P.U.[1] was loudest in the demand for 'compulsory national service for men and women alike'; Lloyd George now possessed the implicit confidence of his old enemies Christabel and Mrs. Pankhurst; he was cheerfully disposed to accept their services. He agreed to receive a women's War Service deputation, to be organized by them on Saturday, July 17th; and to review a great procession which was to march with it. He promised finance for the show out of Government funds, and placed the official War Service registers at the disposal of the W.S.P.U. The Press boomed the function

---

[1] The Women's Social and Political Union: the radical suffragette movement begun by Emmeline Pankhurst, Sylvia's mother, together with Sylvia's sister, Christabel. The WSPU engaged in direct action to further the cause of votes for women and its members were frequently jailed as a result. Lloyd George, the Prime Minister, had long opposed the Pankhursts' efforts. With the outbreak of the war, they became allies, on the understanding the WSPU would suspend its civil disobedience campaign in deference to the war effort and the tacit agreement that the vote would be forthcoming after the war.

as a national event. Women with handbills advertising it were rushing round the East End. A letter signed E. Pankhurst, calling women to the War Service demonstration, was mistaken by some in our district as an appeal from me. That cut me to the quick; for my struggle was to prevent the exploitation of the people in the interests of the war.

Old militants of the W.S.P.U., who had suffered the hunger strike and been forcibly fed, were now interrupting its meetings with cries of 'Votes for Women.' Members of our Federation joined in the heckling. I did not want that; I desired our women to employ themselves in constructive effort, not in the fruitless decrying of those once our comrades, who had departed, as we considered, from progressive paths. If we must attack, let us attack the Government which held the power. At our members' general meeting I got a resolution passed that it was no part of our policy to interrupt the meetings of other Suffrage Societies.

Yet I could not rest content that this jingo demonstration, with its demand for compulsory War service, should stand forth unchallenged as representing the womanhood of the nation. Still less could I let pass, without protest, the new legislation which was so adversely determining the industrial position of women in war time. Our Federation also demanded an interview with Lloyd George and arranged a procession to Parliament for the night of Tuesday, July 20th. *'No National Service under Makers of Private Profit!' 'Down with sweating!*[2] *A Man's Wage for a Man's Job!' 'Down with High Prices and Big Profits!'* Such were our slogans.

Lloyd George refused to receive us, but many both Labour and Liberal Members of Parliament urged us to persevere, including J.R. Clynes, though he was one of the greatest jingoes[3] in the Labour Party, and Philip Snowden, who wrote:

> 'The fight is awfully hard, I know, but you are doing magnificent work.'

How greatly subsequent events were to alter his political attitude!

The big W.S.P.U. procession was produced according to promise. Boomed as it was, it could not have been otherwise. There were two miles of closely massed ranks, a pageant of the nations, led by Belgium

---

[2] Exploitive labor practises.
[3] War-monger.

with bare feet in sandals bearing a tattered flag. There were representations of the trades and professions in which women were called upon to serve. Women who had registered for War work and could not get it, munitions workers and trainees released from the grind of their seven days' work that they might march, warmongers, war workers and soldiers' wives out for a jaunt, women of all sorts and conditions fell in behind the banners and bands, and sang the popular war-songs, 'Tipperary' and all the rest. The procession was lauded as a magnificent achievement, and a proof of the enthusiasm of women for the National Cause.

The significant fact remained that the organization of this demonstration had been paid for by the Government; whereas in the pre-War struggle of the Suffragettes larger and more elaborate demonstrations had been financed by the enthusiasts of the movement itself. Where were those enthusiasts now? Scattered in a hundred directions. Even in the thinned ranks of those who remained supporters of the W.S.P.U. in its changed policy, there was not the disposition to sacrifice all for the Union, which had made it a power in its Votes for Women fight.

Lloyd George received the deputation in the wooden buildings erected for the Ministry of Munitions in the Embankment Gardens, and he and Mrs. Pankhurst went together on to the balcony to speak to the women outside. There was mutual praise and laudation. Mrs. Pankhurst said that the women munitioners should have equal pay with men. Cases of sweating had been brought to her notice and she knew that Mr. Lloyd George did not want that. Having just put through the Munitions Act[4] from which equal pay for women had been deliberately excluded, he repeated to her the pledge he had made to me, and assured her that the munition factories would be controlled and the Government would see that there was no sweated labour.

The *Suffragette*, the lynx-eyed organ of the W.S.P.U., which prided itself on its ability to discern and unmask the subterfuges of politicians, received the evasion complacently:

> Our opinion is that we must see how these assurances work out in practice, and any complaint or criticism made before that would be unreasonable, destructive and injurious.

---

[4] The Act regulated employment in war-related industries. Among other things, it laid out the conditions under which workers could leave their jobs.

Yet the sweating was flagrantly obvious to all who cared to look for it! It was all for the War, and the War before all with the W.S.P.U!

Sylvia Pankhurst fired off a letter to Lloyd George, complaining about the vagueness of his assurances and giving specific instances where women's labor was being exploited. She also objected to the fact that wages were regulated while the price of food was not. She announced a deputation which would march to see him shortly. She received no answer.

Opposing the great engines of war propaganda, as we were, with only the contributions of a small knot of enthusiasts to assist us in printing handbills to make our procession known, we could not hope that night to rival the great sightseer's carnival of the Saturday afternoon. With the factories working overtime, the home workers held more rigidly than ever to their sweated toil by the rising cost of living, the procession surprised me by its size and stirred my heart by its earnestness. The Old Ford Road was alive with the hurrying people. The workers were hastening straight from the factories to march in the ranks, or if they could not march, at least to give the marchers a cheer.

'We would come with you if we could!' Many called to us. 'I wish I could come, but I am too old, too tired, too worn out with standing all day – my feet are too sore! – I am almost dropping with coming this far to see you!' 'I must run home to the children; they have missed me all day; but I came to see you start. I wish I could come!' 'Good luck!' 'Good luck!' 'Bravo!' and 'Bless you all!'

Yet thousands came with us, facing the long march to Westminster after their twelve-hour working day without even staying to get a bite. Some joined our six-deep ranks; some went beside us on the pavement, 'Because my boots are so bad, and the sets[5] in the road hurt my feet.' Folk thronged the roadway from kerb to kerb, because the police charges of recent, pre-war remembrance made our East End crowds prefer to mass together in a swarm. Many of the women were carrying babies, some pushing a child or two in a perambulator. The colourbearer took us along so fast that many could not keep up, and

---

[5] Cobblestones.

were left behind. Yet more held on, swollen feet, varicose ulcers, prolapses and poor health notwithstanding. They were marching for vital needs, and their hearts were full. They carried the banners bravely, though the strong wind tugged at them. A woman told me that she had gone to join the Saturday procession; but she had bought our *Dreadnought* from a paper seller on the Embankment; and on reading it, had left those ranks, convinced that her place was with the workers' procession on Tuesday night. She was making packing cases at Dingwall's from 8:30 am to 7 pm for 12s a week. The man she had replaced got 35s. Home workers spoke of the poor price they got for making and finishing soldier's garments; a mother with little children to maintain got only 3d. for stitching 54 buttons on soldiers' trousers. These women were not urging a point of which they had read in books or heard on platforms; they were the sweated workers come to plead their own cause.

The Bethnal Green contingent awaited us with a big crowd assembled to wish them luck, and the faithful 'Cowboys' band, with their fifes and drums, who had rallied to us in many a Suffragette display. It was dark when we met the Poplar procession at Gardiner's corner. Girls from the biscuit and provision factories, dockers and gas workers with the red regalia of their Union, members of the League of Rights for Soldiers' and Sailors' Wives and Relatives, known by their regalia, 'Suffragette Crusaders' from South-East London, militants who had broken away from the war party, with their gold and purple banners. Masses of people cheered and waved to us. Mounted police galloped around us, their horses rearing.

* * *

We were a large company walking home through the dark streets to the East End that night; with all the power in the land against us, high-hearted in our crusade.

HANNAH WEBSTER MITCHELL
(1871–1956)

Born to a desperately poor family, Hannah Mitchell received only two weeks of formal schooling before she was forced to go to work. Through a combination of talent and perseverance, she went on to become a leader of the Suffrage and Labour movements in the north of England and a member of the Manchester City Council. *The Hard Way Up*, her autobiography, was found among her papers at her death and published posthumously in 1968.

All my life I had hated war. My mother, whose uncles had fought in the Crimean War, had told us of their experiences and how one of them had deserted from the army and remained hidden all the rest of his life. The idea of men killing each other had always seemed so hideous to me, that my first conscious thought after my baby was born was that he should be brought up to resist war. His father fully agreed with me in this resolve. Apart from the ethical point of view, we both believed that war in the main is a struggle for power, territory or trade, to be fought by the workers, who are always the losers.

By 1914 my son was sixteen; it was clear that he might be soon involved in the war, for some of his friends were in the Territorials[1] and as soon as war was declared they were called up at once.

Hitherto I have said little about my son who I now realized might soon be called upon to fight. I had tried to bring him up to believe in the international brotherhood of man, but I don't think I was an ideal mother, being no more inclined to sink my individuality in my child than I had been to do so for my mother or my husband, and I sometimes thought he envied other boys whose mothers were more devoted to them. But he got a good, sound elementary school education and a fair amount of personal freedom. This latter I had to concede, finding him just as determined in his own way as I had been in mine. As he never wanted to do anything really wrong, and I remembered only too well the bitterness and frustration of my own

---

[1] The reserves.

childhood, I thought it best on the whole to let him 'gang his own gait.' One incident will show his strength of mind when quite young, and how his disapproval rather discomfited both his parents. At the time of his birth, we were in the 'anti-religious' stage of thinking, which many of the early Socialists seemed to pass through, so we decided not to have him baptized in church, saying grandly, that we were leaving him free to choose for himself when he grew up. In his early teens he began to attend church, and soon discovered our sin of omission, and was very indignant about it. But to my relief, he accepted my suggestion of a private baptism, and later was confirmed. This brought home to me the folly of parents who try to mould their children to their own pattern. In a way I felt that I had been as mistaken as my mother in her efforts to mould me to her own ideas. But as it happened, his views stood him in good stead later on, when called upon to give reasons for his objections to combatant service.

On the eve of war I attended a protest meeting – one of many[2] – held in Manchester that night. Of those who took part I recall most vividly the Rev. David Dorrity, rector of St. Ann's, who ended a well-reasoned speech with these words:

'Fight if you must, but not until you must.' The war fever spread quickly, and most of the protestors were on the recruiting platform before the week was out. The militant suffragists called off their campaign at once. The Government responded by releasing all the women who were in prison; thus ended a warfare which had gone on for eight years, during which hundreds of women had been sent to prison. At one demonstration in London in 1910, six hundred and seventeen women headed the procession, all in white dresses, carrying long silver staves, tipped with the broad arrow, showing they had suffered imprisonment. This procession was so great that it took an hour and a half to pass a given point, yet statesmen continued to assert that they had no proof that women wanted the vote.

Some of the women were disappointed with Mrs. Pankhurst's support of the war. Personally, I felt the times were so grave that all human beings must decide for themselves where their duty lay. My own views had crystallized into definite opposition, and I spent my scanty leisure in supporting the anti-war organizations, The I.L.P. No Conscription Fellowship and the Women's International League. My friends could not understand me.

---

[2] See Mabel Stobart for an account of a similar event.

'What,' they said, 'you such a fighter and you won't fight for your country?'

Strange that anyone should think that the only way to serve one's country is to fight for her. Surely the best way to serve her is to serve one's fellow men, and to try by hard work and decent living to add something to the common stock. Regarding the soldier as a victim of war, like the rest of us, I spent a good deal of time writing to the boys I knew and sending them such little comforts as I was able to afford. * * *

I took in two soldier boys who were on a gun and searchlight station near us; both were from good homes and were very grateful for a good bed, plain food and hot baths. I felt that bit of war work was of real value, and I was glad to be fully occupied, for I was going through one of the worst times of my life.

My son had withstood all the recruiting appeals of the first months, although, like other generous young hearts, I think he was tempted to volunteer. I waited, in such agony of mind, that I look back on that time as a reprieved man might look back on the time spent in the condemned cell. As the time drew near for his call-up I felt I couldn't bear to live if I knew he had killed another woman's son, but it was for him to decide, and I saw he was slowly making up his mind. He took a course in ambulance work, hoping he might be allowed to join the R.A.M.C. But when he applied for exemption from combatant service, he was told roughly that he could not pick and choose.

Mitchell's son was successful in his application for exemption and was sent off to work first in the countryside, where he suffered an accident that, Mitchell remarks, would have invalided him out of the army and then in Ireland. At the end of the war, he survived a bout of influenza and returned home, no longer the happy young man he had been but under the shadow of the war much as if he had been in active service.

Our friends, the Watsons, got their sons back, but the eldest had a permanently crippled arm, and the second had the seeds of a disease which eventually caused his death. Their daughter's husband never returned; his young wife was left with three children to bring up, one of many in like circumstances. Men came home full of hope for the brave new world which was promised them by the politicians, but which turned out to be even worse than the pre-war England we had tried to imbue with the ideals of Socialism.

SUSANNE R. DAY

(c. 1890–?)

Born in Cork, Ireland, Day wrote several plays that were produced at the Abbey Theatre before serving for twenty months in Bar-le-Duc, France, as a relief worker among the refugees from the fighting at the front. She published *Round About Bar-le-Duc* early in 1918, upon her return to England, at the prompting of her close friend, Carol. It is, she says, rather than 'a book about English women in France, it is mainly a book about French women in their own country ...' Nevertheless, as the following excerpts suggest, she reveals quite a bit about herself as well.

Days lengthen into weeks and still the refugees come through. We now know that Verdun is in danger, that the Germans have advanced twelve kilometres; we wait breathlessly for news, the town is listening, intent, anxious, and every day the crowds at the market grow denser. We spend much of our time there now, we have brought over basins, and soap and towels, we have put a table in the inner room, so that those who will may refresh themselves and wash. The rooms are packed. There must be at least three hundred or four hundred people and still more drift in. Some have been in open cattle trucks for thirty-six hours under rain and snow, for the north wind has become keener and the rain has hardened into fine sleety snow; it is bitterly cold, the roads and streets are awash with mud, women's skirts are soddened to the knee, men are splashed shoulder high. A number of people have fallen ill *en route*, others, seriously ill, have been compelled to leave their beds and struggle as best they might with the healthy in their rush to safety. We hear that the civil hospital is full, that babies have been born on the journey down – been born and have died and were buried by the way. Despair rides on many a shoulder, fear still darkens many eyes. * * *

In spite of all our anxiety as we made our way to the market that second night, laden with basins and jugs, *seaux hygiéniques*,[1] and

---

[1] Slop buckets.

various other comforts, we could not help laughing. We must have cut funny figures staggering along in the darkness with our uncouth burdens. Happily it WAS dark, and then not happily, as someone trips over an unseen obstacle and is only saved from an ignominious sprawl in the mire by wild evolutions shattering to the nerve. At the market we cast what might be called our 'natural feelings' on one side and bored our way into the throng, our strange utensils and luggage desperately exposed to view. *Que voulez-vous? C'est la guerre!*[2] The phrase covers many vicissitudes, but it did not cover the shyest of our coterie when, having deposited her burden on the gallery for a moment in order to help a poor woman, she heard a crash and a round French oath, and turning, beheld a certain official doing a weird cake-walk over things that were never intended to be trodden upon by man. It was the same shy member whose indignation at the lack of proper accommodation bore all her native timidity away and enabled her to persuade the same official to curtain off a small corner at the far end of the gallery and furnish it as a toilet-room for the women, a corner which to our eternal amusement was ever afterwards known as 'le petit coin des dames anglaises.'[3] However, the *petit coin* was not in existence for two or three days and while it was in the process of manufacture we were more than once moved to violence of language, though we realized that physical fatigue may reach a point at which, if conditions be unfavourable, no veneer or civilization can save some individuals from a lapse into primitive ways.

In the inner room the crowd was dense as we struggled in with our apparatus for washing. There was something essentially sordid in the scene. The straw looked dirty, the people were muddier, more wretched. Many were weeping, and very many lying in unrestful, contorted attitudes upon the ground. In such a crowd, no one dare leave her luggage unguarded, and so it was either gripped tightly to the body, even in sleep, or else was utilized as a pillow. And no one of those who came in by train or *camion*[4] was allowed to bring more than he or she could carry.

All the misery, all the suffering, all the heart-break of war seemed concentrated there, and then quite suddenly out of ugliness and squalor came beauty. A tall woman with a resigned, beautiful face detached herself from the throng, a naked baby wrapped in a towel

---

[2] What do you expect? It's the war!
[3] The English ladies' powder room.
[4] Truck.

in her arms. As unconcernedly, as unself-consciously as if she were at home in her own kitchen, she came to the table, filled a basin with warm water, and sitting down, bathed the lusty crowing thing that kicked and chewed its fists, gurgling with delight.

It was the second time she had been evacuated, she told us. She had seven children, her husband was a farmer and well-to-do. Their home destroyed, they had escaped in August 1914, taking refuge in Verdun, where they had remained, gathering a little furniture together again, trying to make a home once more. She neither wept nor complained. I think she was long past both. Fate had taken its will of her, she could but bow her head, impotent in the storm. Her children, in spite of their experiences, looked neat and clean, they were nicely spoken and refined in manner. Soon the dusky shadows of the room swallowed her up and the human whirlpool swirled round us once more * * *.

* * *

Once – it was downright wicked, I admit – two of us, both, be it confessed, wild Irishwomen, with all the native and national love of a row boiling in our veins, hearing the syren one evening, somewhere about nine o'clock, put on our hats and coats, and kilting our skirts, set off up the hill. We left consternation behind us, but we did so want to see a Zeppelin!

The valley was bathed in a soft fitful light. The moon was almost full, but misty clouds flitted across the sky, fugitives flying before a wooing wind. Below us, the town lay in darkness. Not a lamp showing. About us rose the old town, the rue Chavé looming cliff-like high above our heads. We pressed on, pierced the shadows of that narrow street and gained the rue des Grangettes, there to be met by a sight so weird, so suggestive of tragedy I wish I could have painted it. From the tall, grim houses men and women had poured out. Children sat huddled beside them, others slept in their mother's arms. On the ground lay bags and bundles. Whispers hissed on the air. It was alive with sibilant sound. No one talked aloud. They were as people that watch in an ante-room when Death has touched one who relinquishes life reluctantly in a room beyond. In the rue Tribel were more groups. In the rue des Ducs de Bar still more. We thought the population of those old ghost-haunted houses must all have come forth from a shelter in which they no longer trusted. A Zeppelin bomb, it is said, will crash through six stories and break the roof of the cellar beneath. Here in the street there was no safety. But in the woods beyond the town, in the woods high on the hill ... Many and many a poor family spent long night hours in the cold, the wet, and the storm, their little all gathered in bundles beside them during those intense months of early spring. We felt – or at least I know I felt – as we walked through this world of whispering shadow, utterly unreal. I ceased to believe in Zeppelins; earth, material things slid away, in the cloud-veiled moonlight values became distorted. I felt like a spectator at a play, but a play where only shadows act behind a dim, semi-transparent screen.

Then we came to the Place Tribel, and the world enclosed us again. A soldier with a telescope swept the heavens, others gazed anxiously out over the hills towards St Mihiel. That night was very still and beautiful; strange that out there, somewhere in the void, Death should be riding, coming perhaps near to our own souls, with his message written already upon our hearts. In the streets below a bugle call rang out clear and sweet, the *Alerte*, the danger signal ... We thought of the hurried wretches making their way to the woods ... Odd that one should want to see a Zeppelin!

GERTRUDE STEIN

(1874–1946)

Gertrude Stein emigrated from the United States to Paris a decade before the outbreak of the First World War and, with her lover, Alice B. Toklas, was at the center of the international modernist literary movement until her death, shortly after the end of the Second World War. In her memoir, *The Autobiography of Alice B. Toklas*, written from Alice's point of view, she recalls their war-time service driving an ambulance for an American volunteer ambulance group, activities which resulted in their both being decorated by the French government.

Ellen Lamotte and Emily Chadbourne, who had not gone to Serbia, were still in Paris. Ellen Lamotte[1] who was an ex-Johns Hopkins nurse, wanted to nurse near the front. She was still gun shy but she did want to nurse at the front, and they met Mary Borden-Turner[2] who was running a hospital at the front and Ellen Lamotte did for a few months nurse at the front. After that she and Emily Chadbourne went to China and after that became leaders of the anti-opium campaign.

Mary Borden-Turner had been and was going to be a writer. She was very enthusiastic about the work of Gertrude Stein and travelled with what she had of it and volumes of Flaubert to and from the front. She had taken a house near the Bois[3] and it was heated and during that winter when the rest of us had no coal it was pleasant going to dinner there and being warm. We liked Turner. He was a captain in the British army and was doing contre-espionage work very successfully. Although married to Mary Borden he did not believe in millionaires. He insisted on giving his own Christmas party to the women and children in the village in which he was billeted and he

---

[1] Ellen La Motte (1873–1961) wrote *Backwash of War* (1916; 1936), based on her experiences at the Front. The book went into several editions in 1916, then was banned by the British authorities as unhelpful to the war effort. It was republished with an author's introduction in 1936. She also wrote books reporting on her work as a nurse specializing in tuberculosis and on her investigations into the opium trade.

[2] Author of *The Forbidden Zone*, from which the story, 'Blind,' in this collection is taken.

[3] The Bois de Boulogne, a large wooded park in Paris.

always said that after the war he would be a collector of customs for the British in Dusseldorf or go out to Canada and live simply. After all, he used to say to his wife, you are not a millionaire, not a real one. He had british standards of millionairedom.[4] Mary Borden was very Chicago. Gertrude Stein always says that chicagoans spend so much energy losing Chicago that often it is difficult to know what they are. They have to lose the Chicago voice and to do so they do many things. Some lower their voices, some raise them, some get an english accent, some even get a german accent, some drawl, some speak in a very high tense voice, and some go chinese or spanish and do not move the lips. Mary Borden was very Chicago and Gertrude Stein was immensely interested in her and in Chicago.

All this time we were waiting for our Ford truck which was on its way and then we waited for its body to be built. We waited a great deal. It was then that Gertrude Stein wrote a great many little war poems, some of them have since been published in the volume Useful Knowledge which has in it only things about America.

* * *

The little Ford car was ready. Gertrude Stein had learned to drive a french car and they all said it was the same. I have never driven any car, but it would appear that it is not the same. We went outside Paris to get it when it was ready and Gertrude Stein drove it in. Of course the first thing she did was to stop dead on the track between two street cars. Everybody got out and pushed us off the track. Then next day we started off to see what would happen we managed to get as far as the Champs Elysées and once more stopped dead. A crowd shoved us to the side walk and then tried to find out what was the matter. Gertrude Stein cranked, the whole crowd cranked, nothing happened. Finally an old chauffeur said, no gasoline. We said proudly, oh yes at least a gallon, but he insisted on looking and of course there was none. Then the crowd stopped a whole procession of military trucks that were going up the Champs Elysées. They all stopped and a couple of them brought over an immense tank of gasoline and tried to pour it into the little Ford. Naturally the process was not successful. Finally getting into a taxi I went to a store in our quarter where they sold brooms and gasoline and where they knew me and I came back with a tin of gasoline and we finally arrived at the Alcazar d'Été, the then headquarters of the American Fund for French Wounded.

* * *

---

[4] Turner was thinking in pounds sterling, at the time worth $5.00 US.

We had a consultation with Mrs Lathrop[5] and she sent us off to Perpignan, a region with a good many hospitals that no american organization had ever visited. We started. We had never been further from Paris than Fontainebleau in the car and it was terribly exciting.

We had a few adventures, we were caught in the snow and I was sure that we were on the wrong road and wanted to turn back. Wrong or right, said Gertrude Stein, we are going on. She could not back the car very successfully and indeed I may say even to this day when she can drive any kind of car anywhere she still does not back a car very well. She goes forward admirably, she does not go backwards successfully. The only violent discussions that we have had in connection with her driving a car have been on the subject of backing.

On this trip South we picked up our first military godson. We began the habit then which we kept up all through the war of giving any soldier on the road a lift. We drove by day and we drove by night and in very lonely parts of France and we always stopped and gave a lift to any soldier, and never had we any but the most pleasant experiences with these soldiers. And some of them were as we sometimes found out pretty hard characters. Gertrude Stein once said to a soldier who was doing something for her, they were always doing something for her, whenever there was a soldier or chauffeur or any kind of man anywhere, she never did anything for herself, neither changing a tire, cranking the car or repairing it. Gertrude Stein said to this soldier, but you are tellement gentil, very nice and kind. Madame, he said quite simply, all soldiers are nice and kind.

This faculty of Gertrude Stein of having everybody do anything for her puzzled the other drivers of the organization. Mrs Lathrop who used to drive her own car said that nobody did those things for her. It was not only soldiers, a chauffeur would get off the seat of a private car in the Place Vendôme and crank Gertrude Stein's old Ford for her. Gertrude Stein said that the others looked so efficient, of course nobody would think of doing anything for them. Now as for herself she was not efficient, she was good humoured, she was democratic, one person was as good as another, and she knew what she wanted done. If you are like that she says, anybody will do anything for you. The important thing, she insists, is that you must have deep down as the deepest thing in you a sense of equality. Then anybody will do anything for you.

---

[5] The organizer of the American Fund for French Wounded.

It was not far from Saulieu that we picked up our first military godson. He was a butcher in a tiny village not far from Saulieu. Our taking him up was a good example of the democracy of the french army. There were three of them walking along the road. We stopped and said we could take one of them on the step. They were all three going home on leave and walking into the country to their homes from the nearest big town. One was a lieutenant, one was a sergeant and one a soldier. They thanked us and then the lieutenant said to each one of them, how far do you have to go. They each one named the distance and then they said, and you, my lieutenant, how far have you to go. He told them. Then they all agreed that it was the soldier who had much the longest way to go and so it was his right to have the lift. He touched his cap to his sergeant and officer and got in.

As I say he was our first military godson. We had a great many afterwards and it was quite an undertaking to keep them all going. The duty of a military godmother was to write a letter as often as she received one and to send a package of comforts and dainties about once in ten days. They liked the packages but they really liked the letters even more. And they answered so promptly. It seemed to me, no sooner was my letter written than there was an answer. And then one had to remember also their family histories and once I did a dreadful thing, I mixed my letters and so I asked a soldier whose wife I knew all about and whose mother was dead to remember me to his mother, and the one who had the mother to remember me to his wife. Their return letters were quite mournful. They each explained that I had made a mistake and I could see that they had been deeply wounded by my error.

The most delightful godson we ever had was one we took on in Nimes. One day when we were in the town I dropped my purse. I did not notice the loss until we returned to the hotel and then I was rather bothered as there had been a good deal of money in it. While we were eating our dinner the waiter said someone wanted to see us. We went out and there was a man holding the purse in his hand. He said he had picked it up in the street and as soon as his work was over had come to the hotel to give it to us. There was a card of mine in the purse and he took it for granted that a stranger would be at the hotel, beside by that time we were very well known in Nimes. I naturally offered him a considerable reward from the contents of the purse but he said no. He said however that he had a favor to ask. They were refugees from the Marne and his son Abel now seventeen years old had just volunteered and was present in the garrison at Nimes, would

I be his godmother. I said I would, and I asked him to tell his son to come to see me his first free evening. The next evening the youngest, the sweetest, the smallest soldier imaginable came in. It was Abel.

We became very attached to Abel. I always remember his first letter from the front. He began by saying he was not very much surprised by anything at the front. It was exactly as it had been described to him and as he had imagined it, except that there being no tables one was compelled to write upon one's knees.

The next time we saw Abel he was wearing the red fourragère, his regiment as a whole had been decorated with the legion of honor and we were very proud of our filleul.[6] Still later when we went into Alsace with the french army, after the armistice, we had Abel come and stay with us a few days and a proud boy he was when he climbed to the top of the Strasbourg cathedral.

When we finally returned to Paris, Abel came and stayed with us a week. We took him to see everything and he said solemnly at the end of his first day, I think all that was worth fighting for. Paris in the evening however frightened him and we always had to get somebody to go out with him. The front had not been scareful but Paris at night was.

* * *

We did finally arrive at Perpignan and began visiting hospitals and giving away our stores and sending word to headquarters if we thought they needed more than we had. At first it was a little difficult but soon we were doing all we were to do very well. We were also given quantities of comfort-bags and distributing them was a perpetual delight, it was like a continuous Christmas. We always had permission from the head of the hospital to distribute these to the soldiers themselves which was in itself a great pleasure but it also enabled us to get the soldiers to immediately write postalcards of thanks and these we used to send off in batches to Mrs Lathrop who sent them to America to the people who had sent the comfort-bags. And so everybody was pleased.

* * *

Our work in Perpignan being over we started back to Paris. On the way everything happened to the car. Perhaps it had been too hot even for a ford car in Perpignan. Perpignan is below sea level near the

---

[6] Godson.

Mediterranean and it is hot. Gertrude Stein who had always wanted it hot and hotter has never been really enthusiastic about heat after this experience. She said she had been just like a pancake, the heat above and the heat below and cranking a car beside. I do not know how often she used to swear and say, I am going to scrap it, that is all there is about it I am going to scrap it. I encouraged and remonstrated until the car started again.

It was in connection with this that Mrs Lathrop played a joke on Gertrude Stein. After the war was over we were both decorated by the french government, we received the Reconnaissance Française. They always in giving you a decoration give you a citation telling why you have been given it. The account of our valour was exactly the same, except in my case they said that my devotion was sans relache, with no abatement, and in her case they did not put in the words sans relache.

FLORA SANDES

(1876–1956)

The daughter of a Scottish clergyman who deeply regretted not having been a boy, Flora Sandes volunteered for service with an ambulance unit on the Serbian front in 1914, when she was almost forty years old. As the front collapsed, Sandes gradually transformed herself into a soldier, remaining with the Serbian army on its retreat through the mountains of Albania to the sea. In part because of her valor, in part because of her symbolic value as a representative of England, Sandes remained with the army, eventually being commissioned as a lieutenant and after the war, a captain. She married a Serbian sergeant, and lived in Yugoslavia where she was briefly called up, despite her age and the lingering effects of a severe war wound, as a member of the reserves in 1939. Her *An English Woman-Sergeant in the Serbian Army* (1916) aided in her successful fund-raising for the Serbian forces and made her an instant celebrity.

We rode all that morning, and as the Commander of the battalion, Captain Stoyadinovitch, did not speak anything but Serbian nor did any other of the officers or men, it looked as if I should soon pick it up. The staff had also shifted their quarters at the same time, and while we were riding up a very steep hill where Captain S. had to go for orders Diana's saddle slipped round, and by the time some of the soldiers had fixed it again for me I found he had got his orders and disappeared. I asked some of the soldiers which way he had gone, and they pointed across some fields; so I went after him as fast as Diana could gallop. I met three officers that I knew, also running in the same direction, and all the men seemed to be going the same way too. The officers hesitated about letting me come, and said, 'Certainly not on Diana,' who was white and would make an easy mark for the enemy; so I jumped off and threw my reins to a soldier.

'Well, can you run fast?'

'What, away from the Bulgars!' I exclaimed in surprise.

'No, towards them.'

'Yes, of course I can.'

'Well, come on then,' and off we went for a regular steeplechase, down one side of a steep hill, splashing and scrambling through a torrent at the bottom of it and up another one equally steep, a sturdy lieutenant leading us over all obstacles, at a pace which left even all of them gasping, and I was thankful that I was wearing riding breeches and not skirts, which would certainly have been a handicap through the bushes. I wondered how fast we could go if occasion should arise that we ever had to run away *from* the Bulgarians, if we went at that pace *towards* them. Though no one had breath to tell me where we were going, it was plain enough, as we could hear the firing more clearly every moment. We finally came to anchor in a ruined Albanian hut in the middle of a bare plateau on the top of a hill, where we found the Commander of the battalion there before us, he having ridden another way. The Fourth Company, whom we had already met once that morning, were holding some natural trenches a short way farther on, and we were not allowed to go any farther. The Bulgarians seemed to have got their artillery fairly close, and the shrapnel was bursting pretty thickly all around. We sat under the shelter of the wall and watched it, though, as it was the only building standing up all by itself, it seemed to make a pretty good mark, supposing they discovered we were there, which they did very shortly. An ancient old crone, an Albanian woman, barefooted and in rags, was wandering about among the ruins, and she looked such a poor old thing that I gave her a few coppers. She called down what I took at the time to be blessings on my head, but which afterwards I had reason to suppose were curses. The shells were beginning to fall pretty thickly in our neighbourhood, and our Battalion Commander finally said it was time to move on. He proved to be right, as three minutes after we left it the wall under which we were sitting was blown to atoms by a shell. My old crone had disappeared in the meantime to a couple of wooden houses on the edge of the wood. We had to cross a piece of open ground, which we did in single file, to reach this wood, and before we got to it we got a whole fusillade of bullets whistling round our ears from the friends and relations of the old lady upon whom I had expended my misplaced sympathy and coppers. These were the sort of tricks the Albanians were constantly playing on us from the windows of houses, whenever they got a chance.

We got down through the wood to where we left our horses, waited for the Fourth Company to join us, which they presently did, and then rode on, halting for a time, not far from where some of our artillery were shelling the enemy down below in the valley. The officer in charge showed me how to fire off one of the guns when he gave the word, and let me take the place of the man who had been doing it as long as we stayed there.

It was dark when we got to our camping ground that night, close to where the Colonel and his staff were settled, so I sent for my blankets and tent, which I had left with them, and camped with the battalion. After a light supper of bowls of soup we sat in a circle round the camp fire till late, smoking and chatting. The whole battalion was camped there, including the Fourth Company, with whom I had previously spent an evening at their camp in the snow, and I thought it very jolly being with them again. It did not seem quite so jolly, however, the next morning, when we were aroused at 3 a.m. in pitch dark and pouring rain, everything extremely cold and horribly wet, to climb into soaking saddles, without any breakfast, and ride off goodness knows where to take up some new position.

It was so thick that we could literally not see our horses' ears; I kept as close as I could behind Captain S., and he called out every now and again to know if I was still there. We jostled our way through crowds of soldiers, all going in the same direction up a steep path turned into a mountain torrent from the rain, with a precipitous rock on the near side, which I was told to keep close to, as there was a precipice on the other. A figure wrapped up in a waterproof cloak loomed up beside me in the darkness and proved to be the Commander of the Fourth Company. He presented me with firstly a pull from his flask of cognac, which was very grateful and comforting, and secondly a pair of warm woollen gloves, which he had in reserve, as my hands were wet and frozen. * * *

We rode like this till after daylight, and then sat on the wet grass under some trees and had a plate of beans; they tasted very good then, but I've eaten them so often since that now I simply can't look a bean in the face. The asked me if I was going to tackle the mountain on foot with them, or if I would rather stay there with the transport. I went with them, of course.

* * *

Later on the next day the sun put in an appearance, as did also the Bulgarians. The other side of the mountain was very steep, and our position dominated a flat wooded sort of plateau below, where the enemy were. One of our sentries, who was posted behind a rock, reported the first sight of them, and I went up to see where they were, with two of the officers. I could not see them plainly at first, but they could evidently see our three heads very plainly. The companies were quickly posted in their various positions, and I made my way over to the Fourth which was in the first line; we did not need any trenches as there were heaps of rocks for cover, and we laid behind them firing by volley. I had only a revolver and no rifle of my own at that time, but one of my comrades was quite satisfied to lend me his and curl himself up and smoke. We all talked in whispers, as if we were stalking rabbits, though I could not see that it mattered much if the Bulgarians did hear us, as they knew exactly where we were, as the bullets that came singing round one's head directly one stood up proved, but they did not seem awfully good shots. It is a funny thing about rifle fire, that a person's instinct always seems to be to hunch up his shoulders or turn up his coat collar when he is walking about, as if it were rain, though the bullet you hear whistle past your ears is not the one that is going to hit you. I have seen heaps of men do this who have been through dozens of battles and are not afraid of any mortal thing.

We lay there and fired at them all that day, and I took a lot of photographs which I wanted very much to turn out well; but alas! during the journey through Albania the films, together with nearly all the others that I took, got wet and spoilt. The firing died down at dark, and we left the firing line and made innumerable camp fires and sat round them. Lieut. Jovitch, the Commander, took me into his company, and I was enrolled on its books, and he seemed to think I might be made a corporal pretty soon if I behaved myself. We were 221 in the Fourth and were the largest, and, we flattered ourselves, the smartest company of the smartest regiment, the first to be ready in marching order in the mornings, and the quickest to have our tents properly pitched and our camp fires going at night. Our Company Commander was a hustler, very proud of his men, and they were devoted to him and would do anything for him, and well they might. He was a martinet for discipline, but the comfort of his men was always his first consideration; they came to him for everything, and he would have given anyone the coat off his back if they had wanted it. A good commander makes a good company, and he could make a dead man get up and follow him.

That evening was very different to the previous one. Lieut. Jovitch had a roaring fire of pine logs built in a little hollow, just below what had been our firing line, and he and I and the other two officers of the company sat round it and had our supper of bread and beans, and after that we spread our blankets on spruce boughs round the fire and rolled up in them. It was a most glorious moonlight night, with the ground covered with white hoar frost, and it looked perfectly lovely with all the camp fires twinkling every few yards over the hillside among the pine trees. I lay on my back looking up at the stars, and, when one of them asked me what I was thinking about, I told him that when I was old and decrepit and done for, and had to stay in a house and not go about any more, I should remember my first night with the Fourth Company on the top of Mount Chukus.

FLORENCE FARMBOROUGH

(1887–1980)

Farmborough, an Englishwoman teaching English privately in Russia in 1914, immediately offered her services as a nursing sister at the hospital established by Princess Golitsin in Moscow. By 1915, she was at the front in Poland, then Austria and Romania. Soon she found herself part of the Russian retreat and in the end witnessed the outbreak of the revolution. She fled Russia to Siberia, then the United States. After her return to Britain, she went on to become a university lecturer in Spain, where she remained during the Civil War, coming back home to London just in time for the Battle of Britain. Her diary, *Nurse at the Russian Front*, originally intended for her family, was published in 1974.

JANUARY, 1915

A special church service was held to mark the promotion from VAD to qualified Red Cross nurse.

Before each jewelled icon the *lampada* glowed with a ruby light. On the altar the high brass candlesticks held steadily-shining candles; near them stood a silver chalice containing holy water, with the Book of Books alongside; a silver plate, heaped with red crosses had been placed in the centre of the Holy Table. In front of the congregation, standing side by side, were sixteen young women, the first draft of nurses from a class of nearly two hundred. They were wearing the light grey dress, white apron and long white head-veil of the hospital nurse. A priest, in full canonicals, entered and slowly made his way towards the altar. Soon his rich resonant voice was heard reciting the beautiful Slavonic prayers of the Greek Orthodox liturgy. Heads were reverently bowed; a murmur of voices rose and fell. The censer was swung lightly to and fro, emitting trembling breaths of fine grey, fragrant smoke.

Finally there was silence. The golden-robed priest rose from his knees and faced the congregation, crucifix in hand. At a sign from him, the nurses moved slowly, in relays, to kneel at the altar. The priest then pronounced God's blessing on the red crosses in his hand, moved towards the kneeling nurses. Bending down, he asked each one her name; the answers came, softly but distinctly: 'Vera,' 'Tatiana,' 'Nadezhda' ... Over each he intoned a prayer, placed the red cross on her white apron and held his crucifix to her lips. Asya[1] was kneeling at my side. 'Your name?' 'Anna,' she replied. He handed her the red cross and she pressed her lips to the crucifix.

Now he was standing before me. 'Your name?' 'Florence,' I answered. The priest paused and whispered to his deacon-acolyte. A book was brought and consulted, then he consulted me: 'Of the *pravoslavny* [Orthodox] Church?' 'No,' I said, 'of the Church of England.' Again the whispered consultation, again the book was referred to. I felt myself growing cold with fear. But he was back again and resumed the prescribed ritual, his tongue slightly twisting at the pronunciation of the foreign name. 'To thee, Floronz, child of God, servant of the Most High, is given this token of faith, of hope, of charity. With faith shalt thou follow Christ the Master, with hope shalt thou look towards Christ for thy salvation, with charity shalt thou fulfil thy duties. Thou shalt tend the sick, the wounded, the needy: with words of comfort shalt thou cheer them.' I held the red cross to my breast and pressed my lips to the crucifix with a heart full of gratitude to God, for He had accepted me.

One by one, we moved back to our appointed places. On our breasts the Red Cross gleamed. I looked at my Russian sisters. We exchanged happy, congratulatory smiles. As for me, I stood there with a great contentment in mind and spirit. A dream had been fulfilled: I was now an official member of the great Sisterhood of the Red Cross. What the future held in store I could not say, but, please God, my work must lie among those of our suffering brothers who most needed medical aid and human sympathy – among those who were dying for their country on the battlefields of war-stricken Russia.

At the end of January, Farmborough succeeded in having herself posted to a Front Line Surgical Unit then forming in Moscow, though their parents considered her former pupils too frail and too young to join her.

---

[1] Her former pupil.

JANUARY 30TH

Preparations for my departure are well under way. I am breathlessly impatient to be off, but there is much to be done and the Unit itself is not yet fully organized. My nurse's dresses, aprons and veils have been made already, and I have bought a flannel-lined black leather jacket. An accessory to this jacket is a thick sheepskin waistcoat, for winter wear, whose Russian name, *dushegreychka*, means 'soul-warmer.' I hear that our Unit will be stationed for a time on the Russo-Austrian Front in the Carpathian Mountains and that we will have to ride horseback, as direct communication can be established there only by riding; so high boots and black leather breeches have been added to my wardrobe. * * *

But before I joined my Unit, there was one more ceremony in which I was to take part ...

At the moment of my departure, Anna Ivanovna, my Russian 'mother,' bade me kneel before her. Taking from her pocket a little chain, she fastened it round my neck. Then she blessed me, kissed me three times, 'In the name of the Father, of the Son and of the Holy Spirit,' and wished me 'God speed.' I, too, was a soldier, going to war, for thus did all Russian mothers to their soldier sons. The little chain, with a small icon and cross attached to it, has already been blessed by a priest.

* * *

11TH MAY [1917] PODGAYTSY

Today we left Strusuv for Podgaytsy.[2] Our division is back at the front and two of its regiments are already in the trenches. Now and then unexpected skirmishes take place – the initiative always with the Austrians – and a few wounded are brought to us. We notice a strange apathy about them; they lack the spark of loyalty, or devotion to God and their mother-country which has so distinguished the fighting-men in the previous two years. It worries us; we do not need to be told that the Russian soldier has changed; we see the change with our own eyes.

---

[2] Near the Polish–Ukrainian border.

There is an English hospital in Podgaytsy, run by a group of English nurses, under the leadership of an English lady-doctor.[3] I was very glad to chat with them in my mother-tongue and above all to learn the latest news of the allied front in France. * * * They are very nice women, those English and Scottish nurses. They all have several years of training behind them. I feel distinctly raw in comparison, knowing that a mere six-months' course as a VAD in a military hospital would, in England, never have been considered sufficient to graduate to a Front Line Red Cross Unit. They could not believe that I had experienced all those nightmare months of the Great Retreat of 1915, as well as the Offensive of 1916. 'You don't look strong enough to have gone through all that,' said the lady-doctor, 'and too young,' she added,[4] 'I don't think I should have chosen you for my team.' I secretly rejoiced that I had had my training in Russia!

Some of the medical terms they used were Greek to me! I consoled myself with the thought that my Russian was Greek to them! Not one of them spoke Russian – perhaps an isolated word here and there, but quite inadequate to meet the simplest emergency. They invited me to spend my free time with them; I was glad to do so, although my 'work' consists principally in soothing the wounded. The men betray a certain anxiety when they find themselves at the mercy of nurses whose language they cannot understand. I explained to them that they were from England, *my* country, *their* ally; but I saw that suspicion still crept into their untutored minds. So I felt pleased and gratified when some of them whispered to me: 'Stay with me *Sestritsa*.[5] Don't go away! Don't leave me alone!'

Their methods, too, are new to me. I was surprised to note that saline solutions are frequently used, but I was still more surprised and not a little perturbed when I saw that tiny bags, containing pure salt, are sometimes deposited into the open wound and bandaged tightly into place. It is probably a new method; I wonder if it has been tried out on the Allied Front. * * * These bags of salt – small though they are – must inflict excruciating pain; no wonder the soldiers kick and yell; the salt must burn fiercely into the lacerated flesh. It is certainly a purifier, but surely a very harsh one! At an operation, performed by the lady-doctor, at which I was called upon to help, the man had a large open wound in his left thigh. All went well until *two* tiny bags

---

[3] Possibly Dr Elsie Inglis, who died 27 November 1917 upon her return from Russia.
[4] Farmborough was thirty years old at the time.
[5] Sister.

of salt were placed within it, and then the uproar began. I thought the man's cries would lift the roof off; even the lady-doctor looked discomforted. 'Silly fellow,' she ejaculated. 'It's only a momentary pain. Foolish fellow! He doesn't know what is good for him.'

* * *

26TH JULY [1917]

* * * But another story made a deep impression. A Siberian woman soldier had served in the Russian Army since 1915 side by side with her husband; when he had been killed, she continued to fight. She had been wounded twice and three times decorated for valour. When she knew that the soldiers were deserting in large numbers, she made her way to Moscow and Petrograd to start recruiting for a Women's Battalion. It is reported that she had said, 'If the men refuse to fight for their country, we will show them what the *women* can do!' So this woman warrior, Yasha Bachkarova, began her campaign; it was said that it had met with singular success. Young women, some of aristocratic families, rallied to her side; they were given rifles and uniforms and drilled and marched vigorously. We Sisters were of course thrilled to the core.

A woman soldier, or boy soldier, was no unusual sight in the Russian Army. We had even come into contact with a couple of Amazon warriors; one, in her early twenties, who had had a nasty gash on her temple caused by a glancing bullet, had come to our first aid post on the Galician Front. I recalled how, after bandaging her and feeding her, we had had some difficulty in persuading her to stay the night with us in our barn and return to her company at daybreak. I think that she feared that her comrades might think that she had absconded.

* * *

WEDNESDAY, 9TH AUGUST

We housed fifteen wounded in our improvised *Lazaret*.[6] Last Monday, an ambulance-van drove up with three wounded women soldiers. We were told that they belonged to the Bachkarova Women's Death

---

[6] Sick bay.

Battalion. We had not heard the full name before, but we instantly guessed that it was the small army of women recruited in Russia by the Siberian woman soldier, Yasha Bachkarova.[7] Naturally we were all very impatient to have news of this remarkable battalion, but the women were sadly shocked and we refrained from questioning them until they had rested. The van driver was not very helpful but he did know that the battalion had been cut up by the enemy and had retreated.

* * *

SUNDAY, 13TH AUGUST

There was much work in the hospital. Each of us Sisters had her own ward. At dinner we heard more of the Women's Death Battalion. It was true; Bachkarova had brought her small battalion down south to the Austrian Front, and they had manned part of the trenches which had been abandoned by the Russian Infantry. The size of the Battalion had considerably decreased since the first weeks of recruitment, when some 2000 women and girls had rallied to the call of their Leader. Many of them, painted and powdered, had joined the Battalion as an exciting and romantic adventure; she loudly condemned their behaviour and demanded iron discipline. Gradually the patriotic enthusiasm had spent itself; the 2000 slowly dwindled to 250. In honour to those women volunteers, it was recorded that they *did* go into the attack; they *did* go 'over the top.' But not all of them. Some remained in the trenches, fainting and hysterical; others ran or crawled back to the rear. Bachkarova retreated with her decimated battalion; she was wrathful, heartbroken, but she had learned a great truth: women were quite unfit to be soldiers.

After the collapse of the Kerensky Government in 1918, Farmborough made her escape across Siberia to Vladivostok, where she boarded an American steamship headed for the United States. One of her fellow passengers was Yasha Bachkarova.

---

[7] Usually, Maria Bochkareva.

VERA BRITTAIN

(1893–1970)

Certainly the most famous First World War book written by a woman, not least because of its highly successful dramatization which appeared on British and American television, *Testament of Youth* was published in 1933 and based on the journals Brittain kept during the War. Though the book is sometimes criticized for the naivete of its attitudes, it still provides an unparalleled insight into the impact of the War on a young, middle-class woman. The fighting cost Brittain her brother, her fiancé, and every other young man to whom she was close. The experience caused her to become a life-long pacifist.

In the following excerpt, Edward is Vera's brother, Geoffrey and Victor ('Tah') his closest friends. In the first section, Vera discusses the painful memory of a rift between her and her fiancé, Roland Leighton. In the second, about nine months later, Victor has been wounded in the head and lost his sight. Vera is in Malta, serving as a VAD nurse.

Finally, in the third, Vera has returned to London, still nursing, and writes about her response (or lack of it) to the Armistice.

Apart from all these novel experiences, my first month at Camberwell[1] was distinguished by the one and only real quarrel that I ever had with Roland. It was purely an epistolary quarrel, but its bitterness was none the less for that and the inevitable delay between posts prolonged and greatly added to its emotional repercussions.

On October 18th, Roland had sent a letter to Buxton[2] excusing himself, none too gracefully, for the terseness of recent communications, and explaining how much absorbed he had become by the small intensities of life at the front. As soon as the letter was forwarded to Camberwell, I replied rather ruefully.

> Don't get *too* absorbed in your little world over there – even if it makes things easier ... After all the War *cannot* last for ever, and when it is over we shall be glad to be what we were born again – if only

---

[1] The hospital where she trained to become a VAD.
[2] Her hometown.

we can live till then. Life – oh! life. Isn't it strange how much we used to demand of the universe, and now we ask only for what we took as a matter of course before – just to be allowed to live, to go on living.

By November 8th no answer had come from him – not even a comment on what seemed to me the tremendous event of my transfer from Buxton into a real military hospital. The War, I began to feel, was dividing us as I had so long feared that it would, making real values seem unreal, and causing the qualities which mattered most to appear unimportant. Was it, I wondered, because Roland had lost interest in me that this anguish of drifting apart had begun – or was the explanation to be found in that terrible barrier of knowledge by which the War cut off the men who possessed it from the women who, in spite of the love that they gave and received, remained in ignorance?

It is one of the many things I shall never know.

Lonely as I was, and rather bewildered, I found the cold dignity of reciprocal silence impossible to maintain. So I tried to explain that I, too, understood just a little of the inevitable barrier – the almost physical barrier of horror and dreadful experience – which had grown up between us.

'With you,' I told him, 'I can never be *quite* angry. For the more chill and depressed I feel myself in these dreary November days, the more sorry I feel for you beginning to face the acute misery of the winter after the long strain of these many months. When at six in the morning the rain is beating pitilessly against the windows and I have to go out into it to begin a day which promises nothing pleasant, I feel that after all I should not mind very much if only the thought of you right in it out there didn't haunt me all day ... I have only one wish in life now and that is for the ending of the War. I wonder how much really all you have seen and done has changed you. Personally, after seeing some of the dreadful things I have to see here, I feel I shall never be the same person again, and wonder if, when the War does end, I shall have forgotten how to laugh. The other day I did involuntarily laugh at something and it felt quite strange. Some of the things in our ward are so horrible that it seems as if no merciful dispensation of the Universe could allow them and one's consciousness to exist at the same time. One day last week I came away from a really terrible amputation dressing I had been assisting at – it was the first after the operation – with my hands covered in blood and my mind full of a passionate fury at the wickedness of war, and I wished I had never been born.'

No sudden gift of second sight showed me the future months in which I should not only contemplate and hold, but dress unaided and without emotion, the quivering stump of a newly amputated limb – than which a more pitiable spectacle hardly exists on this side of death. Nor did Roland – who by this time had doubtless grown accustomed to seeing limbs amputated less scientifically but more expeditiously by methods quite other than those of modern surgery – give any indication of understanding either my revulsion or my anger. In fact he never answered this particular communication at all, for the next day I received from him the long-awaited letter, which provoked me to a more passionate expression of apprehensive wrath than anything that he had so far said or done.

'I can scarcely realize that you are there,' he wrote, after telling me with obvious pride that he had been made acting adjutant to his battalion, 'there in the world of long wards and silent-footed nurses and bitter, clean smells and an appalling whiteness in everything. I wonder if your metamorphosis had been as complete as my own. I feel a barbarian, a wild man of the woods, stiff, narrowed, practical, an incipient martinet, perhaps – not the kind of person who would be associated with prizes on Speech Day,[3] or poetry, or dilettante classicism. I wonder what the dons of Merton[4] would say to me now, or if I could ever waste my time on Demosthenes again. One should go to Oxford first and see the world afterwards; when one has looked from the mountain-top it is hard to stay contentedly in the valley ...'

'Do I seem very much of a phantom in the void to you?' another letter inquired a day or two later. 'I must. You seem to me rather like a character in a book or someone whom one has dreamt of and never seen. I suppose there exists such a place as Lowestoft, and that there was once a person called Vera Brittain who came down there with me.'

---

[3] Roland had won *all* the prizes when he left school, a matter of considerable pride to him, his family, and of course to Vera.
[4] His Oxford college.

After weeks of waiting for some signs of interested sympathy, this evidence of war's dividing influence moved me to irrational fury against what I thought a too-easy capitulation to the spiritually destructive preoccupation of military service. I had not yet realised – as I was later to realize through my own mental surrender – that only a process of complete adaptation, blotting out tastes and talents and even memories, made life sufferable for someone face to face with war at its worst. I was not to discover for another year how completely the War possessed one's personality the moment one crossed the sea, making England and all the uninitiated marooned within its narrow shores seem remote and insignificant. So I decided with angry pride that – however tolerant Roland's mother, who by his own confession had also gone letterless for longer than usual, might choose to be – I was not going to sit down meekly under contempt or neglect. The agony of love and fear with which the recollection of his constant danger always filled me quenched the first explosion of my wrath, but it was still a sore and unreasonable pen that wrote the reply to his letter.

Most estimable, practical, unexceptional adjutant, I suppose I ought to thank you for your letter, since apparently one has to be grateful nowadays for being allowed to know you are alive. But all the same, my first impulse was to tear that letter into small shreds, since it appeared to me very much like an epistolary expression of the Quiet Voice, only with indications of an even greater sense of personal infallibility than the Quiet Voice used to contain.[5] My second impulse was to write an answer with a sting in it which would have touched even R. L. (modern style). But I can't do that. One cannot be angry with people at the front – a fact which I think they sometimes take advantage of – and so when I read 'We go back into the trenches tomorrow,' I literally dare not write you the kind of letter you perhaps deserve, for thinking that the world might end for you on that discordant note.

No, my metamorphosis has not been as complete as yours – in fact I doubt if it has occurred at all. Perhaps it would be better if it had, for it must be very pleasant to be perfectly satisfied with yourself and life in general. But I cannot ... Certainly I am as practical and outwardly as narrow as even you could desire. But although in this life I render material services and get definite and usually

---

[5] The voice of paternal reason, reproving youthful, especially feminine, emotion.

immediate results which presumably ought therefore to be satisfying, I cannot yet feel as near to Light and Truth as I did when I was 'wasting my time' on Plato and Homer. Perhaps one day when it is over I shall see that there was Light and Truth behind it all, but just now, although I suppose I should be said to be 'seeing the world,' I can't help feeling that the despised classics taught me the finest parts of it better. And I shan't complain about being in the valley if only I can call myself a student again some day, instead of a 'nurse.' By the way, are you *quite* sure you are on 'the mountain-top'? You admit yourself that you are 'stiff, narrowed, practical, an incipient martinet,' and these characteristics hardly seem to involve the summit of ambition of the real you. But the War kills other things besides physical life, and I sometimes feel that little by little the Individuality of You is being buried as surely as the bodies are of those who lie beneath the trenches of Flanders and France. But I won't write more on this subject. In any case it is no use, and I shall probably cry if I do, which must never be done, for there is so much both personal and impersonal to cry for here that one might weep for ever and yet not shed enough tears to wash away the pitiableness of it all.

Roland responded with a letter of passionate apology. He also remarked he has given up any chance of his getting leave before Christmas so that he can remain with his battalion. He was killed the day before that Christmas leave began.

* * *

Following the news of Roland's death, Vera submerged herself in her hospital work. She could, however, take some pleasure in the news of her brother's being awarded a Military Cross. In the summer of 1916, she was posted to Malta, where she got the news first that Victor had been wounded and then that Geoffrey had been killed.

I had just got into bed on May Morning and was drifting into sleep, when the cable came from Edward to say that Geoffrey was dead.

When I had read it I got up and went down to the shore in my dressing gown and pyjamas. All day I sat on the rocks by the sea with the cable in my hand. I hardly noticed how the beautiful morning,

golden and calm as an August in Devon, turned slowly into gorgeous
afternoon, but I remembered afterward that the rocks were covered
with tiny cobalt-blue irises, about the size of an English wood violet.

* * *

All at once, as I gazed out to sea, the words of the 'Agony Column,'[6]
that I had cut out and sent to Roland nearly two years before, struggled
back into my mind.

'Lady, *fiancé* killed, will gladly marry officer totally blinded or
otherwise incapacitated by the War.'

I even remembered vaguely the letter in which I had commented
on this notice at the time:

At first sight it is a little startling. Afterwards the tragedy of it
dawns on you. The lady (probably more than a girl or she would
have called herself 'young lady'; they always do) doubtless has no
particular gift or qualification, and does not want to face the
dreariness of an unoccupied and unattached old-maidenhood. But
the only person she loved is dead; all men are alike to her and it is
a matter of indifference whom she marries, so she thinks she may
as well marry someone who really needs her. The man, she thinks,
being blind or maimed for life, will not have much opportunity of
falling in love with anyone, and even if he does will not be able to
say so. But he will need a perpetual nurse and she if married to him
can do more for him than an ordinary nurse and will perhaps find
relief from her sorrow in devoting her life to him. Hence the
advertisement; I wonder if anyone will answer it? It is a purely
business arrangement, with an element of self-sacrifice which
redeems it from utter sordidness. Quite an idea, isn't it?

I was still, I reflected, a girl and not yet a 'lady,' and I had certainly
never meant to go through life with no 'particular gift or qualification.'
But – 'quite an idea, isn't it?' Was it Geoffrey? Wasn't it? There was
nothing left in life now but Edward and the wreckage of Victor – Victor
who had stood by me so often in my blackest hours. If he wanted me,
surely I could stand by him in his.

---

[6] The personal ads in the London *Times*. The original advertisement had provoked
considerable discussion between Vera and Roland.

If he wanted me? I decided, quite suddenly, that I would go home and see. * * * Much as I liked my hospital and loved the island, I knew that I was not really needed there any more; any one – or no one – could take my place. If I could not do anything immediate for Victor I would join up again; if I could – well, time and the extent of his injuries would decide when that should be.

In the event, Victor took a sudden turn for the worse and died, several weeks after Vera returned to Britain. Fifteen years later, she reconsidered her plan.

Back at home, [Victor's] aunt, kind, controlled, too sensitive to the sorrows of others to remember her own, turned to me with an affectionate warmth of intimacy which had not been possible before and would never, we both knew, be possible again.

'My dear, I understand what you meant to do for Victor. I know you'd have married him. I do wish you could have ...'

'Yes,' I said, 'I wish I could have,' but I did not tell her that the husband of my imagination was always Roland, and could never now be Victor. The psychological combats and defeats of the past two years, I thought, no longer mattered to anyone but myself, for death had made them all unsubstantial, as if they had never been. But though speech had been stifled, thought was less easy to tame; I could not cease from dwelling upon the superfluous torture of Victor's long agony, the cruel waste of his brave efforts at vital readjustment.

As for myself, I felt that I had been malevolently frustrated in the one serious attempt I had ever made to a serve a fellow-creature. Only long afterwards, when time had taught me the limits of my own magnanimity, did I realize that his death had probably saved us both from a relationship of which the serenity might have proved increasingly difficult to maintain, and that I had always been too egotistical, too ambitious, too impatient to carry through any experiment which depended for its success upon the complete abnegation of individual claims.

By the time the Armistice was declared, on 11 November 1918, Vera, now
working in a London hospital, is incapable of rejoicing. All of her close male
friends and relations have perished.

When the sound of victorious guns burst over London at 11.a.m. on
November 11th, 1918, the men and women who looked incredulously
into each other's faces did not cry jubilantly: 'We've won the War!'
They only said, 'The War is over.'

From Milbank I heard the maroons[7] crash with terrifying clearness,
and, like a sleeper who is determined to go on dreaming after being
told to wake up, I went on automatically washing the dressing bowls
in the annex outside my hut. Deeply buried beneath my consciousness
there stirred the vague memory of a letter that I had written to Roland
in those legendary days when I was still at Oxford, and could spend
my Sundays thinking of him while the organ echoed grandly through
New College Chapel. It had been a warm May evening, when all the
city was sweet with the scent of wallflowers and lilac, and I had
walked back to Micklem Hall after hearing an Occasional Oratorio
by Handel, which described the mustering of troops for battle, the
lament for the fallen and the triumphant return of the victors.

'As I listened,' I told him, 'to the organ swelling forth into a final
triumphant burst in the song of victory, after the solemn and mournful
dirge over the dead, I thought with what mockery and irony the
jubilant celebrations which will hail the coming of peace will fall
upon the ears of those to whom their best will never return, upon
whose sorrow victory is built, who have paid with their mourning
for the others' joy. I wonder if I shall be one of those who take a happy
part in the triumph – or if I shall listen to the merriment with a heart
that breaks and ears that try to keep out the mirthful sounds.'

And as I dried the bowls I thought: 'It's come too late for me.
Somehow I knew, even at Oxford, that it would. Why couldn't it have
ended rationally, as it might have ended, in 1916 instead of all that
trumpet-blowing against a negotiated peace, and the ferocious talk
of secure civilians about marching to Berlin? It's come five months
too late – or is it three years? It might have ended last June, and let
Edward, at least, be saved! Only five months – it's such a little time,
when Roland died nearly three years ago.'

---

[7] Ceremonial cannons.

But on Armistice Day, not even a lonely survivor drowning in black waves of memory could be left alone with her thoughts. A moment after the guns had subsided into sudden, palpating silence, the other VAD from my ward dashed excitedly into the annex.

'Brittain! Brittain! Did you hear the maroons? It's over – it's all over! Do let's come out and see what's happening!'

Mechanically I followed her into the road. As I stood there, stupidly rigid, long after the triumphant explosions from Westminster had turned into a distant crescendo of shouting, I saw a taxicab turn swiftly in from the Embankment toward the hospital. The next moment there was a cry for doctors and nurses from passers-by, for in rounding the corner the taxi had knocked down a small elderly woman who in listening, like myself, to the wild noise of a world released from nightmare, had failed to observe its approach.

As I hurried to her side, I realised that she was all but dead and already past speech. Like Victor in the mortuary chapel, she seemed to have shrunk to the dimensions of a child with the sharp features of age, but on the tiny chalk-white face an expression of shocked surprise still lingered, and she stared at me as Geoffrey had stared at his orderly in those last moments of conscious silence beside the Scarpe. Had she been thinking, I wondered, when the taxi struck her, of her sons at the front, now safe? The next moment a medical officer and some orderlies came up, and I went back to my ward.

But I remembered her at intervals throughout that afternoon, during which, with a half-masochistic notion of 'seeing the sights,' I made a circular tour to Kensington by way of the intoxicated West End. With aching persistence my thoughts went back to the dead and to the strange irony of their fates – to Roland, gifted, ardent, ambitious, who had died without glory in the conscientious performance of a routine job; to Victor and Geoffrey, gentle and diffident, who, conquering nature by resolution, had each gone down bravely in a 'big show'; and finally to Edward, musical, serene, a lover of peace, who had fought courageously through so many battles and at last had been killed while leading a vital counter-attack in one of the few decisive actions of the War.

* * *

I detached myself from the others and walked slowly up Whitehall, with my heart sinking in a sudden cold dismay. Already this was a different world from the one that I had known during four life-long years, a world in which people would be light-hearted and forgetful, in which themselves and their careers and their amusements would blot out political ideals and great national issues. And in that brightly lit, alien world I should have no part. All those with whom I had really been intimate were gone; not one remained to share with me the heights and the depths of my memories. As the years went by and youth departed and remembrance grew dim, a deeper and ever deeper darkness would cover the young men who were once my contemporaries.

For the first time I realized, with all that full realization meant, how completely everything that had hitherto made up my life had vanished with Edward and Roland, with Victor and Geoffrey. The War was over; a new age was beginning; but the dead were dead and would never return.

ENID BAGNOLD

(1889–1981)

Bagnold was an art student until she became a VAD during the war. Her *A Diary Without Dates*, from which this excerpt is taken, caused her to be fired from the hospital in which she was working. In her preface to the 1935 edition of the book, she claims to have written it at the age of nineteen, perhaps in order to heighten the impression of the narrator's naivete. She was in fact twenty-nine. Bagnold went on to enjoy a distinguished career as a novelist and is perhaps best known for her children's book, *National Velvet*.

I suffer awfully from my language in this ward. I seem to be the only VAD[1] nurse of whom they continually ask, 'What say, nurse?' It isn't that I use long words, but my sentences seem to be inverted.

An opportunity for learning to speak simple Saxon ...

'An antitetanic injection for Corrigan,' said Sister.[2] And I went to the dispensary to fetch the syringe and the needles.

'But has he any symptoms?' I asked. In a Tommies'[3] ward one dare ask anything; there isn't that mystery which used to surround the officers' illnesses.

'Oh, no,' she said, 'it's just that he hasn't had his full amount in France.'

So I hunted up the spirit-lamp[4] and we prepared it, talking of it.

But we forget to talk of it to Corrigan. The needle was into his shoulder before he knew why his shirt was held up.

His wrath came like an avalanche; the discipline of two years was forgotten, his Irish tongue was loosened. Sister shrugged her shoulders and laughed; I listened to him as I cleaned the syringe.

I gathered that it was the indignity that had shocked his sense of individual pride. 'Treating me like a cow ...' I heard him say to Smiff – who laughed, since it wasn't his shoulder that carried the serum.

---

[1] Voluntary Aid Detachment, a volunteer corps of non-professional nurses' aides.
[2] A nursing sister; i.e. a registered nurse, not a religious sister. VAD's were addressed as 'nurse.'
[3] Enlisted men, as opposed to officers.
[4] To disinfect the needle.

Smiff laughed: he has been in hospital nine months, and his theory is that a Sister may do anything at any moment; his theory is that nothing does any good – that if you don't fuss you don't get worse. Corrigan was angry all day; the idea that 'a bloomin' woman should come an' shove something into me system' was too much for him. But he forgets himself: there are no individuals now; his 'system' belongs to us.

Sister said, laughing, to Smiff the other day, 'Your leg is mine.'

'Wrong again; it's the Governmint's!' said Smiff. But Corrigan is Irish and doesn't like that joke.

There are times when my heart fails me; when my eyes, my ears, my tongue, and my understanding fail me; when pain means nothing to me ...

In the bus yesterday, I came down from London sitting beside a Sister from another ward, who held her hand to her ear and shifted in her seat.

She told me she had earache and we didn't talk, and I sat huddled in my corner and watched the names of the shops, thinking, as I was more or less forced to do by her movements, of her earache.

What struck me was her own angry bewilderment before the fact of her pain. 'But it hurts ... You've no idea how it hurts!' She was surprised.

Many times a day she hears the words, 'Sister, you're hurtin' me ... Couldn't you shift my heel? It's like a toothache,' and other similar sentences. I hear them in our ward all the time. One can't pass down the ward without some such request falling on one's ears.

She is astonished at her earache; she is astonished at what pain can be; it is unexpected. She is ready to be angry with herself, with her pain, with her ear. It is monstrous ... she thinks.

The pain of one creature cannot continue to have a meaning for another. It is almost impossible to nurse a man well whose pain you do not imagine. A deadlock!

One has illuminations all the time!

There is an old lady who visits in our ward, at whom, for one or two unimportant reasons, it is the custom to laugh. The men, who fall in with our moods with a docility which I am beginning to suspect is a mask, admit too that she is comic.

This afternoon, when she was sitting by Corrigan's bed and talking to him I saw where her treatment of him differed from ours. She treats him as though he were an individual; but there is more in it than that ... She treats him as though he had a wife and children, a house and a back garden and responsibilities: in some manner she treats him as though he had dignity.

I thought of yesterday's injection. That is the difference: that is what the Sisters mean when they say 'the boys.'

* * *

It was the first time I had a man sing at his dressing. I was standing at the sterilizer when Rees's song began to mount over the screen that hid him from me. ('Whatever is that?' 'Rees's tubes going in.')

It was like this: 'Ah ... ee ... oo, Sister!' and again: 'Sister ... oo ... ee ... ah!' Then a little scream and his song again.

I heard her voice: 'Now then, Rees, I don't call that much of a song.' She called me to make his bed, and I saw his left ear was full of tears.

O visitors, who come into the ward in the calm of the long afternoon, when the beds are neat and clean and the flowers out on the tables and the VAD's sit sewing at splints and sandbags, when the men look like men again and smoke and talk and read ... if you could see what lies beneath the dressings!

When one shoots at a wooden figure it makes a hole. When one shoots at a man it makes a hole, and the doctor must make seven others.

I heard a blackbird sing in the middle of the night last night – two bars, and then another. I thought at first it might be a burglar whistling to his mate in the black and rustling garden.

But it was a blackbird in a nightmare.

Those distant guns again tonight ...[5]

Now a lull and now a bombardment; again a lull, and then batter, batter, and the windows. Is the lull when *they* go over the top?

I can only think of death tonight. I tried to think just now, 'What is it, after all! Death comes anyway; this only hastens it.' But that won't do; no philosophy helps the pain of death. It is pity, pity, pity, that I feel, and sometimes a sort of shame that I am here to write at all.

Summer ... Can it be summer through whose hot air the guns shake and tremble? The honeysuckle, whose little stalks twinkled and shone that January night, has broken at each woody end into its crumbled flower.

Where are the frost, the snow? ... Where are the dead?

---

[5] The sound of a bombardment at the Front, which could be heard in England.

Where are my trouble and my longing, and the other troubles, and the happiness in other summers?

Alas, the long history of life! There is that in death that makes the throat contract and the heart catch: everything is written in water.

We talk of tablets to the dead. There can be none but in the heart, and the heart fades.

MARY BORDEN

(1886–1968)

A wealthy American from Chicago, Mary Borden worked in a hospital unit she herself set up at the Front from 1914 until 1918. Her short stories and sketches in *The Forbidden Zone* (1929) combine brief vignettes written during or shortly after the War with short stories (among them 'Blind') written later, reflecting her post-war assessment of the meaning of her experience.

BLIND

The door at the end of the baraque[1] kept opening and shutting to let in the stretcher bearers. As soon as it opened a crack the wind scurried in and came hopping toward me across the bodies of the men that covered the floor, nosing under the blankets, lifting the flaps of heavy coats, and burrowing among the loose heaps of clothing and soiled bandages. Then the grizzled head of a stretcher bearer would appear, butting its way in, and he would emerge out of the black storm into the bright fog that seemed to fill the place, dragging the stretcher after him, and then the old one at the other end of the load would follow, and they would come slowly down the centre of the hut looking for a clear place on the floor.

The men were laid out in three rows on either side of the central alley way. It was a big hut, and there were about sixty stretchers in each row. There was a space between the heads of one row and the feet of another row, but no space to pass between the stretchers of the same row; they touched. The old territorials[2] who worked with me passed up and down between the heads and feet. I had a squad of thirty of these old orderlies and two sergeants and two priests, who were expert dressers. Wooden screens screened off the end of the hut opposite the entrance. Behind these were the two dressing tables where the priests dressed the wounds of the new arrivals and got them

---

[1] Barrack.
[2] Members of a service organized for home defense; it enlisted men past the age of active service.

ready for the surgeons, after the old men had undressed them and washed their feet. In one corner was my kitchen where I kept all my syringes and hypodermic needles and stimulants.

It was just before midnight when the stretcher bearers brought in the blind man, and there was no space on the floor anywhere; so they stood waiting, not knowing what to do with him.

I said from the floor in the second row, 'Just a minute, old ones. You can put him here in a minute.' So they waited with the blind man suspended in the bright, hot misty air between them, like a pair of old horses in shafts with their heads down, while the little boy who had been crying for his mother died with his head on my breast. Perhaps he thought the arms holding him when he jerked back and died belonged to some woman I had never seen, some woman waiting somewhere for news of him in some village, somewhere in France. How many women, I wondered, were waiting out there in the distance for news of these men who were lying on the floor? But I stopped thinking about this the minute the boy was dead. It didn't do to think. I didn't as a rule, but the boy's very young voice had startled me. It had come through me as a real voice will sound sometimes through a dream, almost waking you, but now it had stopped, and the dream was thick round me again, and I laid him down, covered his face with the brown blanket and called two other old ones.

'Put this one in the corridor to make more room here,' I said; and I saw them lift him up. When they had taken him away, the stretcher bearers who had been waiting brought the blind one and put him down in the cleared space. They had to come round to the end of the front row of heads; they had to be very careful where they stepped; they had to lower the stretcher cautiously so as not to jostle the men on either side (there was just no room), but these paid no attention. None of the men lying packed together on the floor noticed each other in this curious dream-place.

I had watched this out of the corner of my eye, busy with something that was not very like a man. The limbs seemed to be held together only by the strong stuff of the uniform. The head was unrecognizable. It was a monstrous thing, and a dreadful rattling sound came from it. I looked over and saw the chief surgeon standing over me. I don't know how he got there. His small shrunken face was wet and white; his eyes were brilliant and feverish; his incredible hands that saved so many men so exquisitely, so quickly, were in the pockets of his white coat.

'Give him morphine,' he said, 'a double dose. As much as you like.' He pulled a cigarette out of his pocket. 'In cases like this, if I am not about, give morphine; enough, you understand.'

Then he vanished like a ghost. He went back to his operating room, a small white figure with round shoulders, a magician, who performed miracles with knives. He went away through the dream.

I gave the morphine, then crawled over and looked at the blind man's ticket. I did not know, of course, that he was blind until I read his ticket. A large round white helmet covered the top half of his head and face; only his nostrils and mouth and chin were uncovered. The surgeon in the dressing station behind the trenches had written on his ticket, 'Shot through the eyes. Blind.'

Did he know, I asked myself. No, he couldn't know yet. He would still be wondering, waiting, hoping, down there in that deep, dark silence of his, in his own dark personal world. He didn't know he was blind; no one would have told him. I felt his pulse. It was strong and steady. He was a long, thin man, but his body was not very cold and the pale lower half of his clear-cut face was not very pale. There was something beautiful about him. In his case there was no hurry, no necessity to rush him through to the operating room. There was plenty of time. He would always be blind.

One of the orderlies was going up and down with hot tea in a bucket. I beckoned to him.

I said to the blind one, 'Here is a drink.' He didn't hear me so I said it more loudly against the bandage, and helped him to lift his head, and held the tin cup to his mouth below the thick end of the bandage. I did not think then of what was hidden under the bandage. I think of it now. Another head case across the hut had thrown off his blanket and risen from his stretcher. He was standing stark naked except for his head bandage, in the middle of the hut and was haranguing the crowd in a loud voice with the gestures of a political orator. But the crowd, lying on the floor, paid no attention to him. They did not notice him. I called to Gustave and Pierre to go to him.

The blind man said to me, 'Thank you, sister, you are very kind. That is good. I thank you.' He had a beautiful voice. I noticed the great courtesy of his speech. But they were all courteous. Their courtesy when they died, their reluctance to cause me any trouble by dying or suffering, was one of the things it didn't do to think about.

Then I left him, and presently forgot that he was there waiting in the second row of stretchers on the left side of the long crowded floor.

Gustave and Pierre had got the naked orator back onto his stretcher and were wrapping him up again in his blankets. I let them deal with him and went back to my kitchen at the other end of the hut, where my syringes and hypodermic needles were boiling in saucepans. I had received by post that morning a dozen beautiful new platinum needles. I was very pleased with them. I said to one of the dressers as I fixed a needle on my syringe and held it up, squirting the liquid through it: 'Look. I've some lovely new needles.' He said: 'Come and help me a moment. Just cut this bandage, please.' I went over to the dressing-table. He darted off to a voice that was shrieking somewhere. There was a man stretched on the table. His brain came off in my hands when I lifted the bandage from his head.

When the dresser came back I said: 'His brain came off on the bandage.'

'Where have you put it?'

'I put it in the pail under the table.'

'It's only one half of his brain,' he said, looking into the man's skull. 'The rest is here.'

I left him to finish the dressing and went about my own business. I had much to do.

It was my business to sort out the wounded as they were brought in from the ambulances and to keep them from dying before they got to the operating rooms: it was my business to sort out the nearly dying from the dying. I was there to sort them out and tell how fast life was ebbing in them. Life was leaking away from all of them; but with some there was no hurry, with others it was a case of minutes. It was my business to create a counter-wave of life, to create the flow against the ebb. It was like a tug of war with the tide. The ebb of life was cold. When life was ebbing the man was cold; when it began to flow back, he grew warm. It was all, you see, like a dream. The dying men on the floor were drowned men cast up on the beach, and there was the ebb of life pouring away over them, sucking them away, an invisible tide; and my old orderlies, like old sea-salts out of a lifeboat, were working to save them. I had to watch, to see if they were slipping, being dragged away. If a man were slipping quickly, being sucked down rapidly, I sent runners to the operating rooms. There were six operating rooms on either side of my hut. Medical students in white coats hurried back and forth along the covered corridors between us. It was my business to know which of the wounded could wait and which could not. I had to decide for myself. There was no one to tell me. If I made any mistakes, some would die on their stretchers on the floor under my eyes who need not have died. I didn't worry. I didn't think. I was too busy, too absorbed in what I was doing. I had to judge from what was written on their tickets and from the way they looked and they way they felt to my hand. My hand could tell of itself one kind of cold from another. They were all half-frozen when they arrived, but the chill of their icy flesh wasn't the same as the cold inside them when life was almost ebbed away. My hands could instantly tell the difference between the cold of the harsh bitter night and the stealthy cold of death. Then there was another thing, a small fluttering thing. I didn't think about it or count it. My fingers felt it. I was in a dream, led this way and that by my cute[3] eyes and hands that did many things, and seemed to know what to do.

Sometimes there was no time to read the ticket or touch the pulse. The door kept opening and shutting to let in the stretcher-bearers whatever I was doing. I could not watch when I was giving piqures;[4] but, standing by my table filling a syringe, I could look down over the rough forms that covered the floor and pick out at a distance this one and that one. I had been doing this for two years, and had learned to read the signs. I could tell from the way they twitched, from the peculiar shade of a pallid face, from the look of tight pinched-in nostrils, and in other ways which I could not have explained, that this or that one was slipping over the edge of the beach of life. Then I would go quickly with my long saline needles, or short thick camphor oil needles, and send one of the old ones hurrying quickly along the corridor to the operating rooms. But sometimes there was no need to hurry; sometimes I was too late; with some there was no longer any question of the ebb and flow of life and death; there was nothing to do.

The hospital throbbed and hummed that night like a dynamo. The operating rooms were ablaze; twelve surgical équipes[5] were at work; boilers steamed and whistled; nurses hurried in and out of the sterilizing rooms carrying big shining metal boxes and enamelled trays; feet were running, slower feet shuffling. The hospital was going full steam ahead. I had a sense of great power, exhilaration and excitement. A loud wind was howling. It was throwing itself like a pack of wolves against the flimsy wooden walls, and the guns were

---

[3] Acute, shrewd.
[4] Shots.
[5] Teams.

growling. Their voices were dying away. I thought of them as a pack
of beaten dogs, slinking away across the fields where the dead were
lying and the wounded who had not yet been picked up, their only
cover the windy blanket of the bitter November night.

And I was happy. It seemed to me that the crazy crowded bright
hot shelter was a beautiful place. I thought, 'This is the second
battlefield. The battle is now going on over the helpless bodies of these
men. It is we who are doing the fighting now, with their real enemies.'
And I thought of the chief surgeon, the wizard working like lightning
through the night, and all the others wielding their flashing knives
against the invisible enemy. The wounded had begun to arrive at noon.
It was now past midnight, and the door kept opening and shutting
to let in the stretcher-bearers, and the ambulances kept lurching in
at the gate. Lanterns were moving through the windy dark from
shed to shed. The nurses were out there in the scattered huts, putting
the men to bed when they came over the dark ground, asleep from
the operating rooms. They would wake up in clean warm beds – those
who did wake up.

'We will send you the dying, the desperate, the moribund,' the
Inspector-General had said. 'You must expect a thirty per cent.
mortality.' So we had got ready for it; we had organized to dispute
that figure.

We had built brick ovens, four of them, down the centre of the hut,
and on top of these, galvanised iron cauldrons were steaming. We had
driven nails all the way down the wooden posts that held up the roof
and festooned the posts with red rubber hot-water bottles. In the
corner near to my kitchen we had partitioned off a cubicle, where we
built a light bed, a rough wooden frame lined with electric light
bulbs, where a man could be cooked back to life again. My own
kitchen was an arrangement of shelves for saucepans and syringes
and needles of different sizes, and cardboard boxes full of ampoules
of camphor oil and strychnine and caffeine and morphine, and large
ampoules of sterilized salt and water, and dozens of beautiful sharp
shining needles were always on the boil.

It wasn't much to look at, this reception hut. It was about as
attractive as a goods yard in a railway station, but we were very
proud of it, my old ones and I. We had got it ready, and it was good
enough for us. We could revive the cold dead there; snatch back the
men who were slipping over the edge; hoist them out of the dark abyss
into life again. And because our mortality at the end of three months
was only nineteen per cent., well, it was the most beautiful place in

the world to me and my old grizzled Pépères,[6] Gaston and Pierre and Leroux and the others were to me like shining archangels. But I didn't think about this. I think of it now. I only knew it then, and was happy. Yes, I was happy there.

Looking back, I do not understand that woman – myself – standing in that confused goods yard filled with bundles of broken human flesh. The place by one o'clock in the morning was a shambles. The air was thick with steaming sweat, with the effluvia of mud, dirt, blood. The men lay in their stiff uniforms that were caked with mud and dried blood, their great boots on their feet; stained bandages showing where a trouser leg or a sleeve had been cut away. Their faces gleamed faintly, with a faint phosphorescence. Some who could not breathe lying down were propped on their stretchers against the wall, but most were prone on their backs, staring at the steep iron roof.

The old orderlies moved from one stretcher to another, carefully, among the piles of clothing, boots and blood-soaked bandages – careful not to step on a hand or a sprawling twisted foot. They carried zinc pails of hot water and slabs of yellow soap and scrubbing brushes. They gathered up the heaps of clothing, and made little bundles of the small things out of pockets, or knelt humbly, washing the big yellow stinking feet that protruded from under the brown blankets. It was the business of these old ones to undress the wounded, wash them, wrap them in blankets, and put hot water bottles at their feet and sides. It was a difficult business peeling the stiff uniform from a man whose hip or shoulder was fractured, but the old ones were careful. Their big peasant hands were gentle – very, very gentle and careful. They handled the wounded men as if they were children. Now, looking back, I see their rough powerful visages, their shaggy eyebrows, their big, clumsy, gentle hands. I see them go down on their stiff knees; I hear their shuffling feet and their soft gruff voices answering the voices of the wounded, who are calling to them for drinks, or to God for mercy.

The old ones had orders from the commandant not to cut the good cloth of the uniforms if they could help it, but they had orders from me not to hurt the men, and they obeyed me. They slit up the heavy trousers and slashed across the stiff tunics with long scissors and pulled very slowly, very carefully at the heavy boots, and the wounded men did not groan or cry out very much. They were mostly very quiet. When they did cry out they usually apologized for the annoyance of

---

[6] Grandpas.

their agony. Only now and then a wind of pain would sweep over the floor, tossing the legs and arms, then subside again.

I think that woman, myself, must have been in a trance, or under some horrid spell. Her feet are lumps of fire, her face is clammy, her apron is splashed with blood; but she moves ceaselessly about with bright burning eyes and handles the dreadful wreckage of men as if in a dream. She does not seem to notice the wounds or the blood. Her eyes seem to be watching something that comes and goes and darts in and out among the prone bodies. Her eyes and her hands and her ears are alert, intent on the unseen thing that scurries and hides and jumps out of the corner on to the face of a man when she's not looking. But quick, something makes her turn. Quick, she is over there, on her knees fighting the thing off, driving it away, and now it's got another victim. It's like a dreadful game of hide and seek among the wounded. All her faculties are intent on it. The other things that are going on, she deals with automatically.

There is a constant coming and going. Medical students run in and out.

'What have you got ready?'

'I've got three knees, two spines, five abdomens, twelve heads. Here's a lung case – hemorrhage. He can't wait.' She is binding the man's chest; she doesn't look up.

'Send him along.'

'Pierre! Gaston! Call the stretcher-bearers to Monsieur D–.' She fastens the tight bandage, tucks the blanket quickly round the thin shoulders. The old men lift him. She hurries back to her saucepans to get a new needle.

A surgeon appears.

'Where's that knee of mine? I left it in the saucepan on the window ledge. I had boiled it up for an experiment.'

'One of the orderlies must have taken it,' she says, putting her old needle on to boil.

'Good God! Did he mistake it?'

'Jean, did you take a saucepan you found on the windowsill?'

'Yes, sister, I took it. I thought it was for the casse croûte; it looked like a ragout of mouton.[7] I have it here.'

'Well, it was lucky he didn't eat it. It was a knee I had cut out, you know.'

---

[7] He thought it looked like left-over mutton stew.

It is time for the old ones 'casse croute.'[8] It is after one o'clock. At one o'clock the orderlies have cups of coffee and chunks of bread and meat. They eat their supper gathered round the stoves where the iron cauldrons are boiling. The surgeons and the sisters attached to the operating rooms are drinking coffee too in the sterilizing rooms. I do not want any supper. I am not hungry. I am not tired. I am busy. My eyes are busy and my fingers. I am conscious of nothing about myself but my eyes, hands and feet. My feet are a nuisance, they are swollen, hurting lumps, but my fingers are perfectly satisfactory. They are expert in the handling of frail glass ampoules and syringes and needles. I go from one man to another jabbing the sharp needles into their sides, rubbing their skins with iodine, and each time I pick my way back across their bodies to fetch a fresh needle I scan the surface of the floor where the men are spread like a carpet, for signs, for my special secret signals of death.

'Aha! I'll catch you out again.' Quick, to that one. That jerking! That sudden livid hue spreading over his form. 'Quick, Emile! Pierre!' I have lifted the blanket. The blood is pouring out on the floor under the stretcher. 'Get the tourniquet. Hold his leg up. Now then, tight – tighter. Now call the stretcher-bearers.'

Someone near is having a fit. Is it epilepsy? I don't know. His mouth is frothy. His eyes are rolling. He tries to fling himself on the floor. He falls with a thud across his neighbour, who does not notice. The man just beyond, propped up against the wall, watches as if from a great distance. He has a gentle patient face; this spectacle does not concern him.

The door keeps opening and shutting to let in the stretcher-bearers. The wounded are carried in at the end door and are carried out to the operating rooms at either side. The sergeant is counting the treasures out of a dead man's pockets. He is tying his little things, his letters and briquet,[9] etc. up in a handkerchief. Some of the old ones are munching their bread and meat in the centre of the hut under the electric light. The others are busy with their pails and scissors. They shuffle about, scrubbing, filling hot-water bottles. I see it all through a mist. It is misty but eternal. It is a scene in eternity, in some strange dream-hell where I am glad to be employed, where I belong, where I am happy. How crowded together we are here. How close we are in this nightmare. The wounded are packed into this place like

---

[8] Snack.
[9] Cigarette lighter.

sardines, and we are so close to them, my old ones and I. I've never been so close before to human beings. We are locked together, the old ones and I, and the wounded men; we are bound together. We all feel it. We all know it. The same thing is throbbing in us, the single thing, the one life. We are one body, suffering and bleeding. It is a kind of bliss to me to feel this. I am a little delirious, but my head is cool enough, it seems to me.

'No, not that one. He can wait. Take the next one to Monsieur D–, and this one to Monsieur Guy, and this one to Monsieur Robert. We will put this one on the electric light bed. He has no pulse. More hot-water bottles here, Gaston.'

'Do you feel cold, mon vieux?'

'Yes, I think so, but pray do not trouble.'

I go with him into the little cubicle, turn on the light bulbs, leave him to cook there; and as I come out again to face the strange heaving dream, I suddenly hear a voice calling me, a new far-away hollow voice.

'Sister! My sister! Where are you?'

I am startled. It sounds so far away, so hollow and so sweet. It sounds like a bell high up in the mountains. I do not know where it comes from. I look down over the rows of men lying on their backs, one close to the other, packed together on the floor, and I cannot tell where the voice comes from. Then I hear it again.

'Sister! Oh, my sister, where are you?'

A lost voice. The voice of a lost man, wandering in the mountains, in the night. It is the blind man, calling. I had forgotten him. I had forgotten he was there. He could wait. The others could not wait. So I had left him and forgotten him.

Something in his voice made me run, made my heart miss a beat. I ran down the centre alley way, round and up again, between the two rows, quickly, carefully stepping across to him over the stretchers that separated us. He was in the second row. I could just squeeze through to him.

'I am coming,' I called to him. 'I am coming.'

I knelt beside him. 'I am here,' I said; but he lay quite still on his back; he didn't move at all; he hadn't heard me. So I took his hand and put my mouth close to his bandaged head and called to him with desperate entreaty.

'I am here. What is it? What is the matter.'

He didn't move even then, but he gave a long, shuddering sigh of relief.

'I thought I had been abandoned here, all alone,' he said softly in his far-away voice.

I seemed to awake then. I looked round me and began to tremble, as one would tremble if one awoke with one's head over a precipice. I saw the wounded packed round us, hemming us in. I saw his comrades, thick round him, and the old ones shuffling about, working and munching their hunks of bread, and the door opening to let in the stretcher bearers. The light poured down on the rows of faces. They gleamed faintly. Four hundred faces were staring up at the roof, side by side. The blind man didn't know. He thought he was alone, out in the dark. That was the precipice, that reality.

'You are not alone,' I lied. 'There are many of your comrades here, and I am here, and there are doctors and nurses. You are with friends here, not alone.'

'I thought,' he murmured in that far-away voice, 'that you had gone away and forgotten me, and that I was abandoned here alone.'

My body rattled and jerked like a machine out of order. I was awake now, and I seemed to be breaking to pieces.

'No,' I managed to lie again. 'I had not forgotten you, nor left you alone.' And I looked down again at the visible half of his face and saw that his lips were smiling.

At that I fled from him. I ran down the long, dreadful hut and hid behind my screen and cowered, sobbing, in a corner, hiding my face.

The old ones were very troubled. They didn't know what to do. Presently I heard them whispering:

'She is tired,' one said.

'Yes, she is tired.'

'She should go off to bed,' another said.

'We will manage somehow without her.'

Then one of them timidly stuck a grizzled head round the corner of the screen. He held his tin cup in his hands. It was full of hot coffee. He held it out, offering it to me. He didn't know of anything else he could do for me.

ELIZABETH SHEPLEY SERGEANT

(1881–1965)

Something of a protégé of Willa Cather, Sergeant went to France as a correspondent for the *New Republic*, then a weekly journal of left political commentary. While touring a 'safe' battlefield a few weeks before the Armistice, she was seriously wounded by a grenade in an accident which killed another member of the group and cost their French lieutenant escort his arm. She spent the next six months recuperating in hospitals in France, writing the diaries and notes on which *Shadow Shapes: The Journal of a Wounded Woman* (1920) is based. Her experience in France strained her friendship with Cather, who she felt was romanticizing the war in her best-selling novel, *One of Ours*.

OCTOBER 21, 1918

I am not to be persuaded that love of adventure makes war good, any more than the spirit of sacrifice, or the patient endurance of pain. Is it good for the world, for his mother, or for the boy himself, who is so gifted for life, that Rick[1] should be killed? And for how many individuals of the millions of fighters has this war, after all, been good? To prolong it by one unnecessary day, hour, minute, would be criminally wrong – of that, at least, I am sure, after the evacuation tent.[2]

Like the soldier, I feel no bitterness and very little surprise at my individual lot. At every stage I have said to myself: 'So this is what it is like' – to drive from hospital to hospital, for instance; or to lie on the floor interminably while indifferent people walk about and brush your face with a foot or a skirt. Certainly I did not want to be hurt. But I have still less right than the soldier to complain. Voluntarily, for the sake of my profession I ran a risk – slight it seemed – and luck was against me.

Mine is no more than a pin-point of sharp experience in the vast catastrophe. Yet its stab unites me to millions of other human beings.

---

[1] The son of a close friend. His brother had already died of pneumonia in France before reaching the Front.
[2] Where she was brought immediately following her injury.

To the little *poilu*[3] of the hospital who, under other circumstances might have accepted a franc for carrying my bag across a platform. *Unanimisme*[4]... what potency it has. It is that which keeps the war going. Every American in Europe today, however bad his fate, feels in his heart of hearts glad to be here. Glad not to miss the great adventure of the years 1914–1918. For whether war be good or bad, whether it means purgation or damnation for civilization, it is still the adventure of these years. And if one shares, why not up to the hilt? Why not pay the piper?

But not to let others. Not the little *poilu*. Not the man with no face. Nothing must happen to Ernest, far from his wife and baby. The war must end before Mary loses her second son. Before Rick goes down in flames.[5]

* * *

NOVEMBER 23, 1918

In the American Hospital at Neuilly, a suburb of Paris.

A certain amount of bad pain may be good for the moral character – I may as well think so, though I don't really believe in Purgatory. But pain prolonged is degeneration, not purgation. I am losing, coin by coin, the last of the treasure of 'patience' I have been so carefully hoarding. It has reached the point that I want to remove the head of anyone who merely walks boldly across my floor, thereby causing a faint vibration of my iron bed, which at once communicates itself to my hyper-responsive ankle. I have learned, among my pillows, an art of timid stillness that would give points to a mummy. At moments, as after dressings, it seems quite too perilous to take a long breath.

The reaction of the medical and nursing *entourage* to suffering whose prolongation they see no good reason for – as the infection is clearing up and the fractures presumably knitting – is interesting. Colonel Lambert meets it as a medical man, with specific remedies;

---

[3] A badly wounded enlisted man she observed while she was being treated for her wound.

[4] Literally, 'unanimousism,' the spirit of unanimity.

[5] These were all close friends. Mary was Rick's mother.

he disapproves heartily of my wasting away on hospital chicken broth. Dr. M., who hates suffering, meets it as a surgeon by keeping out of my room save when he is led here for a dressing by one of the nurses who rule his day. Miss O. is very sympathetic that I can't enjoy the hothouse fruit provided by kind friends, but turns prickly when a spasm comes; irritated with herself, I suspect (she is so good and conscientious) because she has not been able to prevent it. A certain gentle, kinky-haired, red-cheeked English night nurse with a cockney accent is the only person who can really arrange my fracture pillows. I begin to understand the New Testament when, after two hours sometimes of weary waiting for her, I feel her healing touch.

She has charge of the babies who occasionally come into the world on the top floor and this morning, against all law and order, she brought one in to me, at the pallid and cynical hour of two. A Swedish baby about three weeks old which, when unrolled from its warm, sweet-smelling blankets, blinked wisely at the light. A miracle of a baby, complete in every detail! Not a bone missing!

What saves me is that I am, even in my worst hours, more concerned with life and its mysteries than with the dykes that fate has built to hem it in and hinder its flow. But sometimes I am aware of what a vicarious version of 'life' I am getting – all through other people's eyes. Even the baby was held up at a distance. I am impatient to touch life again, to feel it swirling hard against my own body.

Life took me at my word. I am still shaken from head to foot by the shock of immersion. Dr. M. (more regardful than Miss O. and I gave him credit for) appeared to announce my immediate departure to 'Number One' to be X-rayed. Before I knew it, the revolution was accomplished: a stretcher with several privates to hoist it had invaded my domain from the garden, and I was lying in an ambulance with keen outdoor air – how rough to the nostrils – rushing in at the open end, and a blurred vision of Neuilly flowing along behind: comfortable, high, brick bourgeois mansions draped, above their discreet gardens, in the flags of victory. The ambulance boy did his best for me – 'I never went so slow before' – but the jolting was excruciating on these boulevards rutted so deeply by four years of ambulances. It took no more than one jolt to translate me again into *unanimisme*.

The sensation of being translated into the body of a soldier, and into the 'system' in which he lives and moves and has his being was further borne out as follows: (*a*) Irksome delay at the next door. (*b*)

Hot altercation between ambulance boy and sergeant in charge. The former claims this entrance will save the patient; the latter 'knows his orders' – so we eventually jolt along to the other one. (*c*) Appearance on the steps, as the stretcher is taken out, of two or three pretty nurse's aides of our best New York families, who gather around (blankets envelop me, and a grey hood like a monk's cowl falls over my head), inquiring in tones whose imperious and patronizing ring make me squirm with indignity, who this poor dear boy is, etc. (*d*) Journey the whole length of the hospital on a jiggly stretcher-cart to an elevator that isn't running. Journey the whole distance back to another that goes up only two stories. Thereafter journey the same distance back again to a long flight of stairs up which I am carried at an angle of forty-five degrees to the X-ray room. (*e*) *Interim* – endless wait by the second elevator (man having his lunch) in a corridor full of French *femmes de service* who are carrying lunch trays to the wards. Unimaginable clatter of dishes, chatter of ten thousand magpies. The new patient intrigues the magpies, especially the youngish specimens, and they close in two or three deep about the stretcher-cart, gazing at the drawn features under the cowl with tilted, frizzed heads and loving, pitying, languorous looks that stifle like a heavy perfume.

Suddenly one soft creature gives away the show: '*On dirait une femme* – you'd say it was a woman,' she breathes.

'It *is* a woman!' I answer furiously.

The ranks simply melt!

The X-ray itself, a skilful doctor in charge, was the least part of the business. But by the time the process *a,b,c,d,e*, etc. had been gone through in reverse order from the top floor on the boulevard Inkermann to the ground floor on the rue Chauveau, I was in a state of acute and agonized exhaustion. There promised to be another wait before I could be moved from the stretcher to the bed – nurses at lunch. But there I spoke up, in the manner of Queen Elizabeth or Amy Lowell, and demanded that the stretcher-boys put me *at once* into the flat, still, waiting bed. (The were only too ready to help, but Miss O. was fearfully shocked.) I then demanded, in the voice of Julius Caesar or Napoleon, a hypodermic. It came too, and quickly (pity I didn't discover earlier how thoroughly it pays to lose one's self-control) and with it a young French nurse with sweet ways and piquant looks, who reminded me of my old friend Annie Wood and who held my hands while the Red Cross nurse – who never holds my hand – we are far too reserved together – had some lunch.

The afternoon was haunted by solicitous faces disappearing into space, and by a queer, faint voice (not at all a royal voice) pleading for silence and solitude: 'Please don't let them come in ... draw the curtains closer ... send them away ... don't let anyone take me out of bed ...'

A pitiable figure of a *unanimiste* I make now.

* * *

JANUARY 2, 1919

* * * The corridor is narrow and dark, and I turned the corner into a very bright gallery which is entirely glass, opening on the garden. There stands the white table of the floor-nurse, with her records; there stand a few inviting wicker chairs (into one of which I was assisted, with trembling knees); and there, above all, on a white bed that seems to grow out of banks of flowers, with a big blue bow on her bobbed black hair, lies one of the most charming young French girls I have ever seen.

My nurse has been telling me much about 'Mademoiselle V.' – how she has been in the hospital since May – that is some eight months – under the care of the Red Cross, with an abscess of the lung due to careless throat treatment in a hospital when she was nursing our soldiers. How she is quite alone in the world, deserted by her French family because she refused to marry the young man of their choice. How she is the *enfant gâtée*[6] of the American Hospital, the friend of the little nurses, the darling of the doctor, the doughboy's delight. How she is often in pain and feverish; how she sometimes cries; how she may never recover, but is intensely social, and manages to stop everyone on the way to the rooms beyond; nurses, doctors, visitors, caught by her perfume as bees are attracted to a flower, forced by her sweetness to give her attention, and kindness, and gifts, and news of the world.

* * * I was helped to a seat beside her and we had a little talk: about New Orleans, where she was brought up (that may account for her revolt against French family tradition) and France where she was born. She came back just before the war, and doesn't know which country she loves better. She speaks with great vivacity, with the prettiest

---

[6] Spoiled child; pet.

gestures of her plump and rounded arms, while the curves of her cheeks flush red out of a skin warm as a white pearl. She radiates health, one would say – something supremely good and sane as well as supremely alluring. But over her pillow hovers a shadow. Where had I seen that shadow before? ... Fate ... Disaster ... I last saw it over the heads of the young soldiers. How blind to suppose that the end of the war had placed timeless youth beyond the reach of that dark wing!

Sergeant sailed for home in May 1919 aboard the troopship *Rochambeau*. About to disembark, she wrote:

For adventure was only the keen edge of the experience with which our slow-moving *Rochambeau* is so heavily laden. Tragedy was its blade. I catch an arrowy flash in the clear American sunshine, where young men in civilian clothes move swift beyond the waiting crowds. Their busy patterns of life are traced in something hard and bright.

 * * * It is tomorrow which cows us, as a high tragedian said long ago. The Coming Thing, greater perhaps than today or yesterday. throbbing out its portent in the dark hospital night, looming and lurking behind the images of a distance shore.

KATHLEEN DAYUS

(b. 1903)

Dayus grew up in the slums of Birmingham, England and left school at the age of fourteen to go to work. Her first job was in a small munitions shop during the First World War. Prompted by a grandchild's curiosity about her life, Dayus wrote the story of her early years, *Her People*, in a school notebook. Some years later, that child showed the book to her history teacher, who arranged for its publication in 1982. Dayus became something of a celebrity, especially after portions of her book became the basis for a television series. She has gone on to complete the story of her life in three more volumes, from one of which, *Where There's Life* (1985) the following is selected.

On the following Monday morning, Mum gave me twopence for a bath at the public ones in Northwood Street where I went now that I was a 'big girl,' and sixpence for my medical which I had to have before I could work in a factory. I bundled up my new clothes and set off. It was heavenly to stretch out in such a big bath and soak in gallons of hot soapy water; I could have stayed there all day, but I knew I had to go out and look for a job before long.

She and her friend Nelly are hired to learn to operate a mechanical press at a factory doing war sub-contracting.

'Please Madam,' I asked, "ow much will the wages be?'
'Twelve and six a week,[1] eight o'clock till six and one o'clock on Saturdays. Yow get fifteen minutes for lunch and one till two dinnertime and yow'll clock in and out. I'll put yow right, an' if yow be'ave yerself and work 'ard you'll get a rise to thirteen shillings at the end of the month.'

* * *

---

[1] About half the nationwide standard for women's factory work in 1917 and a little more than one-third of the wages noted in Rathbone's novel.

At five minutes to eight the next day we were standing outside the gate with several roughly dressed women. They pushed Nelly and me to one side when the gate opened, clocked in and went off up the yard, disappearing up the steps without exchanging a word. We were standing there, hesitant, when a voice boomed out 'Follow me.' It was madam, the forewoman, dressed in a khaki overall. She was elderly, tall and straight, and very serious: I never remember her smiling. She showed us how to clock in with our timecard and then we followed her along the cobbled yard and up the greasy steps into the workshop.

The women who we'd seen previously were already busy operating the presses. At the end of the shop were smaller machines driven by an electric motor on the wall which worked the leather pulleys that ran along the ceiling. The workshop was dirty and reeked of oil. In the centre of the room was a large, battered pipe stove filled with glowing coke, the smoke from which went up the pipe and out through a hole in the roof. Every now and then smoke billowed into the room and when it did Nelly and I began to cough, but no one else seemed to be affected. They just sat there busily swinging the handles of the presses.

We were each handed khaki overalls like the rest had on; mine came almost to the floor and my cap, when I tried it on, kept slipping over my eyes. The forewoman told me it was the smallest they had. Nelly was taller than me and had more hair to fill her cap with.

'Come along you two,' she snapped at us. 'You can work the guillotine,' she said to Nelly.

As soon as she had Nelly settled in she came back to me and showed me how to use the press to cut brass blanks from strips of scrap metal. I soon picked the job up but she came several times that morning to see how I was getting along.

'We don't want any scrap left,' was all she said. She examined the blanks I had made and seemed satisfied, and that made me work harder. Then I noticed the other women along the bench were giving me black looks but I had no idea why.

At break time when I was standing eating my corned beef sandwich, one of the women shouted over to me.

'Yow've got my job an' it's the best in the shop!'

They were all about to join in when Madam appeared and warned them if there was any more trouble they would be reported to the gaffer.[2] They went on eating in silence. One of the women came over

---

[2] The boss.

and offered me her place by the fire but I was too scared to move and anyway it was too late because just then the bell rang for us to start work again. I hadn't finished my sandwich so I wrapped it up and put it in my overall pocket. I was surprised I hadn't seen Nelly but I found out later that she'd walked out because she didn't like the place or the work. But I did. It was satisfying work cutting out the shilling-sized blanks and stacking them in three dozens. Afterwards, I took them to the drilling machine where Minnie, the woman who had offered me her place, showed me how to drill four holes in them. I was proud to be doing my bit for King and Country when I was told they were brass trouser buttons for the Army.

When one o'clock came and I was clocking out, Minnie came up to me and spoke. She was a small, thin woman, very pale, and came, she told me, from the Black Country. I asked her why she couldn't get a job nearer home but she said she had seven children and a husband to keep and this was the best paying job she could find. We became very friendly. She looked as old as my Mum with her lined face but she told me she was not yet thirty. She explained why the other women were nasty to me. Apparently they were on piecework, although I hadn't realized this, and I had one of the best jobs. That made me work harder. But when I got my first week's wages I received a shock. Instead of the twelve and six I expected there was only ten shillings and ninepence. I was too embarrassed to ask the other workers why so I plucked up courage and tapped on the office door.

'Come in!' came the voice of the Battleaxe from within.

I edged in timidly and asked if there had been a mistake in my wages.

'No!' came the reply. 'If you read the notice, you'll find it's correct.'

'What notice?' I asked; this was the first time I had heard about a notice.

'The girls will show you, now be off. Can't you see I'm busy?'

I went over to Minnie and asked her and she pointed to a notice on the wall at the end of the machine shop. It was small and splashed with oil and almost illegible but I could make this out:

STOPPAGES EACH WEEK
TO BE COLLECTED FROM WAGES

6d.   FOR XMAS FUND
3d.   FOR THE SWEEPER

3d.   FOR THE LAVATORY CLEANER
6d.   FOR THE TEA LADY
3d.   FOR THE LOAN OF OVERALLS AND CAP

I thought about it and reasoned that since we all had to take our turn sweeping and cleaning the lav then next time it was my turn I would receive my fair share. When my turn did come I found that they were dirty, smelly jobs but I did them anyway, thinking of my reward at the end of the week. But when the wages arrived I found the same amount as usual. I demanded an explanation from the other women but they just laughed.

'Silly girl. All the money's pooled together for our outing and Christmas party.' Unfortunately for me I went on neither.

When I returned home with that first week's wages I was afraid to tell my Mum because I knew there would be hell to pay. She would have turned workshop and forewoman inside out, so I gave her the ten shillings she expected and made do with the ninepence: not much for a hard week's work.

I went back on the Monday after I'd discovered my error over the deductions but I was determined to find myself another job. However, during the morning the forewoman came over to where I was pressing the brass buttons and offered to put me on piecework like the others, although I hadn't been there as long as you normally had to have been for this to happen. She told me I could earn more money and I deserved it because I was a good little worker. When she'd gone the other women sent Minnie over to find out what she'd wanted and when Minnie told them they started to laugh and titter. I ignored them and set to as hard as I could, so hard that by the end of the week my fingers were bleeding from many cuts I had from the sharp brass discs. The others tried to compete, I suppose because they still resented me, but I worked even harder. I even slipped back in, unknown to them all, including the forewoman, and worked through my dinner hour; at the end of that week, I'd earned fifteen shillings and fourpence clear. I didn't tell the others but the following Monday the forewoman told me how pleased she was with my 'output.' I didn't tell Mum either; she still had her ten shillings and the rest I hid under the floorboards.

The following week the pace began to tell and I had to slow down because I was tired and lifeless. All I wanted when I finished work at six o'clock was my bed. I was in more trouble at work as well. The women crowded round me, jostling and shouting, making all kinds of threats. I had no idea why until Minnie told me that the piece rates were being cut and it was my fault. And sure enough at the end of the week all I had earned was seven shillings and threepence. It was not even the day rate. That was it! I decided there and then to leave, and I did. I was only glad I had enough to make up Mum's ten shillings.

IRENE RATHBONE

(1892–1980)

When the Great War began, Rathbone was a young actress. She volunteered for war service, working at two YMCA camps in France and as a VAD in London. Her novel, *We That Were Young* (1932), draws upon those experiences as well as upon those of her close friend, Ruby Wyld, who worked in a munitions factory. The following excerpt, while not, strictly speaking, autobiographical, nevertheless provides a convincing account of the life of women munitions workers.

Rows of blue-overalled girls in unbecoming jelly-bag caps sat or stood all day in the long light shed of Staple and Studd's munitions works at Willesden. Two hundred and fifty girls divided into sections according to the different jobs they were doing; three hundred men in other parts of the same vast shed. From eight to five, with an hour's break for lunch, they worked unceasingly.

Many of them came long distances. Liz Fanshawe, whose people kept a small shop in Brixton, took an hour to come. Nellie Crewe, ex-kitchenmaid in a boarding-house, took about the same time from her crowded home in Battersea. Pamela Butler,[1] who sat between them, was luckier. If she caught the right trains and trams she could do the distance from her aunt's door in Curzon Street to the door of the 'shop' in forty-five minutes.

These three, with twenty-seven others, sat at the drilling machines. Perched on high stools, their feet on the cross-bar of the bench in front of them, their left hands held pieces of steel, six inches square, which were to become the backs of signal lamps; their right hands worked the levers which drilled into the plates five holes on five marked places. From the machine up to the ceiling ran broad leather belts which flapped and whirred. The noise made by all the belts together was like a flock of nightmare birds. Added to it was the noise of the drilling of the plates; and from all parts of the shop came a mixed din

---

[1] The middle-class character based on Ruby Wyld.

of rasping, filing, cutting, hammering. Clang, clang, zzz, whrr. Deafening, stupefying, brain-shattering.

Down came Pamela's lever: once, twice ... five times. The plate was thrown on to a pile beside her. Another was picked up, held steady, punched, dropped. She could do thirty to the hour now, like Liz Fanshawe on her right; for the first fortnight she had only been able to do twenty-four. The present pace meant keeping hard at it. Incidentally it meant extra pay on to one's £3 a week, and that was not to be despised.

* * *

At three o'clock, tea was brought round. Pamela never took it. At the best of times she disliked tea, and only drank it if it was expensive China, and extremely weak. Liz swallowed hers at a gulp.

'That's better!' she sighed. 'Now come on, girls! "*Take* me back to dear old *Bli-ghty,* Tum te, tum te, tum te, tum te, *tum*." Lor' that tea ain't 'alf made me sweat! Funny! Think I'll take me cap orf for a minute. Where's old Dick?[2] Don't want '*er* after me body!'

She pulled off the detested head-gear – though it was strictly against orders – and fluffed out her wiry black hair. The breeze from the flapping belt about her blew pleasantly on her hot forehead. She seized her lever.

'"Tiddely-iddely-ighty, carry me back to *Blighty, Blighty – is* the – *place – for – me.*"' The last five notes were considerably slowed down to enable her to punch her plate in time to them.

'Put your cap on again!' shouted Pamela; but the din from the whole shop, and Liz's strident singing, drowned her cry. She waved her hand, pointed to her neighbour's head, and then to her own.

'Not much! I shan't be seen! I feel fine like this!' Her hair was blowing about. '"Birmingham, Leeds or Manchester, I *don't – much – care!*"'

In a second it had happened. She had leant a fraction too far forward, and the wind from the flapping belt had blown her hair into the wheel of the drilling-machine. There was a yell which pierced even the usual racket of the shop, and then big Liz was on her feet, her eyes starting from their sockets, both hands to her head. The front part of it – from the forehead back – had been ripped raw.

---

[2] Miss Dixon, the forewoman.

The belt whirred on. The wheel continued to revolve; but now it had grown a wiry black beard which at each revolution flicked up into sight.

'All right, Liz,' cried Miss Dixon, who had materialized from nowhere, and was holding the screaming girl beneath the arms. 'Steady, steady now. You're all right.'

The girls round about had leapt to their feet; Pamela being nearest was best able to give assistance. But they were all ordered off.

'Get back to your stools!' thundered Miss Dixon, in the voice of a sergeant-major. 'All right, Liz, I'm with you.'

The next minute Liz, with a long moan, had crumpled up, and two St. John Ambulance men, arriving from other parts of the shop, lifted her up and carried her away.

* * *

A week later the interior of the shop presented a much gayer appearance. Gone were the dingy overalls and the shapeless caps. Miss Dixon, with sound instinct about every detail that made for more efficient work from females, had introduced overalls of different colours, and gay handkerchiefs that tied tightly over the head with a knot behind. The place looked like a herbaceous border, and the difference in the spirits of the girls was surprising.

Pamela had been moved from the drills and put, at her own earnest request, on to shell-cases. This was particularly heavy work, and only two women besides herself were engaged on it – the rest were men. It would have been balm to Pamela, in her present temper, to feel that she was dealing with actual explosives – to be filling shells, for instance, instead of merely cleaning and measuring cases – but in these works, in which she had been taken on, there was no active stuff, and she had to be content with the nearest approach to the real thing which obtained.

The fact of having to stand all day – as you had to at the lathes – was wearing enough, but the lifting of the heavy brass shell-cases became back-breaking after a time. Nothing but the energy lent by her revengeful despair[3] could have kept a girl of Pamela's physique at this job for more than a month. Pamela stuck it for nearly two.

Six shell-cases to the hour ... eight cases to the hour ... ten cases to the hour. That was her maximum – and a pretty high one. Beyond

---

[3] The death of Pam's fiancé, Ian, had precipitated her decision to quit nursing and work in munitions.

that she was unable to go. And all the time she thought of Ian. It was a shell like one of these that had splashed his brains into the soil of the Somme country, shattered the arms that had held her so tight, and blown his whole strong, beautiful body into nothingness. She had been given details of his death in a letter – an unimaginative but well-meaning letter from one of his friends – and never, never would she forget. Each time that she heaved one of the shell-cases from the floor on to the fixture in front of her; each time that she turned the great wheel which sent the fixture driving through the case, clearing and hollowing it to the required dimensions; each time that she measured carefully across the diameter of the top to see that the cap would fit exactly, she sent wishes of death with the shell. 'Do the same, my beauty, do the same to the enemy who killed *him*!' Sometimes she felt she was going a little mad.

In her ears the roar of the machinery; under her feet a sodden mat of iron filings mixed with oil and the milk-like 'Gippo' in which the machines were soaked; on her fingers, so delicately kept till now, filth and grit. And hour by hour the shell-cases were removed, and taken to Woolwich to be filled for the Front.

By Christmas Pamela reluctantly and disgustedly had to give it up. She asked for a lighter job.

GRACE MORRIS CRAIG

(1891–1987)

Grace Morris Craig was born in Pembroke, Ontario into a middle-class family of Scots descent. She was the eldest child and only daughter in a family of three children. She was refused admission to the University of Toronto's School of Architecture on the grounds of gender. When the War broke out, her brothers Ramsey and Basil both enlisted and she involved herself in volunteer work at a nearby military base. In 1981, at the age of ninety, she wrote this memoir, *But This Is Our War*, for her grandchildren.

When news reached us that Ramsey was in hospital at Manchester, threatened with blindness,[1] it caused consternation. My parents were able to accept the situation when I announced my plans to go to England as soon as possible to be with him. In reply to my cable, 'Do you want me to come?' Ramsey had wired, 'Please come.'

After a few days of consideration my mother decided to accompany me. When they heard of our venture, Welland's mother, Mrs Williams, and her sister Ada Dickson agreed to come along as well. We needed only passports in order to make the trip, and we obtained these easily from Ottawa within the week. Within ten days we were all on board the Canadian Pacific liner *Missanabie,* sister ship of the *Metagama* on which Basil had sailed at the beginning of the year, bound for England from Montreal.

For me it was an exciting first trip across the Atlantic. But there were dangers as well. In May of the previous year the Cunard liner *Lusitania* had been sunk off the British Isles by a German submarine with the loss of over a thousand lives. Passenger liners were still going back and forth in late 1916, but some of them were known to be carrying troops and therefore liable to enemy attack. The *Missanabie* was itself torpedoed toward the end of the war.

The ship was very crowded, another sailing having just been cancelled. The four of us had to share a modest stateroom and, to add

---

[1] Ramsey was suffering from 'shell-shock'; his blindness was temporary and evidently the result of the stress of serving at the front. It had the fortunate result of keeping him from the Battle of the Somme.

to the discomfort, the sea was very rough. The majority of the passengers were women and children, the families of men in the Canadian forces who had connections in the British Isles, many having been born there. The only 'military' on board was a group of young men in civilian clothes who were going to England to be trained in the Royal Flying Corps. They made life interesting for some young women I knew, who came to my cabin each day begging me to join them and play the piano; when I remained in my berth they borrowed my music and even some of my clothes. I was too seasick to care.

On reaching the Irish Sea, where submarines were successfully sinking many ships, our lifeboats were swung out on davits ready for a quick abandonment of the ship. This proved unnecessary as a great storm was raging which made it difficult for the enemy 'subs' to operate. Some of the lifeboats were blown away. The captain ordered the passengers to remain in the lounges and listen for the siren. The order was obeyed by all except the very seasick, including me, who remained in their berths and wished the ship would sink.

On landing at Liverpool the nightmare of the voyage quickly faded. There at the dock to meet us was a fine-looking soldier. Ramsey had just been released from hospital to spend a long sick leave while his blindness gradually vanished as he recovered from shell-shock. With our mother, we now travelled to London where we would stay until Basil would have leave from the front and could join us.

* * *

One evening early in December Basil arrived at our hotel in Bedford Square. A group of people were chatting beside the fire in the reception room after dinner and I had joined them. I became aware that a soldier was standing in the darkened hall, smiling quietly, with tousled hair, a haversack on his back. A rush and a hug and I quickly led him to our mother's room. Ramsey was there and the reunion for all of us was an ecstatic occasion. It was as if he had come back from the dead.

First he must remove some of the mud and grime from the trenches. He opened the haversack he had been carrying and was amazed to discover a collection of ferocious-looking war souvenirs; obviously he had picked up the wrong haversack on the channel boat. There was a cudgel studded with nails, a leather thong to slip over the wrist, useful for trench raids, and, the most frightening object, a very large grenade equipped with a wooden handle and streamers. Ramsey, an expert in such things, thought the grenade might not be detonated. The question was how to dispose of this dangerous object. We went out into the darkened streets to find the Thames River, but better than that, after wandering for a while, we found a London 'Bobbie.' He was not overjoyed with the present we gave him but decided it was his duty to take it. Returning to the hotel we were joined by our mother and set out to find a restaurant with good food and music.

Carefully we planned Basil's precious eight-day leave. We decided to go by train to Scotland, the home of our ancestors, which proved to be a perfect place for a holiday. We stayed in Edinburgh at the Caledonian Hotel, which was then in its hey-day, in rooms which looked across the park to the castle on the hill. It was all we had hoped for: the romantic castle, the beautiful park, the ancient streets leading to Holyrood Palace with its bloody history, the shops with familiar Scottish names. We felt at home.

* * *

One day we travelled to Stirling. Looking from the battlements of the castle toward Bannockburn and recalling the famous battle,[2] we felt our Scottish blood stirring, though several generations had passed since our ancestors had crossed the sea. As children we had delighted in stories of the Middle Ages, and now, being alone on the battlements, we amused ourselves playing the parts of ancient warriors, thus forgetting for a little while the war that had brought us all across the Atlantic. As we were leaving to catch our train back to Edinburgh, Basil stopped for a moment to look at an ancient tomb. There lay an effigy of a knight with crossed legs showing that he had been to the Crusades. He stooped to read the inscription and a chilling shadow seemed to pass as he looked up and said, 'Perhaps he is the parfait gentil knight that Chaucer wrote about. He was only twenty-five.'

We travelled back to London by a day train and spent the night in our hotel. Our mother did not sleep that night and wakened us early in the morning. It was raining heavily and with difficulty we secured a horse-drawn cab to take us to the station. As we passed Buckingham Palace we noticed that many rooms were lighted and we wondered if the king got up so early. There were bright lights too in Victoria Station, and much confusion as soldiers rushed to have papers signed before boarding the 'leave' train for the channel port. Basil secured

---

[2] In which Robert the Bruce defeated the English forces under Edward II on June 23, 1314.

a place in the dining-car for breakfast, then came to the end of the car to wave us goodbye. We watched in sadness as the train pulled slowly away, and our one thought was, 'Would we ever see him again?'

It was now December and a few days before Christmas. Ramsey received orders to be ready to rejoin his battalion.

* * *

For a number of reasons I wanted to remain in London. It was exciting to be at the centre of activities and it would mean a great deal to Ramsey and Basil to have me there when they had leave. But there was another reason, which I did not disclose to anyone. Stuart Thorne, whom I had so greatly admired, had not come for Christmas as I had hoped. I had not even heard from him, for his letter was forwarded to me later when I was at home in Canada.

In order to stay in London I had to have a useful job to help support myself and to contribute to the war effort. For some reason which I never learned, my brothers did not wish me to become a V.A.D., doing voluntary work in the hospitals. With a letter to General Thacker, supplied by Colonel G.V. White, I applied for a job at Argyle House, Canadian headquarters in London. At my interview I learned that if I had been able to do shorthand, I would have been welcomed with open arms, but not having this skill, all they could offer me was a filing clerk's job. A quick decision had to be made, as the last ship to Canada on which women would be allowed to travel, because the North Atlantic was becoming so dangerous, would be leaving in a few days. At this moment a cable arrived from my father, begging me to return home with my mother, as there soon would be important work to be done in Canada. Within a few days I was on the *Scandinavian* with my mother and Mrs Williams sailing from Liverpool for home.

* * *

The weeks spent in England had opened our eyes to some of the realities of trench warfare. Adventure and glamour obviously had no part in it. The intelligent young men with whom we had talked over the dinner table in London avoided all reference to the unspeakable horrors and wretched discomforts. These were things they endured. Their only hope and purpose was to survive and to bring it all to a successful conclusion.

I found that the letters from France, which had been kept with care, meant even more to me now that I understood better the conditions under which they had been written.

* * *

In March 1917, Basil was killed. On the intervention of a cousin, a general, Ramsey was safely posted to Scotland, having lived through the Battle of Vimy Ridge. At home, Grace threw herself into the struggle over conscription.[3]

For the first time, women would be allowed to vote, but they would be a very select group – the mothers, wives, and sisters of the men in the overseas forces. The job my father had chosen for me, which he had had in mind many months before when he begged me to return from England, was to organize the women voters of the riding. Upon my return I had taken a course in Isaac Pitman shorthand from a nun at the convent, and I asked several of my friends who had been in the business class there to help me form a committee. We were provided with a well-equipped office on Main Street in Pembroke. Through the nominal rolls of the overseas units we learned who the voters would be and we got in touch by mail with every one of them throughout the large riding. There were no women's meetings called, but it was explained to all of them by letter that the only way they could hope to see their men again was to vote for the Union government and conscription.

On the night of the election, December 17, 1917, people crowded the armouries to hear the results, which came first by telephone in the riding and then by wire from the rest of Canada. The tension was great and angry looks were exchanged; but we had the great satisfaction of having helped to elect a coalition government that would bring in conscription, which we felt was our way of helping to win the war. We expressed our delight in loud cheering and scornful looks for the group of young men who did not like the results.

* * *

---

[3] The Great War was not universally popular in Canada, especially in Quebec and in some of the western provinces with a high proportion of German and Eastern European immigrants. In the hope of solidifying support for a Conscription Act, the women in the category mentioned here were allowed to vote in the Federal election in 1918.

Basil's was not to be the only loss Grace would suffer as a result of the War. After the Armistice, she fell in love with and became engaged to Stuart Thorne, a mining engineer, who had served with her brother Basil.

Before undertaking a strenuous job, a doctor in Toronto suggested [Stuart] should enter a hospital for an examination to locate the source of a continual feeling of fatigue. Nothing definite was found, but it was suggested that he take a holiday in Florida. * * * When he returned to Toronto in the spring of 1920 he accepted the position of mine manager for a new mine being opened by the Trethewey company in Gowganda in northern Ontario. I was not at all deterred when he told me he could offer only complete isolation, and for entertainment a canoe on a nearby lake. It seemed to me a most wonderful adventure.

The rough, strenuous life took its toll after a few months and he began to doubt whether he was strong enough to carry it through. At his request I went to Cobalt and spent a few days as a guest of Mary Rogers while he came down from Gowganda to discuss the situation with me. We walked over the rocky hills and one evening, in bright moonlight, we found ourselves on a foot-bridge close to what had once been Cobalt Lake but was now filled by 'tailings' of the Nipissing Mine. Almost a moonscape, it gleamed like quicksilver, and reminded Stuart of an incident that had happened to him during the war. His unit had been 'dug-in' in a cemetery in France when suddenly the enemy subjected them to an intense artillery bombardment, showering them with skulls and bones and splinters of ancient coffins. It had been horrible – the living and the dead all mixed up – and it remained in his mind as his most gruesome experience of the war. He felt that perhaps he should not have told me about it, but to share the memory with me was a relief.

When I realized the pressure under which he had been living, I offered to marry him the next day in Cobalt and go into the mine with him at once. As the log cabin being built for us was not ready, he could not accept my offer * * *.

Preparations for my arrival were going forward, the cabin nearing completion, when disaster struck in the form of a great forest fire. For days Stuart and his men fought to save the mine workings, but finally he was overcome with exhaustion and had to be taken south to a hospital. There it was found that he had a mysterious and unusual illness which the doctors were unable to diagnose, but they assured him that with rest he would recover. They advised him to give up his mining career and find less strenuous work.

* * *

Stuart did come to spend several months at my home in Pembroke. A symptom of his illness was a persistent cough which my mother diagnosed as bronchitis and treated as she had always done with her children; she made sure also that he had nourishing food and plenty of rest. The result of her nursing was a great improvement in his general health, and in the spring he accepted a job with Ontario Hydro. He found and rented a pretty little house with a garden at Niagara-on-the-Lake.

Our future now looked bright and we planned our wedding for the month of June. The day approached and only the last minute details remained to be completed: final fittings for the wedding dress, invitations to be mailed to close friends. Arrangements for our wedding trip to Quebec City were to be made by the groom on a weekend in Toronto; beautiful roses sent to the bride expressed the joyousness of the approaching day.

It was while attending church with his aunt during his weekend in Toronto that Stuart collapsed. A heart specialist was called and at last the cause of his fatigue was diagnosed. Stuart was dying of endocarditis, an infection in the lining of the heart, resulting from his attack of trench fever at the front in the late spring of 1916; the doctor said, 'He has been killed in action just as if a German bullet had pierced his heart.' Because penicillin had not been discovered, there was no possibility of a cure.

Is all this a dream? A glimmering through the dream of things that were? Or is it the shadow of a dream? The room is filling, mostly with young people. It is heavy with the perfume of masses of flowers. The clergyman, handsome in his white surplice, stands close to the young officer, who appears to be asleep. His eyes are closed. On his khaki tunic gleams a row of bright ribbons. Voices are hushed, the service begins. The words are beautiful but they are not the words I expected to hear at my wedding. Everything is confusing. It must be the shadow of a dream. Now it is finished. They go away.

Alone I wander to the edge of the country, into a quiet valley where a stream flows gently. I sit near the water and listen to its murmuring. Is it deep enough?

The hours slip by. I am alone still, but the anguish is subsiding. The evening sunlight pours through the golden leaves of the delicate birches; I feel overwhelmed by its beauty. In this tragic world, there must be purpose. Perhaps for me it is that I must live to see that the names of the men who gave their lives for this beautiful country should not be forgotten.

IDA B. WELLS-BARNETT

(1862–1931)

Born in Mississippi a slave and the daughter of slaves, Ida B. Wells-Barnett grew up to become a distinguished journalist, a founder of the NAACP, the leader of an effective anti-lynching campaign waged both in the United States (where it had the support of Susan B. Anthony) and in England, and a vigorous defendant of civil rights. When the United States entered the First World War, she was living in Chicago, where she waged militant opposition to racial oppression. Her autobiography, *Crusade for Justice*, written shortly before her death, was published in 1970.

Nineteen seventeen, the year our country went to war, found Chicago and Camp Grant alive with soldiers and with those who had been drafted. Some had already gone overseas and the boys of the regular army were in Texas awaiting transportation. Word was flashed through the country that they had run amuck and shot up the town of Houston, just as a few years before the Negro soldiers were accused of shooting up Brownsville and had been discharged by President Roosevelt for doing so.

The result of the court-martial of those who had fired on the police and the citizens of Houston was that twelve of them were condemned to be hanged and the remaining members of that immediate regiment were sentenced to Leavenworth for different terms of imprisonment. The twelve were afterward hanged by the neck until they were dead and, according to the newspapers, their bodies were thrown into nameless graves. This was done to placate southern hatred.

It seemed to me a terrible thing that our government would take the lives of men who had bared their breasts fighting for the defense of our country. I felt that a protest ought to be made about it, and I feared that unless the Negro Fellowship League did it it would not be done.

Accordingly, we decided to hold a memorial service for the men whose lives had been taken and in that way utter a solemn protest. We felt that the government itself could not help but heed if we had a crowded outpouring of our people, at a meeting which would reflect dignity and credit upon us as a race. My first act was to put in an order with a button manufacturer downtown in order to have the buttons ready for distribution at our coming memorial service.

I then called the pastors of several of our large churches and asked which one of them would donate us the use of a church for the Sunday afternoon. I had imagined they all felt as I did about the matter but was again given one of the many surprises of my life when every single pastor refused to let us have the use of the church. I felt it all the more keenly because almost every church in town had military services urging the boys to go to war and every congregation had done its bit by organizing nurse training classes, by meeting trains with cigarettes and sweets to give our boys who were passing through, by patriotic demonstrations, by Liberty Loan drives, by every sort of means which could fire the hearts of our young men to offer their lives if need be in defense of this government. The churches all did their bit along that line; yet they couldn't see that it was a duty which they owed to the youth of our race to protest to the government when they had been badly treated.

Of course when I could not get a church in which to have the kind of meeting we wanted to stage, there was nothing for me to do but distribute the buttons to those who wanted to buy them and thus reimburse us for the money we had spent in having them made.

One morning very soon after we began distributing those buttons, a reporter for the *Herald Examiner* came into the office and asked to see one. I gave it to him and told him that the purpose was to give to every member of our race who wanted to wear one in protest an opportunity to do so. I did not tell him that I was distributing them in this way because I was unable to get a church in which to hold a meeting. I didn't want the white people to know that we were so spineless as to not realize our duty to make a protest in the name of the black boys who had been sacrificed to race hatred. And I am telling it here for the first time.

The reporter went away with a button, and in less than two hours men from the secret service bureau came into the office with a picture of the button which I had given to the reporter. They inquired for me, showed me the button, and told me that they had been sent out to warn me that if I distributed those buttons I was liable to be arrested. 'On what charge?' I asked. One of the men, the smaller of the two, said, 'Why, for treason.' 'Treason!' said I. 'I understand treason to mean giving aid and comfort to the enemy in time of war. How can the distribution of this little button do that?' 'Why,' he said, 'if you were in Germany you would be shot; and we have to have your assurance that you are not going to distribute any more of them.' I said, 'I can't give you any such promise because I am not guilty of treason; but if you think I am, you know your duty – only you must be very sure of your facts.'

The other fellow said, 'Well, we can't arrest you, Mrs. Barnett, but we can confiscate your buttons. Where are they? Weren't you showing one to a man as we came in?' 'Yes,' I said, 'but he has gone and he must have taken the button with him.' He said, 'I told my partner on the way out here that I thought I knew you people and that we would have no trouble with you. Will you give us the buttons?' I said no. 'Why,' he said, 'you have criticized the government.' 'Yes,' I said, 'and the government deserves to be criticized. I think it was a dastardly thing to hang those men as if they were criminals and put them in holes in the ground just as if they had been dead dogs. If it is treason for me to think and say so, then you will have to make the most of it.'

'Well,' said the shorter of the two men, 'the rest of your people do not agree with you.' I said, 'Maybe not. They don't know any better or they are afraid of losing their whole skins. As for myself I don't care. I'd rather go down in history as one lone Negro who dared to tell the government that it had done a dastardly thing than to save my skin by taking back what I have said. I would consider it an honor to spend whatever years are necessary in prison as the one member of the race who protested, rather than to be with all the 11,999,999 Negroes who didn't have to go to prison because they kept their mouths shut. Lay on, Macduff, and damn'd be him that first cries "Hold, enough!"'

The men looked at me as if they didn't know what to do about it, but finally asked me to consult my lawyer, for he would probably advise me differently. They went away, but they didn't take the buttons with them.

Both of the daily papers came out next day with a most respectful notice touching this incident. The *Herald Examiner* had reproduced a picture of the button, and both of them said that Mrs. Barnett said anybody who felt as she did about it and wanted to wear a button in protest of the treatment the government had meted out to those soldiers could get one from her. The men did not come back, and I continued disposing of the buttons to anybody who wanted them; and strange to say, I was never molested and no further reference was made to the incident.

While the reporters and secret service men were in my office, I took them back and showed them tables filled with candy boxes, cigarettes, pipes, tobacco, and other things which we were preparing to send to Camp Grant for gifts for the Negro soldiers.

Major General Barnum had me come to Camp Grant and had asked if I would undertake to see that the colored soldiers there would have some Christmas remembrances. He said the white ones had already been taken care of; but that some of the colored boys had come from far South and that Christmas would be a very blue day for them unless someone could be interested to see that they too had some Christmas.

I laid the matter before the City Federation of Colored Women's Clubs and asked the appointment of a committee to work with me in seeing that twelve hundred soldier boys of the regiment each had a Christmas token. Our committee found that we had bitten off more than we could chew, for to get each one of those twelve hundred men a half-pound box of candy netted six hundred pounds. The estimated cost for that one item, candy and cartons, was nearly two hundred dollars.

While we were worrying over this problem, an appeal was made through the *Chicago Tribune* for help. The first response came from Miss Fannie R. Smith, dean of girls at the Wendell Phillips High School, in which she tendered us one hundred dollars of the money that had been raised by a bazaar at the school. With this help and that of a few others, we were able to send three large boxes of Christmas cheer to the men at Camp Grant.

ADDIE HUNTON

(1875–1943)

and

KATHRYN M. JOHNSON

(b. 1878)

Churchwomen and social workers, Hunton and Johnson succeeded against considerable opposition in going to France in 1918 as YMCA workers specifically to administer to the needs of the African-American troops, most of whom were systematically denied access to the services provided to white soldiers. Their book about their year abroad, *Two Colored Women with the A. E. F.* (1920), uncompromisingly records the atmosphere of racism and discrimination which they observed and encountered and seeks to set the record straight regarding the service of black troops and their officers, whose courage and capabilities were being publicly attacked, especially by Southern white officers.

Although written in the third person, the book represents an autobiographical account of Hunton and Johnson's experiences.

Press and pulpit, organizations and individuals were beseeching and demanding in 1918 that the Red Cross add some of our well-trained and experienced nurses to their 'overseas' contingent, but no favorable response could be obtained. Meantime, the Paris Headquarters of the Young Men's Christian Association cabled as follows: 'Send six fine colored women at once!' This call diverted from the Red Cross issue that had been uppermost in all minds.

Six women! A small number to be sure, but the requirements for eligibility were not so easy to meet and one must not have a close relative in the army. Many questions were asked. 'Was there a real need for women over there?' 'Could they stand the test?' 'Would they not be subjected to real danger?' 'Were not gruesome stories being told relative to terrible outrages perpetrated on women who had gone?' To these questions and to others there seemed to be but one reply. It was that if hundreds of other women had answered the call to serve the armies of the Allies, surely among the thousands of colored troops already in France and other thousands who would soon follow there would be some place of service for six colored women. A few leaders were far-visioned enough to see the wisdom of colored women going overseas. Mr. Fred R. Moore, Editor of the *New York Age*, worked untiringly to help secure the required number, while W.E.B. Du Bois, Maj. R.R. Moton, and Mr. Emmett Scott strongly endorsed the sending over of colored women.

Almost immediately Mrs. James L. Curtis and Mrs. William A. Hunton were invited to go to France. These were the days when sailing dates were kept secret and orders for departures came at the last moment. When the first call to sail came, Mrs. Hunton could not easily be released from the war work she had undertaken for the Young Women's Christian Association. But the following week, Mrs. Curtis, keenly anxious for the adventure, was permitted to go alone. Meanwhile, Miss Kathryn Johnson had been called from Chicago, and three weeks later sailed with Mrs. Hunton.

For all the period of the war and the dreary winter that followed it, there were just these three colored women with the American Expeditionary Forces in France. Time and time again they were lifted up by rumors that other canteen workers were on the way. Whenever they saw women arriving fresh from America, they would at once inquire if there were any colored women in their party. Always the rumors proved false and the answer negative. Two hundred thousand colored soldiers and three colored women in France! So it was for many months. But finally the dream of help was realized when in the spring of 1919[1] sixteen canteen workers reached France. Only sixteen, to be sure, but to the three who had waited and served so long alone, they seemed a mighty host.

What a wonderful spirit these sixteen women brought with them! They had been impatiently waiting, some of them for many months, to answer the call. They knew how their soldiers needed their presence in France so they arrived eagerly ready for that last lap of Y service, the importance and significance of which can hardly be over-estimated. The Armies of the Allies had won the war, but there was

---

[1] Although the Armistice was signed in November, 1918, many American troops were retained in Europe awaiting the conclusion of a peace treaty. African-American soldiers were employed largely on graves detail, reburying casualties in the vast war cemeteries.

a moral conflict for the war-weary men hardly less subtle and deadly than the conflict just ended. It required a program of compelling interest to hold the soldiers against the reaction of war's excitement and ghastly experiences, and the new thirst for home and friends.[2] Therefore the coming at that time of the sixteen canteen workers for our soldiers was wonderfully opportune.

But just what of the canteen service for all the months that had preceded their coming? How had just three of us managed to be mothers, sisters and friends to thousands of men?

The first colored woman who reached France had been sent to Saint Sulpice in the great Bordeaux area, and though she was quickly returned to Paris, the few days she had spent in the camp made a bright spot for the men there in that veritable wilderness of hardships. That she made ice cream and other 'goodies' for them, and best of all, let them open their hearts to her, was never forgotten by the men of that camp. Reaching Paris, we found her with a group of men secretaries[3] ordered home. It was then for the first time that we questioned the wisdom of our adventure. Surely we had not given up home, friends and work for such an experience! Would blind prejudice follow us even to France where men were dying by the thousands for the principles of truth and justice? There had been no slackening of the impulse to serve, when as part of a mighty procession, we crossed the periled deep; no lessening of our enthusiasm for war work as we looked for the first time upon war's dark picture. But somehow this incident, with its revelation of the fact that prejudice could follow us for three thousand miles across the Atlantic to the very heart of the world's sorrow, tremendously shocked us in those first days. But it was a challenge to a heroic sacrifice, and we realized the significance of the challenge more deeply as the months receded.

* * *

Over the canteen at Brest meant hut activity from early morning till midnight. It was part of what came to be known as the 'Battle of Brest,' which Miss Watson, the Regional Secretary, declared 'Ofttimes more terrible than that of "No Man's Land"' because less open. Every minute almost meant keeping men free from the despair of long waiting and hope deferred. Eight regiments of Pioneer Infantries, three

---

[2] This problem was not confined to black soldiers. American, British, and Canadian troops all rioted or mutinied demanding demobilization.
[3] YMCA workers.

labor battalions, many groups of casuals[4] and several depot companies were among those whom we bade *bon voyage* during our days at Pontanezen. Here, as at St. Nazaire, the huts were crowded and the canteen lines unending. Men made 'seconds,' as an additional helping was called, but rarely unless they were fortunate to slip into other men's places. Those were busy but happy days at Brest! The men were not strange, for we had met them in the Leave Area or along the devastated highways. We closed our work there so happy that nothing could take away the joy of it.

Over the canteen in France we learned to know our own men as we had not known them before, and this knowledge makes large our faith in them. Because they talked first and talked last of their women back home, usually with a glory upon their faces, we learned to know that colored men loved their own women as they could love no other women in all the world. Their attitude of deep respect, often bordering on worship, toward the colored women who went to France to serve them only deepened this impression. The least man in camp assumed the right to protect his women, and never, by word or deed, did they put to shame the high calling of these women. But they were intensely human and their longing for their women showed itself in a hundred different ways. One night a Red Cross parade on Fifth Avenue, New York City, was being passed on the screen. When a group of colored women were shown marching, the men went wild. They did not want that particular scene to pass and many approached and fondled the screen with the remark, 'Just look at them!' Mrs. Curtis, in whose hut this occurred, tells how it brought tears to her eyes. One man came to us saying, 'Lady, do you want to get rich over in France?' We gave an affirmative reply and questioned how. He said, 'Just get a tent and go in there and charge five cents a peep. These men would be glad of even a peep at you.' Another man stood near the canteen one day, but not in line. He stood so quietly and so long that we finally asked if we could serve him. He simply gave a negative shake of the head. After several minutes we said, 'Surely you desire something,' only to be met by another shake of the head. The third time we inquired he said quietly, 'Lady, I just want to look at you, if you charge anything for it I'll pay you – it takes me back home.' Hundreds of incidents gave evidence of the love of these men for their women. Sometimes they shed tears at their first sight of a colored woman in France.

---

[4] Men not part of specific units.

We learned somewhat of their matchless power of endurance and of their grim determination to be steady and strong to the end in spite of all odds. We came to know, too, that what was often taken for ignorance, was a deep and far-thinking silence. They were sympathetic and generous, often willing to risk the supreme sacrifice for a 'buddie.' * * *

We learned to know that there was being developed in France a racial consciousness and racial strength that could not have been gained in half a century of normal living in America. Over the canteen in France we learned to know that our young manhood was the natural and rightful guardian of our struggling race. Learning all this and more, we also learned to love our men better than ever before.

HELEN THOMAS

(1877–1967)

Her two memoirs, *As It Was* and *World Without End* were, according to her daughter Myfanwy, written as a form of therapy to lift the depression which settled over her after her husband, Edward, was killed at the front in 1917. Her tender, yet frank, account of their married life apparently violated the conventional standards of respect due the heroic dead. Although the original volumes appeared with the names of all the characters disguised, Robert Frost, a good friend of the Thomases, was so appalled by their sexual honesty that he dropped a dedication to Helen that appeared in a volume of his poetry. The book was, moreover, banned in Boston. Nevertheless the two accounts rapidly found an appreciative audience and have remained steadily in print, usually as one volume. The latest edition (Carcanet, 1987) contains the text of both with the real names restored and with the addition of letters and further reminiscences by Helen and selections from Myfanwy Thomas's autobiographical account *One of These Fine Days* (1982).

One day when [Edward] was in London ostensibly looking for work, he sent me a telegram telling me he had enlisted in the Artists' Rifles.[1] I had known that the struggle going on in his spirit would end like this, and I had tried to prepare myself for it. But when the telegram came I felt suddenly faint and despairing. 'No, no, no,' was all I could say; 'not that.' But I knew it had to be and that it was right. He was – so the telegram said – to come home in a few days a soldier.

During our life there had been many bitter partings and many joyous homecomings. The bitterness of the partings has faded from my consciousness; I knew it was so, but I forget how and why. But the memory of the joy and hope and happiness of the reunions has stayed with me, and forever, so it seems to me, part of me will stand at the gate and listen for his step, watch for his long stride; feel the strong embrace of his arms, and his kiss.

After a terrific furbishing of the house, so that wherever you looked everything – the floors, the crockery on the dresser, the brass

---

[1] A volunteer regiment open, as its name suggests, to men associated with the arts.

candlesticks – shone with cleanliness and neatness, I went to meet him at the station. As I hurried along the country road I caught up village people in twos and threes, all in their best, evidently out on some festive errand; they called to me as I passed, 'Going to welcome the V.C.?'[2] 'No,' I called back gaily. My soldier has no medals yet.' As I got nearer the station the road was fringed with people from the villages round, some of whom I knew. 'You'll get a good view of him if you stay here,' said one. 'Oh no, I must be there when the train comes in,' I replied; and flushed and excited I rushed on. The platform was crowded, the town band was there, with the town officials. It seemed right and natural to me that there should be all this fuss, and it accorded with my own joyous excitement, but I stood away from the crowd at the end to the platform. The crowd could have their hero, but I wanted my soldier all to myself. The train came in.

I did not see the official welcome of the V.C., for Edward got out just where I stood. I noticed with a shock that his hair was cut very short, and that the thinness of his face was accentuated, but that he looked trim and soldierly in his uniform.

As he stooped to kiss me I smelt for the first time that queer sour smell of khaki, so different from Edward's usual smell of peaty Harris tweed and tobacco. What a difference the clothes made! The stiffness and tightness too were so strange after his easy loose things. I could not now walk with my hand in his pocket and his hand over mine.

I looked up at his face as we walked along, and in a flash I saw the sensitiveness, the suffering, the strength and the sincerity which had determined for him the rightness of this step. I was proud of him, and my heart silently responded to the cheers with which the crowd welcomed their hero. I passed again the woman who had spoken to me. 'You be luckier than us,' she said, 'with a V.C. all your own.' Edward saluted her, and I nodded in acknowledgement of the truth of what she said.

The children[3] were excited and eager to hear all about soldiers and after tea, as we sat round the table polishing his buttons and badges and buckles, he told us about enlisting, and how he was not a soldier for the duration of the war. He had already learned some soldiers' songs which had good choruses in which we all joined.

The three days he had before joining his regiment were busy with gardening, and putting papers and books in order in the hill-top

---

[2] A winner of the Victoria Cross, Britain's highest award for military valor.
[3] There were three – a son, Merfyn, and two daughters, Bronwen and Myfanwy.

study and making preparations for a long absence from home. We had one glorious walk together. On that day he discarded his khaki, and but for his short hair, which I could not get used to, was his old self. We talked of ways and means, of the children and the garden, of the men mostly painters and writers like himself who were to be his companions and to learn with him the uncongenial business of warfare. Sometimes, walking though familiar country which we loved, we talked of that, and sometimes in the old way we walked silently. I remember thinking, 'Oh if only we could walk on like this for ever, and for ever it be summer, and for ever we be happy!' And then I remembered that, after all, the war itself was the reason for this very walk, and had its part in the depth of our deep content with the English country and with each other. Because of the war our souls were now drawn into the circle that was our love, and we understood and loved each other completely.

The war ruthlessly made clear the difference between the various people who lived in the village. All the able-bodied village men had enlisted – the young men out for life and adventure, the older because they felt it their duty to do so. Only the old and infirm were left.

The school[4] as a whole stood for pacifism, and though the roll of honour in the school hall lengthened as old boys fell,[5] the spirit of the place was anti-war. Young athletic men in sweaters and shorts carried on the great work of co-education, and at the village debating society tried to hold their own against the onslaughts of the more instinctive villagers and landed proprietors. I could hardly believe in the sincerity of the men who said they would not fight for anything and if they were sincere I thought them even more contemptible. When I told a leading member of the staff that Edward had enlisted, he said disapprovingly, 'That's the last thing I should have expected him to do.' How I hated him for that remark, and hated more the schoolmaster smugness from which it came. So by degrees I became antagonistic towards the school people and all they stood for. I felt stifled – especially at that agonizing time – by the self-confident righteousness, by the principles which proved so irresistible to hypocrisy, by the theories which remained in the head and never reached the heart. A meeting was called at the school at which it was decided that, as the men of the village were all at the war, the cottagers' gardens would

---

[4] Bedales, a progressive co-educational boarding school where Helen taught and her children were day pupils.

[5] The list of graduates who had died in the War.

be dug and planted by the pacifist members of the staff, 'for we realize,' they said to the women who composed the audience, 'how much you depend on your gardens, and that the soil is too heavy for you to tackle.' The women clapped at the vote of thanks, but were not much impressed with the magnanimity of this offer, because being wiser than their betters they knew that if they did not dig their gardens themselves no one else would. And so indeed it turned out.

* * *

[1916] Christmas had come and gone. The snow still lay deep under the forest trees, which tortured by the merciless wind moaned and swayed as if in exhausted agony. The sky, day after day, was grey with snow that fell often enough to keep the surface white, and cover again and again the bits of twigs, and sometimes large branches that broke from the heavily laden trees. We wearied for some colour, some warmth, some sound, but desolation and despair seemed to have taken up her dwelling-place on the earth, as in our hearts she had entered, do what we would to keep her out. I longed with a passionate longing for some sign of life, of hope, of spring, but none came, and I knew at last none would come.

The last two days of Edward's leave had come. Two days and two nights more we were to be together, and I prayed in my heart, 'Oh, let the snow melt and the sky be blue again!' so that the dread which was spoiling these precious hours would lift.

The first days had been busy with friends coming to say good-bye, all bringing presents for Edward to take out to the front – warm lined gloves, a fountain pen, a box of favourite sweets, books.

This was not a time when words of affection were bearable; so they heaped things that they thought he might need or would like. Everyone who came was full of fun and joking about his being an officer after having had, as it were, to go to school again and learn mathematics, which were so uncongenial to him, but which he had stuck to and mastered with that strange pertinacity that had made him stick to all sorts of unlikely and uncongenial things in his life. They joked about his short hair, and the little moustache he had grown, and about the way he had perfected the Guards' salute. We got large jugs of beer from the inn near by to drink his health in, and an end to the War. The hateful cottage became homely and comfortable under the influence of these friends, all so kind and cheerful.

Then in the evenings, when just outside the door the silence of the forest was like a pall covering too heavily the myriads of birds and little beasts that the frost had killed, we would sit by the fire with the children and read aloud to them, and they would sing songs that they had known since their babyhood, and Edward sang new ones he had learnt in the army – jolly songs with good choruses in which I, too, joined as I busied about getting the supper. Then, when Myfanwy had gone to bed, Bronwen would sit on his lap, content just to be there, while he and Merfyn worked out problems or studied maps. It was lovely to see those two so united over this common interest.

But he and I were separated by our dread, and we could not look each other in the eyes, nor dared we be left alone together.

The days had passed in restless energy for us both. He had sawn up a big tree that had been blown down at our very door, and chopped the branches into logs, the children all helping. The children loved being with him, for though he was stern in making them build up the logs properly, and use the tools in the right way, they were not resentful of this, but tried to win his rare praise and imitate his skill. Indoors he packed his kit and polished his accoutrements. He loved a good piece of leather, and his Sam Browne and high trench-boots shone with a deep clear lustre. The brass, too, reminded him of the brass ornaments we had often admired when years ago we had lived on a farm and knew every detail of a plough-team's harness. We all helped with the buttons and buckles and badges to turn him out the smart officer it was his pride to be. For he entered into this soldiering which he hated in just the same spirit of thoroughness of which I have spoken before. We talked, as we polished, of those past days: 'Do you remember when Jingo, the grey leader of the team, had colic, and Turner the ploughman led her about Blooming Meadow for hours, his eyes streaming with tears because he thought she was going to die? And how she would only eat the hay from Blooming Meadow, and not the coarse hay that was grown in Sixteen Acre Meadow for the cows? And do you remember Turner's whip which he carried over his shoulder when he led Darling and Chestnut and Jingo out to the plough? It had fourteen brass bands on the handle, one for every year of his service to the farm.' So we talked of old times that the children could remember.

And the days went by till only two were left. Edward had been going through drawers full of letters, tearing up dozens and keeping just one here and there, and arranging manuscripts and note-books and newspaper cuttings all neatly in his desk – his pace pale and suffering while he whistled. The children helped and collected stamps from the envelopes, and from the drawers all sorts of useless odds and ends that children love. Merfyn knew what it all meant, and looked anxiously and dumbly from his father's face to mine.

And I knew Edward's agony and he knew mine, and all we could do was to speak sharply to each other. 'Now do, for goodness' sake, remember, Helen, that these are the important manuscripts, and that I'm putting them here, and that this key is for the box that holds all important papers like our marriage certificate and the children's birth certificates, and my life insurance policy. You may want them at some time, so don't go leaving the key about.' And I, after a while, 'Can't you leave all this unnecessary tidying business, and put up that shelf you promised me? I hate this room but a few books on a shelf might make it look a bit more human.' 'Nothing will improve this room, so you had better resign yourself to it. Besides, the wall is too rotten for a shelf.' 'Oh, but you promised.' 'Well, it won't be the first time I've broken a promise to you, will it? Nor the last, perhaps.'

Oh, God! melt the snow and let the sky be blue.

The last evening comes. The children have taken down the holly and mistletoe and ivy, and chopped up the little Christmas-tree to burn. And for a treat Bronwen and Myfanwy are to have their bath in front of the blazing fire. The big zinc bath is dragged in, and the children undress in high glee, and skip about naked in the warm room, which is soon filled with the sweet smell of the burning greenery. The berries pop and the fir-tree makes fairy lace, and the holly crackles and roars. The two children get in the bath together, and Edward scrubs them in turn – they laughing, making the fire hiss with their splashing. The drawn curtains shut out the snow and the starless sky, and the deathly silence out there in the biting cold is forgotten in the noise and warmth of our little room. After the bath Edward reads to them. First of all he reads Shelley's *The Question* and *Chevy Chase*, and for Myfanwy a favourite Norse tale. They sit in their nightgowns listening gravely, and then, just before they kiss him good night, while I stand with the candle in my hand, he says: 'Remember while I am away to be kind. Be kind, first of all, to Mummy, and after that be kind to everyone and everything.' And they all assent together, and joyfully hug and kiss him, and he carries the two girls up, and drops each in her bed.

And we are left alone, unable to hide our agony, afraid to show it. Over supper, we talk of the probable front he'll arrive at, of his fellow officers, and of the unfinished portrait-etching that one of them has done of him and given to me. And we speak of the garden, and where this year he wants the potatoes to be, and he reminds me to put the beans in directly the snow disappears. 'If I'm not back in time, you'd better get someone to help you with the digging,' he says. He reads me some of the poems he has written that I have not heard – the last one of all called *Out in the Dark*. And I venture to question one line, and he says, 'Oh, no, it's right, Helen, I'm sure it's right.' And I nod because I can't speak, and I try to smile at his assurance.

I sit and stare stupidly at his luggage by the wall, and his roll of bedding, kit-bag, and suitcase. He takes out his prismatic compass and explains it to me, but I cannot see, and when a tear drops onto it, he just shuts it up and puts it away. Then he says, as he takes a book out of his pocket, 'You see, your Shakespeare's *Sonnets* is already where it will always be. Shall I read you some?' He reads one or two to me. His face is grey and his mouth trembles, but his voice is quiet and steady. And soon I slip to the floor and sit between his knees, and while he reads his hand falls over my shoulder and I hold it with mine.

'Shall I undress you by this lovely fire and carry you upstairs in my khaki greatcoat?' So he undoes my things, and I slip out of them; then he takes the pins out of my hair, and we laugh at ourselves for behaving as we so often do, like young lovers. 'We have never become a proper Darby and Joan, have we?'

'I'll read to you till the fire burns low, and then we'll go to bed.' Holding the book in one hand, and bending over me to get the light of the fire on the book, he puts his other hand over my breast, and I cover his hand with mine, and he reads from *Antony and Cleopatra*. He cannot see my face, nor I his, but his low, tender voice trembles as he speaks the words so full for us of poignant meaning. That tremor is my undoing. 'Don't read any more. I can't bear it.' All my strength gives way. I hide my face on his knee, and all my tears so long kept back come convulsively. He raises my head and wipes my eyes and kisses them, and wrapping his greatcoat round me carries me to our bed in the great, bare ice-cold room. Soon he is with me, and we lie speechless and trembling in each other's arms. I cannot stop crying. My body is torn with terrible sobs. I am engulfed in this despair like a drowning man by the sea. My mind is incapable of thought. Only now and again, as they say drowning people do, I have visions of things that have been – the room where my son was born; a day, years after, when we were together walking before breakfast by a stream with hands full of bluebells; and in the kitchen of our honeymoon cottage, and I happy in his pride of me. Edward did not speak except now and then to say some tender word or name, and

hold me tight to him. 'I've always been able to warm you, haven't I?'
'Yes, your lovely body never feels as cold as mine does. How is it that
I am so cold when my heart is so full of passion?' 'You must have
Bronwen to sleep with you while I am away. But you must not make
my heart cold with sadness, but keep it warm, for no one else but you
has ever found my heart, and for you it was a poor thing after all.'
'No, no, no, your heart's love is all my life. I was nothing before you
came and would be nothing without your love.'

So we lay, all night, sometimes talking of our love and all that had
been, and of the children, and what had been amiss and what right.
We knew the best was that there had never been untruth between us.
We knew all of each other, and it was right. So talking and crying and
loving in each other's arms we fell asleep as the cold reflected light
of the snow crept through the frost-covered windows.

Edward got up and made the fire and brought me some tea, and
then got back into bed, and the children clambered in, too, and sat in
a row sipping our tea. I was not afraid of crying any more. My tears
had been shed, my heart was empty, stricken with something that tears
would not express or comfort. The gulf had been bridged. Each bore
the other's suffering. We concealed nothing, for all was known
between us. After breakfast, while he showed me where his account
books were and what each was for, I listened calmly, and unbelievingly
he kissed me when I said that I, too, would keep accounts. 'And here
are my poems. I've copied them all out in this book for you and the
last of all is for you. I wrote it last night, but don't read it now ... It's
still freezing. The ground is like iron, and more snow has fallen. The
children will come to the station with me; and now I must be off.'

We were alone in my room. He took me in his arms, holding me
tightly to him, his face white, his eyes full of a fear I had never seen
before. My arms were around his neck. 'Beloved, I love you,' was all
I could say. 'Helen, Helen, Helen,' he said, 'remember that, whatever
happens, all is well between us for ever and ever.' And hand in hand
we went downstairs and out to the children, who were playing in
the snow.

A thick mist hung everywhere, and there was not sound except,
far away in the valley, a train shunting. I stood at the gate watching
him go; he turned back to wave until the mist and the hill hid him. I
heard his old call coming up to me: 'Coo-ee!' he called. 'Coo-ee!' I
answered, keeping my voice strong to call again. Again through the
muffled air came his 'Coo-ee.' And again went my answer like an echo.
'Coo-ee' came fainter next time with the hill between us, but my

'Coo-ee' went out of my lungs strong to pierce to him as he strode away from me. 'Coo-ee!' So faint now it might only be my own call flung back from the thick air and muffling snow. I put my hands up to my mouth to make a trumpet, but no sound came. Panic seized me, and I ran through the mist and the snow to the top of the hill, and stood there a moment dumbly, with straining eyes and ears. There was nothing but the mist and the snow and the silence of death.

Then with leaden feet which stumbled in a sudden darkness that overwhelmed me I groped my way back to the empty house.

Edward Thomas was killed by a shell in the battle of Arras on Easter Monday, 1917.

MYFANWY THOMAS
(1910–)

Myfanwy Thomas was the youngest child and second daughter of Edward and Helen Thomas (q.v.). Although she claims 'not to be good at English,' her autobiography, *One of These Fine Days* (1982) was well received and went into several editions. In the following excerpt, she recalls the day the news of her father's death at the Front came by telegram.

After saying goodbye to my father, every night for weeks I prayed for his safety on the ship, which seemed to me the most dangerous part of going to war. I imagined huge waves dashing against a small tug-boat, which mounted to the crest and then slithered down. My eyes screwed up tightly could not dispel this terrifying picture. The only other prayer I knew was one which Joan Farjeon, Joe's daughter, had taught me. This prayer was a puzzle but I did not like to ask Mother about it; we were not a praying family. But seeing Joan kneel by her bed enchanted me and I became a regular kneeler. The prayer I learned from her was:

> Gentle Jesus meek and mild
> Look upon a little child
> Pity mice and plicity
> Suffer me to come to Thee
> Four corners to my bed
> Four angels round my head
> One to watch and one to pray
> And two to bear my soul away.

To pity mice seemed logical and proper, disliked and trapped as they were, but what in the world was *plicity*? I came across the prayer many years later and felt a great fool to have pitied mice ....

The time came for me to go back to High Beech. The dangers of the sea were over now, and I had no further fear. One saw funny pictures by Heath Robinson of soldiers at the Front, and occasionally we saw overhead white bursts of anti-aircraft fire. But mother's terror and anxiety for my father's safety were carefully hidden so as not to distress us. She was making me an emerald green coat with a set of small brass Artist's Rifles buttons down the front. We walked up to the post every day, which I dreaded as we had to pass the school playground which bordered the road. The boys would shout 'Hullo four-eyes' or 'Gig-lamps, there goes gig-lamps.' I could tell by the jeering tone of their voices that it was something unpleasant, but I had to ask Mother what it meant. How I hated my offending spectacles!

The second and last letter I had from my father came from France with the FIELD POST OFFICE postmark dated 24 March 1917 and overstamped with the oval red mark saying PASSED FIELD CENSOR – 4227.

The letter is written in pencil on paper torn from a notebook and has two sketches.

My dear Baba,

One day I saw a house or a big barn in the country where the Germans were, with a little roof over a pump or a well alongside of it, like this: [sketch].

But the next morning when I looked, all I could see was the little roof like this: [sketch].

All the trees were gone and the house was gone. Also the Germans have gone and since then I have been right up there and seen Cockneys and Scotchmen but no Germans. It is a funny country. Now I expect the French people will be coming up to that village to see if there are any walls left of their houses and anything in their gardens.

Now you have come back to your house and found all the bricks there and perhaps some new things in the garden You are going to have Joy, too, aren't you? I wish I could see you in the forest. There is no forest here and no copses even very near, and no hedges at all, so that there are not so many birds, but plenty of chaffinches and larks, no peacock, no swans. There are lots of little children about as old as you are, but without specs, living in the cottages here.

Now I hear I have to get up early and do a hard day's work tomorrow, so I must go to bed.

Good night, *Nos da y chwi.*[1]

Daddy

Sometimes I would walk to the corner on my own to sit on a log and wait for Bronwen walking back from school at Loughton. I was joined on one occasion by a very respectably-dressed man, who began to chat to me. To forestall any offerings of sweets which I felt might be an embarrassment to both of us, I quickly ventured the information that my father was a policeman, and felt quite safe. The man walked off after that and I knew I was in control.

But on that bright April day after Easter, when mother was sewing and I was awkwardly filling in the pricked dots on postcard with coloured wool, embroidering a wild duck to send to France, I saw the telegraph boy lean his red bicycle against the fence. Mother stood reading the message with a face of stone. 'No answer' came like a croak, and the boy rode away. Mother fetched our coats and we went shivering out into the sunny April afternoon. I clutched her hand, half-running to keep up with her quick firm step, glancing continually up at the graven face that did not turn to meet my look. There were no children in the playground as we hurried to the post office, no calls which I could not have borne – for although I knew the shouts of 'Four Eyes' were aimed at me, Mother also wore spectacles. I waited, with dry mouth and chilled heart, outside the post office, while wires were sent off to Mother's sisters, to Granny and to Eleanor.

The day after, before arrangements were made for us to go to London to stay with Auntie Mary, I was looking at my favourite picture in a story book, an engraving which Bron had delicately coloured for me. Suddenly I ripped it out, screwed it up and flung it on the fire in a rage of tears – for what couldn't possibly happen to us had happened. My father would never come back. Why had I only prayed for his safety crossing the stormy sea? No answer.

---

[1] 'A good night to you.' (Welsh)

ANNA EISENMENGER

Her book, *Blockade: The Diary of an Austrian Middle-Class Woman, 1914–1924*, is less a diary than a memoir based on her notes from those years. It primarily concerns the years between 1918 and 1924, since her daily life was, she says, hardly affected by the war, though her husband, a doctor, died of overwork during those years and one son was killed at the Front, another son and her son-in-law gravely wounded and maimed for life, and her daughter became seriously ill from malnutrition. The book provides an excellent insight into the impact of the war and the peace on the middle classes on the losing side and sheds some light on why the Austrian middle class was to welcome Hitler with such enthusiasm.

NOVEMBER 8, 1918

We housewives have during the last four years grown accustomed to standing in queues; we have also grown accustomed to being informed after hours of waiting that the supplies are exhausted and that we can try again in a week's time with the pink card, section No. so-and-so; in the meantime, we are obliged to go home with empty hands and still emptier stomachs. These disappointments are the order of the day. Only very seldom do those who are sent away disappointed give cause for police intervention. One hears a little grumbling there, and then but it is rare for any of them to adopt an aggressive attitude. On the other hand, it happens more and more frequently that one of the pale, tired women who have been waiting in a queue for hours collapses from exhaustion and has to be taken away from the Food Centre in an ambulance. The turbulent scenes which occurred today inside and outside the large market hall seemed to me perfectly natural. In my dejected mood the patient apathy with which we housewives endure all our domestic privation seemed to me blameworthy and incomprehensible. Karl[1] immediately tried to profit by my state of mind to win me over to his communistic views:

---

[1] Her son, wounded in the head and invalided home. He became a Communist during the war, much to his mother's horror. Later, a political argument between them would end in his shooting her in the chest, a wound she survived.

'Abolition of the present incapable bourgeois form of government, war on capitalism, war profiteers and exploiters of the starving people, etc.'

But my inherited bourgeois outlook made me see and fear in these familiar catchwords merely a provocation to fresh war and hatred and I protested immediately against Karl's introduction of communistic propaganda into my house. My own state of mind made me realize, however, how easy it must be to upset the moral equilibrium of whole classes of the population who have been forced out of their ordinary habits of life by this unhappy war and now fall an easy prey to the political agitator. Although the German armies are still fighting on the western Front, the war is ended for us Austrians and has given place to an armistice. The terrible massacre of human lives has ended as far as we are concerned. After four years that seemed as if they would never end, I have to mourn a terrible war sacrifice: my husband and Otto dead, Erni for the time being deprived of his sight; Rudi a cripple with only half a leg; Karl utterly changed owing to his head wound and perhaps not sane; Liesbeth weak and ailing for lack of nourishing food, Aunt Bertha bedridden with bone-softening due to under-nourishment. Since the hospitals are full to overflowing and no longer take civilians unless their lives are in danger, there was nothing else to be done but to have Aunt Bertha conveyed to my flat, so that I could nurse and look after her.

Wolfi, who is now in his sixth year, is healthy and always in high spirits as well as good and intelligent, though he is very small for his years.

Five of my nephews and one of my nieces were sacrificed to the war fury, but as to them I cannot go into greater detail here.

The result of these four most terrible years I have ever experienced is, as regards my immediate family, consisting of eight persons (I do not include Aunt Bertha, who had hitherto lived by herself), namely Victor, my husband; Karl, Otto and Ernst, my sons; Liesbeth, my daughter, Rudi, my son-in-law, and Wolfi, my grandson:

2 dead
3 seriously wounded
1 invalid
Out of eight people six clawed by the devilish talons of war.
Of these six, two torn from us for ever (Victor, Otto).

Of the remaining four: Erni, at 19 years of age, condemned to lifelong darkness through loss of his sight; Karl, with his moral equilibrium seriously disturbed as a result of his head-wound; Rudi, a poor helpless cripple owing to the loss of both legs; Liesbeth, his wife, suspected of tuberculosis as the result of insufficient nourishment.

Wolfi at a tender age in constant danger of infection.

The eighth, myself, still in health, but nervously overstrained and in need of a rest. Fully conscious of my heavy obligations, and firmly resolved to withstand the tempests of fate and, under these melancholy circumstances still to make the best of everything. I want to fill my dear invalids with resignation and courage to bear their fate. I want to try as far as possible to gather together the scanty remnants of their shattered lives and to make those lives worth living. I want to try, under these bitter, altered circumstances, to procure for them some meagre joys, without which such terrible blows of fate could not be borne for long, until time, that infallible though often cruelly relentless physician, has transformed even the most crushing losses into habit.

I lay aside my pen and fold my hands. 'God Almighty! Give me strength to go on fighting for the happiness of my children!'

NOVEMBER 20, 1918

Our flat consists of six rooms, with kitchen, maids' room and bathroom. As eight persons live in these rooms, we have nothing to fear from the Government Control Commissions, which are rigorously commandeering unused rooms. Erni and Wolfi are sleeping in my bedroom. Karl has his own room. Aunt Bertha is in the writing room. Liesbeth and Rudi I have put in what used to be our dining-room, since, in view of the difficulty of heating, we make do with one room as sitting room and dining-room. This is the large room which used to be the drawing-room, looking on to the garden and containing the piano. Up to now I have been able to keep this room at a tolerable temperature of 12–14 degrees Réaumur by means of a small iron stove. The room has two windows and a double glass door leading on to the verandah. As we all get the winter sunshine on this side, we have even now heat and light.

* * *

The bedrooms were only heated a very little and according to the outside temperature. Not until the temperature sank to freezing point did Kathi heat the bedrooms a little after she had tidied them. As in other years, I had during the summer saved up a little stock of coal in the cellar. When the decree was issued that no one must possess or consume more than $^1/_2$ cwt.[2] of coal per week and that it must be used exclusively for cooking purposes, I ought to have notified the authorities of my little supply of coal, which amounted to about $1^1/_2$ tons. Probably it would be requisitioned; possibly I should be fined. During the War there had been no Government restrictions in regard to wood and coal. The prices were very high compared with peace prices, but it was possible to secure considerable quantities from a coal-merchant if one had been a regular customer. Now the difficulty of supplying coal for household needs has suddenly become very painfully aggravated, for the Czechs have completely stopped the export of coal to Austria and Germany and the German coal-mining districts are occupied by the French or the Poles, who likewise refuse to supply any coal to the vanquished nations. My simple woman's brain tries in vain to understand why the victors have adopted these measures. The temperature has fallen considerably during the last weeks. Heating of the living rooms has been forbidden by the authorities. A new struggle, which we were spared during the War, is being imposed upon us housewives: the struggle against the winter cold in our homes.

Since I, like most other housewives, had already infringed the law by resorting to complicated and forbidden methods of procuring the most necessary articles of food, I resolved to run the further risk of keeping my little stock of coal and, in consequence, of coming into conflict with the new authorities. As the cellars were to be searched by the Volkswehr[3] for supplies of wood and coal, I had to act at once. I came to an understanding with our good-natured house-porter, promising him 2 cwt. of coal if he would quietly transfer onto the verandah the stock of coal in my cellar. The other people living in the house must not see it, for how often it had happened that an envious and less fortunate neighbour had secretly given information to the authorities! At eleven o'clock at night, when everyone else was asleep, I began, aided by Kathi[4] and the house-porter, to transport to our verandah the supply of coal in the kitchen. The porter used the Viennese 'Holzbutte,' a large wooden pail carried on the back. Kathi and I together carried the washing-basket. As we live on the third floor,

---

[2] 50 pounds.
[3] A semi-military group rather like the Home Guard.
[4] The maid.

we had to go up and down four storeys each time, for there is no lift in our house. By two o'clock in the morning, Kathi was so exhausted that I had to send her to bed. At four o'clock we had almost all the coal on the verandah. But both I and the porter were utterly worn out. I hastily gave the old man a glass of plum brandy, washed myself clean of the coal dust, and crept quietly to bed, so as not to disturb Wolfi and Erni.

That I should one day, in order to escape freezing in my own home, carry up my coal and thereby constitute myself a criminal, was something that no one had prophesied at my cradle. But this is war, the war of the housewives against that lack of primary physical necessities which is evidently not to cease even after the cessation of the Great War in the trenches.

THE SECOND WORLD WAR

MARY BORDEN

(1886–1968)

Borden met and married her second husband, Major-General Sir Edward Spears, while both were serving on the Western Front. Between the wars, Borden continued her successful and prolific literary career, but when Germany invaded France in 1940, she rushed to be of service, organizing a field hospital service similar to the one she had run in the Great War. *Journey Down a Blind Alley*, published in 1946, records her disillusionment and anger at the French, whom she accuses of moral cowardice and collaboration with the Germans, as well as the opportunities and political complexities she faced as the wife of a highly-placed British official.

* * * It was the war that had taken me to France. I had spent it with the French Army, had met B.[1] for the first time during the Battle of the Somme, and we had given up the house in Paris in '21 to come home to England, when he resigned his commission, thinking that the world would have peace at least for his lifetime. But now in '39 we were at war again, and to the word 'war,' my answer was France. Instantly, inevitably, twenty-five years of crowded life were as if they had never been and a great wave of emotion out of the past swept me back to France of 1914.

Dunkirk, a dingy hostelry in a cobblestone square filled with dapper French officers in sky-blue tunics and scarlet breeches. It is warm, its beds are enormous and soft and deep; the smell of succulent food pervades its stuffy corridors. A siren screams from the church tower, there is a confused scramble for the cellars, a tram making along the windy beach to the ugly suburb of Malo-les-Bains stops; and out on the sands a swarm of tiny figures fall flat on their faces like frantic worshippers; Big Bertha, the great gun beyond the sand dunes in Belgium, is shelling the town.

Convoys are lumbering along the road to Poperinghe and Ypres. Columns of men in heavy gray-blue coats that are too big for them are staggering across the mud of Flanders, a woman in a gray army

---

[1] Her husband, Edward Spears.

cape turns into the sodden field outside the village of Ruysbrock, between gateposts that carry a sign marked '*Hôpital Chirurgical Mobile No. 1.*' That woman is myself. I cannot see her face, but I can see the rows of wooden sheds that house the wounded, the nurses in their white caps hurrying from one to another, and the small square hut in the center of the compound that was my home.

That was the World War – the war to end war. We were young in those days and full of nonsense. But how strange to realize now looking back that when I landed on the quay at Dunkirk in 1914 I could not look forward and observe what was to happen there twenty-five years later. How frightening to think that when I took the tram each day along the beach to the derelict casino at Malo-les-Bains no glimmer shone back out of the future to my tiny present to reveal what that beach was to witness of disaster and heroism. * * *

It is fascinating and instructive to contemplate in retrospect one's minute blind burrowing progress through the dark night of events which we imagine to have been vivid and luminous. I see myself as a very small mole nosing its way with comic assurance through the roaring gloom of that old war zone. And then, presto, I am at it again doing precisely the same thing in exactly the same way in a new, different, but even more terrible war. And so, though I gained much useful experience in the first that stood me in good stead in the second, by way of wisdom I would seem to have acquired less than nothing.

And now that both wars are over they tend already to blend into one. Soon, if I am not careful, I shall confuse their events, mistake the road I followed in 1916 on my way down from Flanders to the Somme for the one I took in 1940 from Paris to Lorraine, or transpose frail Miss Warner with her eye-glasses and gray hair who came to Dunkirk from Philadelphia in 1915 as my head nurse and put her down on her slender feet in one of the wards at St. Jean le Bassel behind the Maginot Line. What more natural? Miss Warner, if she still lives, is old, but the valiant women who answer the call of pain, disease and death are all like her; the giant poplars lining the roads of France are the same today as yesterday; the soil of France does not change, and her fields, her rivers, her forests are timeless as human beings mark time.

* * *

It is strange to look back and observe how little I understood during those days of what was going on in Paris behind the façade of military activity. Why, I ask myself, had I no inkling of what was about to happen, no suspicion of the fate that was awaiting the French Army? * * *

It was all there for those who had eyes to see and ears to hear. The defeatism, the corruption, the treachery that had been eating away at the foundation of France and was to bring about the collapse of her armies. I said to myself: 'These people don't count. They represent nothing. France hasn't changed since 1914' – and I would hurry for comfort to the woman whom I trusted above all others, who was, and is, one of the most brilliant French women of her time.

She was grim during those days. She saw, I believe, what was coming and didn't flinch, she had a fearless mind, but she would ask about England, her eyes doubtful and dark with distress. Was it true that we had been caught unprepared? When would we be able to put a great army into the field? Did Chamberlain have his heart in the war? I could not give her the answers she longed to hear.

I have seen her again. And I shall tell of how I found her when the iron curtain was lifted. We have talked together since the liberation of France almost as we used to talk – almost but not quite. We had had in common a great liking for truth and an immense zest for life, could disagree with enjoyable violence respecting each other's passionate prejudices and we never lied to each other. Nor did we lie when we met again after the four years' silence, but there were questions I dared not put, fearing she would not tell me the truth, or if she did, that I would be unable to bear it. Something enormous, you understand, happened to divide us, something that we cannot talk about without fear or prevarication. I haven't lost her. It is still possible for us to enjoy being together, but it will never be quite the same. So she must remain nameless.

And the others whom I loved, they too must be nameless, for they are gone. They seemed to me in '39 to be as close to us as they had been in 1918. They were full of interest and sympathy with my project. They said how gallant it was of these English girls to go to the front to nurse their wounded. Then they would shudder or change the subject. I should have known what they meant, should have realized. But how could I? They were a part of the best years of my life, belonged to the time when I was young and in love and lived on the left bank of the Seine. We had won a world war together then and our hearts were light because they had been brave. How could I doubt these old friends now? Why should I? They were the same people. I thought them unchanged.

I was wrong. They were graceful and kind. They expressed admiration but were not really interested in my venture. They didn't want to be interested. They were giving their sons to the army, but unwillingly. They hated the war, but not as we hated it, for they did not admit that it was inevitable, and they wished to have as little to do with it as possible.

I remember sitting after luncheon with a group of these friends, shortly before I left for Lorraine. I remember the sunlit room, the wood fire in the grate, the delicious aroma of the coffee in my cup, and the plaintive charm of my hostess. I admired her quality more than that of almost any woman I had ever met. Frail, very slender, with a mocking tenderness in her voice, she had always charmed me. Now she said, 'How can you do it, May?'

'I did it before.'

'But that was different, *chère amie.*'

'You mean the war was different?'

'But of course.'

'I don't understand.'

She gave an impatient shrug, then laughed, a gentle mocking apologetic laugh.

'I'm afraid,' she said, 'that all I want is peace – peace at any price.'

I didn't believe her. It didn't occur to me to take her seriously as meaning literally what she said.

Now I am afraid to ask what became of that charming group when the monstrous thing happened. Because they were friends. I cannot pry into their secrets. Perhaps it is even true that I never knew them.

But we used to be intimate, that is the queer thing. It used to seem almost as if we belonged to the same race. Now we are strangers.

It may be that I shall meet them again in the streets of Paris or London; if I do, if they speak and smile at me, it will not alter the fact that I have lost them.

VERA BRITTAIN

(1893–1970)

As she feared, Brittain was fated to experience not one, but two devastating wars. Unlike *Testament of Youth*, which was written years after the war it describes, *England's Hour*, from which the following selection is taken, was written immediately following the Battle of Britain, when the outcome of the war was still in doubt. In later years, Brittain was to question the wisdom of her decision to send her children abroad, but at the time she clearly felt she had little choice. At the end of the book, Brittain surveyed the ruins of London and was able to spare a thought for the ruins of Cologne, Hamburg, Frankfurt and Munich and hope that the knowledge of the mutual destruction on both sides would help Britons learn to forgive the sufferings inflicted on them by German bombers.

Towards the end of June, many conscientious parents throughout England find themselves confronted with a heartbreaking dilemma.

Simultaneously with the collapse of France, the government announces an official scheme to send thousands of British children to the Dominions. Canada, South Africa, Australia, and New Zealand broadcast enthusiastic offers of hospitality. In the United States, a Committee is formed under the chairmanship of Marshall Field of Chicago to rescue Europe's children;[1] it is even possible, we learn, that the adamant immigration laws may be modified in order to admit a hundred thousand boys and girls of British stock to America.

We feel certain that the Government would not sponsor so large a scheme unless it was convinced that horror and dislocation would come to this country with the downfall of Europe. The announcement of the plan seems to thousands of anxious parents a warning of 'things to come.' Earlier evacuation schemes have made no special appeal to them, for moving children from the town to the country was merely a method of redistributing the population; it assured neither safety, freedom from chaos, nor that sense of security which is the

---

[1] Not, however, Europe's *Jewish* children, who were systematically barred from both Canada and the United States. Whether Brittain was aware of this is uncertain, though her reference to 'adamant immigration laws' suggests she may have been.

birthright of childhood. Emigration to the Dominions or America, where real freedom from war will be a gift from new territories unhampered by the evil nationalistic traditions of the quarrelsome Old World, is a proposition more hopeful and far more imaginative. The most resourceful and energetic parents decide to register their children immediately.

* * *

Sick at heart, conscious that our obligations as parents may demand a sacrifice of a kind we had never contemplated, Martin[2] and I debate the question for a weary weekend. Richard is at school in a so-called 'safe' area, but Hilary, at Swanage,[3] has already been summoned to the air-raid shelter and her headmaster has finally concluded that no place nearer than Canada can now offer a stable life and an uninterrupted education. We ourselves have lived in the United States for long periods during fifteen years; we have friends tested by a decade of loyal affection. Shall we not be sadly remiss as parents if we fail to take advantage of circumstances so favourable?

'It's a terrible thing to do,' I protest, unable, after twelve years of careful rearing, to face giving up the children just when their personalities are developing and their fascination is growing every day.

'You're only thinking of yourself,' Martin replies inexorably. 'It's the children's interests that matter, not your feelings.'

I agree with him miserably. 'I know that. I'm only trying to decide whether it's better for them to have danger with me or security without me. As you feel so certain, you're probably right.'

After one more night of agonized indecision, I accompany Martin to the offices of the Children's Overseas Reception Board. Two humble units in a long line of troubled questioning parents, we make our inquiries. The woman Member of Parliament who answers them happens to be a personal friend.

'Don't hesitate,' she advises us. *'Get them out!'*

She hands us several alternative application forms; one is a request for permission to make private arrangements without waiting for the government scheme to come into operation.

---

[2] The name the author uses for her husband, G.E. Catlin.
[3] The names the author gives to her two children, John and Shirley, to protect their privacy. Shirley (now Williams) went on to become a prominent left-liberal political figure.

'Look here,' she adds, 'you could afford to pay for their passage, couldn't you?'

We admit that we could. 'The children have been to the United States before,' we continue. 'They both hold re-entry permits.'

'Well, then, there's nothing to wait for. They're in quite an exceptionally favourable position. Fix up their passages yourselves, and you'll be making room under the government scheme for two more children whose parents can't afford to send them on their own.'

We decide to take her advice and book provisional berths for Richard and Hilary, never dreaming that in three weeks time, when the operation of the government scheme has been impeded by the loss of the French fleet and the resulting shortage of convoys, we and other middle-class parents who have acted with similar promptitude will have our distress increased by accusations that we have abused our 'class privileges' at the expense of children from state-aided schools whose interests under the scheme we believed ourselves to be serving.

When we visit the Passport Office to obtain passports for Richard and Hilary, there is certainly no evidence that the queue of parents which stretches to the end of Dartmouth Street is composed of 'wealthy escapists.' For over an hour we stand waiting in the company of an ex-army corporal, who is using his savings to send his family to a Canadian sergeant whom he knew in World War No. 1.

'Yes,' he explains. 'I'm sending the wife and kid. She doesn't want to go, but I tells her: "You mark my words, it'll be the only life, after this war. The boy won't 'ave 'arf a chance here, compared with over there. When it's all over," I says to her, "I'll come out and join you."'

* * * I feel I cannot face this separation; cannot endure to submit Richard and Hilary for one terrible week to the intensive danger of torpedoes in order that they may be removed from the long-drawn risk of bombs and economic dislocation. I have work to do, and cannot accompany them; how shall I confront the suspense of that week? Even though I do not know that while my son and daughter are on the ocean, the *Arandora Star* will be sunk five days before I learn that they are safe and well, I cannot find in myself sufficient strength and courage to let them go in such circumstances as these. Late that evening, I have arrived at so fierce a stage of desperation that the sudden wail of the air-raid siren over midnight London comes as an unexpected relief. It is the first time that we have heard it in town for many months, and though no raid comes to our district, the threat pulls me together with its reminder of the ordeal before this country.

The next day, the children are to return from their schools. All the arrangements have been completed, but with only twenty-four hours to spare, any last-minute hitch will destroy the whole plan. Their lives, and perhaps their entire future, may depend on the punctual catching of a train and its safe arrival.

Hilary is due first, and we meet her at Waterloo. She seems undisturbed by her impending emigration, and is interested only in relating her recent adventures.

'We were in an air-raid shelter for *three* hours last night,' she tells me triumphantly. 'And we were there for two the night before! Susie says she saw a German bomber brought down!'

I examine her carefully, but as yet her little sunburned face shows no sign of fatigue. How soon, I speculate, would the shadows have come under her eyes? How quickly would those interrupted nights have ceased to have seemed adventurous? Two hours later, Richard arrives at Paddington. In his safer area he has heard no alarms but he accepts our decision with the philosophic stoicism of twelve years old.

'It's all right,' he confides, 'so long as Hilary's going to America too!'

'Then you don't mind Daddy and me not coming with you?'

'Oh, no! It's half the fun, being by ourselves.'

The children have brought their hastily packed school trunks with them. It is already tea-time; I have only two hours in which to re-pack for both before I help them to get to bed. All the necessary clothes that I can lay hands on go in first; then, with a sudden overwhelming nausea, I pack their personal treasures – Richard's stamp collection and Hilary's private zoo. How long before I see those treasured possessions again? Six months? Two years? A lifetime?

'O God, I cannot bear it.'

Whose voice was that? Surely not mine! Yet swift as thought, from nowhere, comes the reply.

'You've got to bear it. This is War. You know already from your own experience that war takes the dearest human relationships and tramples them ruthlessly into the dust. It has no concern for love and marriage, for maternity and childhood. If you want to save your children, you must pay its price.'

* * *

We join the waiting boat train at Euston, our luggage-laden taxicab hemmed in a long cavalcade of vehicles which threads its way laboriously through the newly barricaded entrance to the station.

Just in time we board the train and discover that it is crowded with children – children of both sexes and all ages, babies whose fortunate mothers are justified in leaving an invasion-threatened country and going with them, older children who vary from five or six years old to the school ages of fourteen and fifteen. Most of them are being accompanied to the boat by their parents – miserable mothers and fathers of whom some are even now torn cruelly with indecision. On the way back to London we are to meet an unhappy father whose departing wife, right up to the moment of embarkation, announced her intention of returning to London with her boy and girl.

Like the rest of the children on the train, Richard and Hilary remain philosophical, even with regard to the dangers they may encounter on the way to Montreal.

'Wonder if we'll meet any submarines?' speculates Richard, voicing with no inhibition of fear the secret dread that tears at our hearts, challenging our resolution, making us perpetually uncertain whether we have acted for the best. It is the parents, not the children, who are suffering; at least we can thank God for that. As the crowded train mills inexorably onwards, the hackneyed verse of a familiar hymn seems to beat into my brain with the roar of the wheels.

> If Thou should'st ask me to resign
> What most I prize, it ne'er was mine.
> I only yield Thee what is Thine.
> Thy will be done.

* * *

A cold rainy wind blows suddenly over the docks. Beyond the enclosure we see now the grey-painted hulk of the anonymous liner, waiting to carry away from us the dearest possessions that are ours on earth. No – not our possessions. We never possessed them; they have always possessed themselves.

The CPR[4] official approaches again. His manner is discreetly sympathetic.

'I'm afraid you'll have to say good-bye to the children now.'

'Very well,' we reply with outward equanimity. I remember then that I have brought no farewell gifts for either; that I was packing throughout the two hours that the children went shopping with their

---

[4] Canadian Pacific Railroad.

father. Oh, dearest Richard and Hilary – will you think of me as the careless mother who never gave you a parting present, when you brought her such a lovely bunch of scarlet carnations?

'Good-bye, Mummie! Good-bye, Daddy!'

'Good-bye, my own darlings. You'll look after Hilary, won't you, Richard? And you, sweetheart – you *will* do what Richard tells you on the boat?'

'We'll be quite all right, Mummie. Don't worry about us. We promise we'll look after ourselves until you come across too.'

'Good-bye, then, my loves!' ('*If Thou should'st ask me to resign What most I prize ...*')

With the gallant pathetic courage of children, Richard and Hilary kiss us and leave us as calmly as though they are departing for a week-end visit to a familiar relative. Their eyes are bright; their faces do not change and they go with their guide to meet the unknown adventure.

At the entrance to the gangway, they turn and wave cheerfully. Then the tarpaulin flaps behind them, and they are gone.

STORM JAMESON

(1891–1986)

Storm Jameson was a prominent novelist and essayist and an active anti-Fascist. Over a long literary career, she published at least forty-five novels, one of which, *Company Parade* (1933), is set at the end of the First World War. In 1942 she edited a collection of pieces by London writers, *London Calling*, which was intended to demonstrate that the spirit of Britain had not been extinguished by the Blitz and to serve also as a kind of thank-you to America for its aid during the difficult period of 1940–41.

It is not a story of an air-raid, but of something which took place inside an air-raid. At this date it is superfluous to describe a raid: you have only to read any of the admirable accounts by the Americans who were here. Or Noel Streatfeild's diary in this book: disregard the last sentence – dear Noel ... she did not tell her friends she felt low, not even when her flat was blasted out of existence and she, thank goodness, on duty that night, was nearly but not quite killed in the street: one of my hopes, if we were defeated, was to find myself in the same concentration camp with her instinctive gaiety, and conscienceless and equally instinctive contempt for the enemy: you can imagine the nightmare it would be to find oneself behind barbed wire in company with this or that famous Left philosopher, or poet ...Very well, it was a moderately bad raid. A woman[1] arrived in London by a late train, long after dark. The darkness was naturally relative; there were fires, tracer bullets, flares, and the rest of it. She could have sheltered in the tube,[2] but she had a tic about sleeping in her bed. There was a lull in the raid, a something enough like silence to be mistaken for it. She set out to walk home. Turning into one street, she saw that it had caught it earlier in the night; there was a crashed house lying partly in the road. She was too tired to take a longer way round and went forward hoping to be allowed to scramble past. Men had been digging, and they had stopped. Just as she reached this, in

---

[1] Jameson herself, one presumes.
[2] The London Underground, used as a shelter during the raids. Many Londoners spent night after night sleeping on the station platforms.

those days very ordinary place, a raid warden separated himself from the rubble and said, 'Can anyone here sing?' A moment of stupefied silence. Someone said, 'Nay, I can't.' But the question seemed to make the woman's presence there respectable. She asked, 'What do you want?' In a matter-of-fact voice the warden explained that a child was alive under the house, a little girl, she did not seem to be hurt at all – at any rate, when he asked, she said No – and she was not frightened, but she kept asking for someone to sing to her. The woman had no singing voice at all, oh not at all. But she had been used, she said, to sing to her son when he was a baby. 'That would perhaps do,' the warden said.

'Very well, where shall I go?'

'Here. You don't mind the chance of the rest of the wall coming down on you, I suppose.'

It was a quite unwarranted supposition. The woman was thoroughly alarmed. She lay down where she was told, on the rubble, to bring her mouth to the end of the way by which the child's voice had reached the upper world. There is no other way to describe it. Imagine yourself hearing a voice from the ground you are crossing at night ... The warden crouched down. 'You're all right, you're not hurting?' he said gently. The reedy voice came up. 'No.'

'What shall I sing?'

'Sing about the old woman,' the child said.

'*There was an old woman who went up in a basket?*' the woman said, 'do you mean that one?'

'Yes.' The child sounded impatient that anyone could doubt that she meant that old woman and no other.

'They're going to try digging at the other side,' the warden said, 'this here looks like coming down on her.'

> *There was an old woman went up in a basket*
> *Ninety times as high as the moon,*
> *And where she was going I couldn't but ask it,*
> *For in her hand she carried a broom.*
> *Old woman, old woman, said I*
> *Whither, O whither, away so high?*
> *To sweep the cobwebs out of the sky*
> *And I shall come back again by and by ...*

This woman's mother had taught her the tune and the words; she in turn had taught them to her son, who very likely did not remember them. All these memories have to end somewhere, or the world would be choked with them. The almost tuneless old tunes, the rubbed stone of old walls, the innocent curve of old lanes, must be effaced to make room for the future. And if the future is less charming? So much the worse for it ... The raid had started again, but her voice, thin as it was, reached the child by a line shorter than the lines joining the German planes to the houses and streets of London. She sang it through once and stopped. She knew what the child would say. The child said it.

'Again.'

It is one of the first words a child learns. Why? Perhaps it guesses that there are not enough new joys to go around. She sang it again.

'Again ...'

She sang it three, four, five times. This time there was no answer. 'Shall I sing something else?' No answer. She twisted round to speak to the warden. 'I think she is dead.'

He was suddenly and bitterly angry. 'Oh, no she isn't! She'll have dropped off to sleep.'

It was daylight when the men digging were able to lower a doctor and another man into the cellar. The first thing to be brought back was a curious monster, formed of two women crushed together and covered thickly with plaster. Then the dead child. The lower half of her little body had been crushed. How had she lived for four hours? The warden was angry again.

'You're not going to tell me ...' he sputtered.

Tell him what? That the night sky is less innocent than it was in the days of old women in baskets, or that death is not death? He bent stubbornly over the stretcher. It is impossible that a child lives in such circumstances or dies after demanding again and again something quite idiotic. But everything, the woman wanted to tell him, is impossible in an air-raid. It is impossible that brave young men have been trained to crush the bodies of children, it is impossible that a song which served to put one child to bed serves just as well to put another one to die, it is impossible that a young girl has just come out of that windowless house, tilting her hat over one eye, patting the back of her hair, going off on high-heeled shoes to her day's work. Human nature is impossible. Once a long time ago we knew that. We have been forgetting it, and forgetting has not improved us much.

VICTORIA MASSEY

The fifth of six children and the only girl, Victoria Massey was born in a small industrial village in the north of England, where her father was employed in the soap works. After the village suffered a series of heavy air-raids, she was evacuated to Wales, along with her elder brothers Edward and Joe. After the war, she won a scholarship to Liverpool College of Art. Her account of those years, *One Child's War*, became the basis for a BBC Woman's Hour serial, first broadcast in 1978. She is currently writing a biography of the eighteenth-century Lady Diana Spencer and is pursuing an MA English Literature course.

We children, Jenny, Daphne, Bob Hyde, Joe and I collected gun metal on the way to school, vying with each other for the largest pieces. We had been warned against picking things up, but to no avail. The enemy was likely to drop a bomb in any disguise – a box of matches, a handbag, to say nothing of cobwebs, might blow us to smithereens, or burn us to a cinder. The war brought its own superstitions. We were all pale and jaded from disturbed nights, although after a raid we were allowed to go to school late. I happily lost some puppy fat, but Joe could ill afford his. There were blue rings under his eyes which now blinked sharply in a putty white face. Then through obscure conversation, at times directed at us, we became aware of some secret and massive campaign in operation.

Not an articulate family, we were seldom told anything clearly or directly, and indeed we all went out of our way to be as vocally indistinct as possible. To be voluble was considered as showing off, and followed by such remarks as, 'Hark at him!' or 'mind your tongue or it might trip you up one of these days!' Anyone given to vocal expression, such as a visiting Southerner, was looked upon in silence and with an almost sullen contempt. So it was that we had to use all our wits to discover what was afoot, sharpening our senses, and becoming pretty adept at asking vague questions and making sense from the inexplicit answers. We pointed at the three haversacks on the floor, half packed.

'Wot's them for, eh?'

'What do you think, our kid?'

'I dunno, do I?'

'Ask no questions and you'll be told no lies.'

It turned out that we were to be evacuated, not to Canada this time,[1] but to a country where we would understand even less than in our own what was said to us – to Wales, in fact. We found the prospect of a foreign language amusing at first, and gabbled to one another in a made-up language. We also caught hold of the idea (probably rumours arising from the first evacuations from big cities at the very beginning of the war) that when we arrived in this strange country we would have to go from door to door, knocking and begging to be taken in. This prospect was not so funny, and we eyed our luggage with mixed feelings.

Perhaps if I burst into tears on the doorstep? As the only girl in the family, tears seldom failed me, and usually got me my own way. Yet somehow I knew that tears would not stop the war nor stop my being evacuated. These were things that just happened.

One day we were hushed and told to listen to the radio. Princess Elizabeth and Princess Margaret Rose were to speak to all evacuees. This was a magic moment: a real princess speaking to us all with a voice like a blackbird. I listened enchanted, not so much at the words, they were over my head, but at the sound itself. If only I had a voice like that, I was sure that anyone would take me into their home, delighted to have me. As it was, I doubted my charm.

We were to travel first by coach from the village school to the station, then by train to North Wales. A trail of mothers and children with bags and gas masks slung over shoulders, and with packages under arms, labels flapping in buttonholes, made their way along the dock road towards the village school, to be swallowed by the gate in the wall, and like the Pied Piper's children, perhaps never to return.

It was strange to see a great charabanc outside the school, and I wondered how it had managed to force its way in through the narrow gateway, not realizing at the time that there was a road entrance to the village. There were few private cars in those days, and only one small shop took deliveries, so most of us had never seen a large vehicle in the village before. We were bustled up the steps into the coach, and told to hold on to our luggage, and gazed down from our seats to our mothers below. My own mother looked small, like a mole with two wet blue eyes peeping out. She smiled up at us but

---

[1] An earlier plan to send the children to a grandmother in Canada was abandoned following the torpedoing of a ship carrying child evacuees.

with a desperate look as though she was within two minds to climb on to the coach and take us out and not let us go at all. I felt this strongly, and half waited for her to do so, but knew in my heart she could not make such a show of herself in front of everyone.

Ellie Hyde, the mother of Daphne and Bob, a handsome woman, gipsy-like, with red cheeks and small bright black eyes, circled the coach and tapped on the windows calling 'chin up!' in her high voice. She laughed as she rapped on the windows, but tears flowed down her cheeks unchecked.

'Come on, give us a smile! That's right, luv – now look after your little brother, and mind you don't get separated. Thumbs up now! Keep your thumbs up!'

I turned my thumbs in my pockets and kept them like that till they ached. Her words, 'Mind you don't get separated' were an echo of my mother's 'Keep with our Joe. Don't let them part you.'

My mother was anxious not to have us split up as she had been from her own brother all those years ago.[2] There was a lump in my throat. I hoped our Joe wouldn't start yelling and start me off. He was pale, the freckles standing out on his face, and his mouth sulked, but he seemed hardly aware of what was happening. My mother mouthed some words but I could see she dared not shout for fear of weeping. Jenny James's mother stood beside her rocking the pram, very thin and strained, her hair blowing wispily in the wind. She was still young and pretty, and her husband had been called up. It was hard for her with no man about. Bob Hyde was crying, unabashed, the tears slipping down his cheeks like sleighs on a bob-run. Daphne sat beside him, red-eyed but grim.

The mothers would cry all the way home, returning to cold houses where the fires had not yet been lit. Some of them had small infants who were too young for evacuation, but my mother was able to share life alone with my father for the first time. After their marriage twenty years earlier, they had lived with Nanny till Norman was born, and a succession of five more children saw to it that they were never alone when they moved to their own house. Now with Norman in the Air Force, and Joe, Edward and myself on our way to an unknown destination in Wales, it would seem that they could have a much belated honeymoon. But things never worked out like that.[3]

---

[2] During the First World War. Regardless, the children were billeted separately and rarely saw one another over the next several years.

[3] Two other brothers had died before Victoria was born. Soon after she was sent to Wales, her father died.

Meanwhile the coach wheeled toward Rock Ferry station and the singing began:

> Ten green bottles
> Hanging on the wall
> Ten green BOTTLES
> Hanging on the wall
> And if ONE green BOTTLE
> Should accidently fall ...

The railway station was noisy and bewildering, but somehow Edward, who had departed from his own school at Woodsleigh, managed to be in the same railway carriage as Joe and me, and this was a comfort. There were several other labelled, quiet, and unknown children in the carriage with us, and Edward's teacher, Miss Johnson. She was a plump, pink-faced woman with sandy hair beginning to grey, and drawn back into a bun. She had a large circular tin on her lap, and a small square one with a picture of a white bear on an ice cube. We were like live parcels in a guards van, with brown paper labels in our buttonholes.

There was a screech and the train lurched forward. I suddenly felt sick and Joe began to wail. Miss Johnson hurriedly gave out Horlicks tablets and glacier mints from her tin. After a few shunts the train left the platform and came to a standstill at a junction. Several lines away another train drew parallel to us and the windows were crowded with soldiers in khaki uniforms. They whistled and yelled across to us children and we in our turn crowded at our own windows and waved to the soldiers. The soldiers began to pelt us with brightly coloured sweets in crackly wrappers, some falling between the lines. We replied with a shower of brown Horlicks tablets and mints. Brown tablets and bright fruit drops lay between the tracks, and suddenly without warning a fast train screeched and thundered between us crushing the sweets like children or soldiers on a battlefield. Then our train shunted forward and we shouted and cheered across to the soldiers who set us singing, 'It's a long way to Tipperary ...!'

Joe forgot to cry and the sick feeling I had felt became just a small ache in my stomach as I sucked hard at a mixture of Horlicks and fruity chocolate. It seemed a long journey and I wondered if we would arrive in Wales in the dark. Again I imagined myself knocking at doors and asking to be taken in, with the tears rolling down my face. I must hold Joe's hand so we would not be parted – and Edward was with us. He would see we were all right. Joe now sat with his feet just reaching over the edge of his seat, his face set in a deep sulk.

A second coach awaited us at Phwllheli. Wales looked as dull and as wet as England, but it was daylight still. The streets of the small Welsh town were tabby coloured and uninviting in the rain. The coach took us away from this, and the scene gave way to green fields and mountains, and marshland, and suddenly the sea. Our eyes opened wide at this. Miss Johnson's comforting figure remained with us, and the older children shrilly overturned several hundred more green bottles as the coach heaved over hillocks and came at last to a grey village with a harbour and one or two disused boats. We crossed a narrow bridge where stood a black and white hotel with Pen-y-Bont written on its wall, and so through the narrow village to the Abersoch Memorial Hall. Here the coach stopped.

It was a single storey building with several cars lined up outside, more cars than I had ever seen parked at one time. I caught a glimpse of Daphne and Bob Hyde pushing into the hall ahead of me where a babble of voices could be heard. Daphne's face was pale and sharp and determined.

We must have looked a sorry sight with pixie-hoods drooping and our identity labels flapping sharply into our faces, the string of our gas mask boxes cutting sharply into shoulders and our arms aching from the weight of haversacks. Our faces were thin and white after long nights spent in shelters and it was perhaps no wonder that the people who awaited our arrival thought they had got what they feared – a bunch of kids from the city slums. As we entered the hall we in our turn felt we were being pounced upon by a babbling bunch of savages. I saw a glimpse of Jenny James's bright hair submerge under a shroud of Sunday hats. I glanced around desperately for Joe and Edward. A greedy arm shot out at Daphne who still pushed purposefully ahead of me, but she ducked, then, just as though these savages were playing oranges and lemons at a Sunday School treat, down came the chopper and chopped off the last man's head, and that head was mine.

A face floated towards me mouthing through the general din and peered at the label in my lapel.

'Well now, Vicky Massey is it? Would you like to come along with me, bach?'

The crowded room whirled and tipped, and screamed in my ears. My mouth was open, and my feet stamping up and down, and I was shrieking: 'I-I-w-w-hant our Edward!'

Edward was suddenly with me. I had caused quite a stir even in this general havoc.

'You're OK our Vicky. We'll soon find out where you're going to. You're all right!'

I gulped down my shame and still involuntarily sobbed, allowing myself to be led by a hand that seemed to emerge from a mass of people, and so out into the road. The mass separated, parts of it running along the lines of cars, gabbling and hooting in Welsh. Car doors were opened and slammed shut. The hand still holding mine belonged to a small woman with bright eyes who, despite a genteel appearance, talked more shrilly and more Welshly than the others, pulling open car doors and slamming them shut in a way I thought shockingly impertinent. Suddenly there was a cry of success and the parts of the bundle converged again inside one of the cars, myself part of the bundle. I glanced out towards the hall once more. Joe and Edward were nowhere to be seen.

I found myself squashed, but was aware of the luxury smell of leather seats, while the slim lady, apparently my part of the bundle, leaned forward and talked rapidly in Welsh to a stout woman with a hooked nose and a grey bun, who had pushed in at the back from the other door. All the time the small lady squeezed my hand, but my heart fluttered like a caged canary as the front door of the car opened again and a man heaved himself into his place behind the wheel, grunting in reply to a torrent of Welsh from the women.

The door slammed, I breathed hard. It was the first time that I had ever been driven in a car and I held my breath as the beast shuddered into life. I glanced sideways and suddenly my heart leaped up. Toppling forward from the bunch of people beside me was a head of rust coloured ringlets, and a pair of orange eyes that laughed across from me. It was Jenny.[4]

---

[4] Jenny James, her best friend.

DIANA MURRAY HILL

According to an author's note which prefaces the book, the factory described and all the workers in it are fictional, 'though based on first-hand experience.' The disclaimer perhaps allowed the author of *Ladies May Now Leave Their Machines*, which was published during the war, to feel at greater liberty to speak more frankly about munitions work than she might otherwise have.

The CLOCK became more of a feature in our lives. That large white square dial hanging over the material stores began to dominate our thoughts, so that we were forever glancing up to see what it marked, and if we weren't looking at it, it was there, a white milky disc at the back of the brain. The rituals that we went through each day, before we could start work, before we could change our job, before we could have a meal, became more and more an automatic part of our behaviour. The different people and officials in the shop all took shape and fell into their different categories – their personalities and their relation to the business of production and to the workers, their positions and how they got there, and their relationships to one another. Even the very words used by the workers, and their conversations started to work themselves into your being, till all this went to make up the unchanging whole, which is the pattern of the munition-worker's existence:

This is a brief outline of our day's routine: –

7.50 a.m.	Having had breakfast, set off for the bus park and get into waiting works bus.
8.15	Arrive at factory gates.
	Produce identity disc at Police Checking Station and pass through into factory grounds. Enter shop, giving groan under stale yellow atmosphere, take time-card out of rack and clock-in.
8.20	Mount stone steps to cloakroom, take purse out of bag, insert locker key, take out overall and mug. Shut locker, replace key in bag (find handkerchief is left in drawer, take key out again, insert in locker, etc.).
	Hang coat on numbered peg.

Put on overall.

Push into vantage point among crowd round mirrors, put bag on floor and comb in teeth.

Do hair and make-up.

8.30   At place on machine.

Start up machine.

If job is in progress, find job-book form from inspection-wall, fill in name and date and join queue at time-office for clocking on job. (This has to be repeated with every new batch. If job has run out a new routine is necessary: receiving drawing and process and gauges at drawing stores, in return for checks, and getting recs for necessary tools, signing on for new set, etc.).

Operator then starts on job, getting setter to adjust the machine as soon as he is free, till a good enough component is produced to be placed in a queue on inspection-wall, together with respective job-book, route-card and gauges, to be passed for a First-Off.

The operator then gets to work, turning them out, and putting them up on the wall, till, with one eye on the clock and the other up the bay, she sees the welcome approach of the tea-trolley, about 10 a.m.

Here there is a ten-minutes' respite from handle-turning, and the operators rush with their mugs – and often those of the setters – to collect a liquid that tastes like a mixture of oil with a touch of tannin, also to eat some cake if she has brought any.

She then resumes the handle-turning, with usual interruptions from inspection, and appeals to setter, till lunch-time.

At 10:30, 'Music While You Work ' blares forth from a loud-speaker which has to be strident enough to be heard above the noise of the machinery.

12.55   Girls leave machines to get ready for lunch.

1.0–2.0   Lunch interval

Queuing up 'first,' outside canteen doors; inside canteen to obtain lunch tickets at shop, and then again at food-hatches, followed by scramble for space at table.

1.55   Clock-in and make-up in the cloakroom.

2.0   Start up machine and resume work.

3.0   'Music While You Work.'

4.15	Tea for girls in canteen (more queuing up).
4.30	Resume work.
7.20	Clean down machines.
	Clock off job.
	Repeat morning programme in cloakroom, reversed.
7.30	Clock out and pass through checking station. Queue for bus and home by 8.

THE STATE OF BEING BROWNED-OFF

It is in this way, and the doing of these things over and over again, ten hours a day, six days a week (Saturday is a half-day, Thursdays you get out at five) that BROWNED-OFFNESS begins to creep in on the munitions worker. Scarcely perceptible at first, and then steadily and more steadily growing till, aided by other factors like lack of sleep, petty illnesses, and factory disturbances, it permeates and then predominates your whole life. Those glowing figures of the posters and the documentaries can laugh away and bend their shoulders to the wheel, and handle their machines with eagerness and skill; but the browned-off man has his fingers on you, and after he has had you in his insidious grip for a year, two years or more, unless your morale and health are very sturdy, he can make you very poor shadows of the War Effort girls.

Always there is one eye on the clock, to see if it has moved an inch nearer to tea-time, or 'Music While You Work,' and at last to 7.30 and the release to go home, eat, sleep and return.

The objects of conversation and the vocabulary in a munitions factory are very limited.

The stock phrases are 'Browned-off,' 'Tear-Ass,' 'Roll on 7.30,' 'How's the job going' 'Get cracking,' 'bonus,' 'it's in the bag.'

If a statistician took the trouble to record how many times the word 'browned-off' was used in a munitions factory, he'd get so browned-off himself that he'd give it up. 'Browned-off,' as anyone unfamiliar with the word must have guessed by now, means totally, and without any reservations, bored. Bored through to the very core, so bored that nothing has any significance to you but being bored. Bored with turning handles, bored with seeing the same old faces round you, and with doing the same old thing the same old way at the same old time. Bored with life, bored with your setter and your companions; bored with the same old dried peas and rissoles made

of left-overs that you know you are going to get in the canteen; bored
with rinsing your knife and fork after lunch; bored with the woman
supervisor and the operators asking the same old questions; bored
with washing your hands at the same old basin and drying them on
the sodden towels; bored with taking your mug and penny to the tea-
up man; bored with stepping up to get a drink at the drinking fountain
to stop yourself from being bored; bored with the same old buns you
get for tea, and having to get tickets for them at the desk; bored with
night-shift, bored with day-shift; bored with getting into the works
bus and with going to bed at the same time and getting up at the same
time to come to work again – in fact thoroughly and whole-heartedly
BROWNED-OFF.

* * *

From time to time the management used to get together and think
up new ways of adding to the wealth of routine which was already
making the munition-workers' lives such a burden. So, as the result
of somebody's bright idea, restrictions and regulations would be
tightened up, or new ones put in. There were a hundred little ways
that could be thought of for irritating operators. Among these were
the locking of cloakroom doors between the start-up of work and
lunch-hours, chivvying in cloakrooms, lavatories and rest-rooms,
and the periodic tightening up of restrictions of clocking-off times,
cleaning-down and leaving machines, the washing of hands and
general preliminaries to meals. These took place presumably after
meetings of the Production Committee or some other kind of
committee, when new tricks were put into practice which had been
devised to raise the output. These were generally put into force one
morning without any preliminaries and very stringently policed, so
that at first this had effect. They then continued, generally with
decreasing effect, with a long life or short life, according to how
practicable the 'improvements' were, how firmly enforced and by
whom, or how quickly the operators could get round them.

* * *But the stock regulation, which caused more tearing out of hair
than anything among the charge-hands, foremen and women
supervisors, was the one which forbade operators to leave their work
till five minutes before the lunch hour.

By law, women operators are allowed five minutes to wash their
hands, do their hair and make up, before going into meals (the same
before leaving for home). The general practice was to ooze out to the
cloakroom at anything varying from half an hour to ten minutes

before that time, as inconspicuously as possible. Sometimes this was managed by girls going out one by one at different times and returning to work as if nothing at all had happened. Sometimes they managed it carelessly and all went in a bunch so that the whole section was left bare. It was very difficult to keep check on them; setters were called upon to co-operate, but they found it as difficult, and anyway, they were generally too busy to notice. Finally the management decided on a huge round-up.

At about 25 minutes to the hour, the woman supervisor was posted at a vantage point between the bays and the cloakroom to guard against any premature hand-washings. She was in such a position that the foreman in charge could watch her from the other end of the shop, to see that she let no one through. To put a check on anyone dodging this, the cloakroom door was locked, and the forewoman kept the key in her pocket till the legitimate five minutes to. A colleague was sent on a continual tour of the lavatories and rest-rooms, to turn out and report any hardened malingerers.

To make the cordon finally foolproof, the police had orders to keep the doors of the canteen locked till 1 o'clock on the dot. This meant that the men and women were squeezed up into such a serried mass down the narrow wire-bordered passage that led to the canteen, that when the doors were finally swung open – or more often, half the double door cautiously pushed open a few inches (they opened outwards) – the solid stream that heaved its way forward nearly broke the door off its hinges, apart from crushing the trapped women to death.

Luckily, on one of these occasions, a girl's spectacles were knocked out of her hand and trampled upon and she sued the firm for damages. This is one of the few things that never fails to make the firm act instantaneously. From that day on, girls were allowed inside the canteen five minutes to the hour, while the men were held back snarling by the police till the hour struck and the lock-gates opened. The women could then form up into a comparatively small and peaceful queue, get their food and be sitting before the men rushed in like wolves on the fold.

But one institution dating from this round-up left its mark. This was a man's voice which suddenly, causing much delight to all, and at exactly five minutes to the lunch hour, issued with a mellow ring from the loudspeakers in the shops, announcing:

'THE LADIES MAY NOW LEAVE THEIR MACHINES!'

MARY LEE SETTLE

(b. 1921)

When she was twenty-one, in 1942, Mary Lee Settle left her home in Washington, DC to join the British Royal Women's Auxiliary Air Force. Twenty-five years later, she remembered her experiences in her book *All the Brave Promises*, dedicated 'to the wartime other ranks of the Women's Auxiliary Air Force, Royal Air Force – below the rank of sergeant.' Her American sensibility was affronted by the class distinctions she observed and by the arrogance of the authority which controlled her life and the lives of her fellow airwomen. After the war, Settle lived in Britain for a number of years, eventually returning to the United States, where she is a highly-regarded novelist.

But outside of the secret and accidental connections, a sort of stumbling together through taste or individual circumstance, the taboos between groups on such a large station were unbridgeable gulfs, to be crossed only in times of crisis and with great force. These crossings were punishable. The isolation between the ranks was traditional. To break it was to suffer. Sometimes this punishment took on all the methods of a small, organized martyrdom against which there was no built-in protection in the wingless parts of the Air Force, as there was in the Army and the Navy.

There were eight of us on a train, and one soldier in full kit. He sat and listened to us complain – not about ill-treatment necessarily, but about a sense of wrong we could not put into words, could only blast about in ineffectual stories which sounded too unimportant to tell; it is hard to make a plot of indifference. He said, 'Our officers would never treat us like that. They've got to go into action with us – and we have this.' He patted his rifle.

We, too, had a weapon – silence – and all too seldom a kind of solidarity of despair or anger that could shoot up through the other groups, as isolated from each other as we from them in the military hierarchy. Sometimes it was done individually.

Viv did it through sturdy innocence. During the year between initial training and her posting to Turnbull St Justin, she had been in a small, proud, independent balloon barrage unit. She had gone through the hard, concentrated discipline of training, but she had never faced the debilitating discipline of isolation, boredom and neglect, within which we made our small, fiercely protected worlds on the station. We suffered more often from the attrition of threats of unnamed punishments, meted out in secret, unknown to the officers, than we did from direct contact with power. It was the secret threats which taught us the patience of fear.

Viv would have none of it. For some weeks before she came, the airwomen's mess had suffered in charge of our food one of those obscene, loud-mouthed, filthy men; whose small power had grown in the cookhouse until he ruled as a tsar in a food-streaked apron over the few frightened cook-house girls who could not fight back because he was a corporal. In their jobs, he was the only NCO[1] they came into daily contact with. They fought him only by neglecting the food, so that their lowered morale seemed to poison it. It was thrown onto our plates as we held them out over the steaming cauldrons of swill which were set on a serving table beside two open garbage bins. When we had finished eating, we took our plates back and scraped them into the bin. By the time the mess had been open half an hour, the smell of the thrown garbage had mingled with the smell from the cauldrons to form a thick, scummy miasma over the mess.

One day the stew was actually sour. Girl after girl, not daring to speak, brought it back untouched and scraped it back into the garbage under the satisfied smile of the fat corporal, who, because he had to work in the heat of the cauldrons, wore his filthy cookhouse apron over a pair of once-white overalls; he had a naked look about him.

That day, as Viv and I sat down with our plates, a neat, pert little WAAF officer came in and marched from table to table in a sort of formal, blind inspection, stopping at each table to say, 'Any complaints?'

We could hear her coming through the silence. She stood at the end of the table.

'Any complaints?' I heard her say, bored, above my head, bowed, like all the others, into my sour-smelling plate.

I felt Viv get up. There was a little gasp from the other women and then a deeper silence.

'Airwoman!' the little WAAF officer said.

'Smell it, ma'am,' Viv said and sat down.

---

[1] Non-commissioned officer.

The officer seemed, for the first time to realize where she was. She did make a close inspection of the food, the filth, and as she started to leave, she stopped again at the table.

'Thank you, Airwoman,' she said to Viv's embarrassed head. 'If you other girls would have the courage to speak out as she has done, we could do something.' I thought she sounded a little lost.

When she had left, one of the women across the table looked at Viv. 'You should have known better.'

'This ain't fit to eat!' Viv turned the food over on her plate. 'Why shouldn't we complain? That's wot they're for, in'it?'

'You'll find out,' the WAAF told her.

She did. Viv had committed the unpardonable sin of going over the head of an NCO directly to an officer in a channel opened by King's Regulations but completely closed by tradition, which formed one of the strongest of the deep, unspoken barriers between officers and other ranks. It was formed by an agreed recognition of the need, within the hidden world of other ranks, to stick together against authority, the enemy, and it was perverted into a kind of silent dictatorship by ourselves, from not the destruction but the gradual erosion of dignity that can be caused by too long exposure to indifference and fear.

Like a disease, one could not know it was happening until the first warning signs appeared: a quickening of the heart, a closing of the facial expression to stone on being spoken to by an officer, a learning to take up as little space as possible, as if to be noticed were to bear a punishment in itself. Viv had been one of the lucky minority in active units small enough for names to be known instead of numbers; she had had the simple communal job to do of raising the barrage balloons. She had experienced no personal attrition, but rather, an expansion and acceptance she had not known before in her life. When she did face indifference, it came too quickly, and it did not quite 'take' with her. Time had not robbed her of her freedom.

For a few days after the incident of the complaint, the mess was clean, the food was better, the corporal even changed his apron. Then circumstances, as if they were too heavy to be shored up so late and in such a tired time, collapsed back to normal; the corporal's apron collected new stains day after day, the food went back to its combined smells of dead animals and tannic acid. All went along as before, and from time to time the officers marched through it chanting, 'Any complaints? Any complaints?' like a litany with no response.

Through it all, the return to normal, Viv took her punishment. She got nothing to eat. We were not allowed to touch the ladles in the food.

We held out our plates to have it dumped on them in assembly line as we moved from vat to vat. Viv's plate was ignored. The other girls at the table would share with her when they weren't being watched by the corporal, but our rations were small – two-thirds that of the men – and Viv's strong muscular body needed as much food as any of the men on the station.

Anger, a sense of injustice, turn inward at the punishment of 'being sent to Coventry.' Viv could not answer. She only moved within a worrying silence, ate in the NAAFI[2] when she got paid, and waited – and presented her plate at every meal.

On the tenth day, Viv's plate was filled. The punishment was over, the unspoken order given – not a word or a glance showed the change – just the flinging of the inevitable stew from the ladle. Her stomach, shrunk from the rationing anyway, then forced to fast, could not take it. She ate a few bites, then waited for me, and together we took our plates to dump the remains in the open garbage bins.

The fat corporal had watched her all through dinner. He stood waiting in front of the bins. When Viv's hands went forward over the bins to scrape her plate, he reached forward and grabbed her wrist.

'No you don't,' he told Viv. 'Eat it.'

'Not bloody likely,' Viv answered, watching his fingers around her wrist. She let the food, plate and all, fall into the swill.

'We'll see about this,' I heard the corporal mutter. He turned away from her.

Viv's foot came up and caught him in the seat of his dirty overalls. His arms went wide, but there was nothing to catch at but the steaming air. He went spread-eagle into the bins – garbage and corporal were splayed over the floor.

'You struck an NCO. You'll get a court martial.' He was trying to pick himself up off a slick floor.

'Not likely.' Viv looked at him, not bothering to smile at the sight. 'King's Regulations. Don't lay hands on an other rank.' She added happily, 'I 'ad to defend meself.'

She never heard officially of the incident again, but her action, for a few days, cleared the air. The voices of the WAAF were heard in the mess, calling across the tables with a new ease.

Morale was so delicate, so barometerlike in its exposure to circumstance, that an incident like this could make it shoot up. We gathered courage from each other. One action was done for us all, one

---

[2] The recreational club for enlisted personnel.

injustice depleted us again. Just as delicately, morale could slip lower and lower – a bad officer, an unjust or blind action, a death in flying threatened us all.

Coming back off leave a month later, I sensed, as I signed in, that lowering of temperature, the silence of one of those barometric tumbles so subtly caused that often no one could say what is was, how it had started. We could only suffer it until the temperature changed again. Being American – more frenetic, more anarchic by the training of my past to the quick violence of stepping forward, to what we like to think of as initiative – I had a heightened sense of such a lowered atmosphere. It made me impatient to the point of feeling trapped at the quiet, almost bucolic patience of the people around me. It seemed negative, dead. I was wrong. It was only a different way of action. It even had a name, the silent mutiny of the British other ranks. It was called dumb insolence. At the time, signing in that evening, I only registered the silence.

At the billet Viv told me that there was a new WAAF commanding officer on the station and that, at the last inspection, she had insisted that the coal in the coal bins be washed piece by piece. There needed be no more facts about the woman. The brutality that sticks in one's craw forever is not that of quick passion or even of active cruelty, perhaps because the sane are, themselves, capable at some time of such action and therefore understand it. The brutality that diminishes is that of circumstance, of the insane moments of obedience to folly simply because folly has power – the perfect absurdity of following form when the sane substance is at odds with it. Looking back, I can forgive and understand being attacked by the women and thrown down the stairs,[3] but I can never reconcile my own cowardice, my own state of diminished pride, in which I followed a sergeant on her bicycle, running along behind her, simply because I was ordered to. To Viv and to the others who had done it, the turning point, the obscenity, had been the washing of the coal in the bins.

After it the new WAAF CO, a tall, awkward woman with a heavy chin and sullen, beaten eyes, walked through corridors of silence. To counteract it, she tightened discipline, as if the one protection the women had was subject to command.

Two days later she instituted WAAF pack drill as a punishment. The order broke what morale was left on the station, affecting us all,

---

[3] Settle was attacked early in her service by airwomen who thought she was acting superior.

at the same time connecting us all like the lines of breakage starred out on glass.

WAAF pack drill differed from the pack drill for the men in one respect. Our full kit was lighter. We had no arms. We wore for it packs, helmets and gas equipment, and we marched on punishment at the double, alone, before the yelled commands of a sergeant, around the otherwise empty parade ground in full view of the whole station. There was little physical brutality in the punishment, but the English are fairly used to corporal punishment. They are slapped as children if they are working class and beaten if they are 'educated.' The one Anglo-Saxon torture which goes beyond physical brutality is humiliation. For a nation whose deepest emotion is embarrassment, it is almost unbearable. The first WAAF given the punishment deserted.

The second girl received the punishment for coming back two hours late off leave. She appeared behind the sergeant, her head hanging, her kit strapped on, at 1700 hours. It was usually an active, busy time around the parade ground. Airmen and women were crowding the doors of the mess and the NAAFI on one side of the square. The sergeants' mess on the left side of the square was full of noise, and on the other side, at the airmen's barracks, men leaned out to call to each other from the windows. The blare of the Light Programme[4] came from the buildings, its sound permeating the atmosphere at tea-time.

On that day, two hours before blackout time, without, so far as I could tell, a single word being said, every blackout curtain that abutted the parade ground was drawn – in the mess, in the sergeant's mess, the barracks windows. There was not a soul to be seen. The station had a dead, waiting silence about it. I saw, only by a glance, the WAAF, tiny on the huge square, and heard, far away, the faint voice of the sergeant drilling her, and, as the others did, I turned away quickly.

Three civilian workmen from the maintenance unit on the station stopped beside the parade ground to see what was going on. I saw, in the distance, three men walk out of the sergeants' mess and take them by the arms. In dead silence, they moved along through the yellow evening mist to the barracks gate, their bodies slow and heavy.

There was no more WAAF pack drill. For a week after the incident the station rested in a kind of uneasy silence, waiting to see if the

---

[4] Of the BBC, programmed to appeal to popular taste.

trouble was over. Women fought over trifles. Barracks cots were left unmade. People sat in movies, dim, tired, without reaction. Having reached a dangerous, still point, it was taking time for the barometer to rise, for the station to come alive again. When it did, it exploded – but still in complete silence – mutinous, communal dumb silence.

* * *

The explosion was triggered by the unjust punishment of an airman, a volunteer from Canada, who had remarked in a letter home that the WAAF punishment was the sight that had finally sickened him. Charged with 'spreading dissension in a major Dominion,' he was sentenced to twenty-eight days in a punishment barracks. But the incident, and the collective, if silent, response to it caused certain changes to be made. The WAAF CO was transferred and morale began to lift.

* * *

After the incident it was too late for me to deny the possibilities of where I was, the recognition that I was trapped among the thousands within a system where, if we were protected from the cruder psychopathic actions (and often not from those – authority, let loose, finds its own excuses), we were exposed naked to the illogical flicks of the human mind that forced us into diminishing situations, anonymity, debility of soul. The awareness of being at the mercy of such caprice was boglike in its uncertain threat. Authority, to the anonymous, had long arms but no discernible, respected head. What strength I found, I found in the surviving underground, among my friends.

Shortly thereafter, Settle was invalided out of the service, unable to perform her job due to 'signals shock,' a kind of aural overload. She went to work in London for the Office of War Information. She never again saw any of the women with whom she had served.

MARY MEIGS

(1917–)

After spending a considerable part of her life as a painter in Wellfleet, Massachusetts, Meigs developed a second career in her sixties as a writer of a number of works based on her life and relationships on the Cape, in France and in Montreal, where she now lives. In her seventies, she was a featured player in a popular NFB film, *Company of Strangers*. During the Second World War, Meigs enlisted in the WAVES, the women's naval service, as an officer. Her recollections of those years were written especially for this volume.

With our eyes reverently fixed on Old Glory hanging beside the interrogating officer, each of us said, 'No,' to his perfunctory question, 'Are you a homosexual?' Don't tell is still the law in the USA, and it takes a very courageous woman like Gretta Cammermeyer to risk her career by saying, 'I'm a lesbian.' For me in 1943, 'No' was not quite an outright lie. I had not yet engaged in the sexual activity classified as 'homosexual' and I did not yet think of myself as a lesbian, yet I knew perfectly well that saying 'No' was the only way you could become a WAVE.

My sister-trainees, many of whom could have said yes, had evidently made the same prudent decision. We were billeted in the wonderful old Northampton Inn where the peacetime staff still ran the kitchen and dining-room (we were served lobster thermidor for our farewell dinner). I was keenly aware of the vibrations of suppressed sexuality between officers and trainees and among the trainees themselves. We were assigned eight to a room which was crowded with four double-decker bunks. Above me was a woman ambiguously named Preston; she had a caressing Mississippi accent and curly hair that sprouted defiantly in every direction from under the confines of her WAVE hat. After lights-out I heard a stealthy sound as some of my roommates climbed into upper bunks, or occupants of upper banks climbed down. The sound of giggles and cautious movements was accompanied by the whispered confidences of straight WAVES who had changed bunks in order to talk. It surprises me still that the straight WAVES didn't squeal on us. I, too, climbed up to Preston's welcoming arms one night, was surprised by the ardour with which she wrapped them around me, and wriggled out and down. I had conjured up the spectre of an officer-on-watch bursting in, and of our subsequent dishonorable discharge.

When I graduated as an Ensign, I was assigned to the Bureau of Communications (BuComm) in Washington, DC, where I was aware only of WAVES who took themselves and their patriotic duty with appropriate seriousness. I was transferred after a period of incompetence to the Bureau of Personnel (BuPers) across the Potomac, to the Artists' Unit. The Post Office Department where I worked in BuComm was run by a crusty sergeant who shouted at us in the time-honored male way; now I was with compatible artists and writers, with civilian hearts unchanged by their uniforms. I fell in love with a russet-haired lesbian WAVE who gave me my first lesson in sex. I also fell in love with a WAVE lieutenant whom I passed sitting at her desk every time I walked up the corridor. When a round-eyed, round-faced sailor gave me an envelope with, inside, a big studio photograph of my WAVE lieutenant, of her twinkling eyes and smiling mouth, I felt discomfited and uneasy. Was this a way of saying, 'I know, and can denounce you at any time?' or (but this only occurred to me recently) was he telling me that he was gay and understood why I stopped so often in front of the WAVE lieutenant's desk? The necessity for secrecy made us suspicious of everybody. I shunned the sailor with the round eyes, and would look away when we passed each other, for I read a kind of sly suggestiveness in his face. 'We're buddies, you and I,' it said. I was glad when I fell in love with men, too, even if these loves were never consummated. The russet-haired WAVE fell in love with a succession of sailors and was briefly married to one of them. It was standard practise for lesbians to hint at male lovers in their lives or claim to be mourning a lover who had been killed in the war.

The spy system in the services got underway when the mother of an enlisted WAAC surprised her daughter in bed with her lesbian lover and sounded the alarm. Enlisted lesbians who took the risk of sleeping together in barracks were likely to be denounced by informers, whereas officers, who lived in houses and apartments were neither identified as lesbians nor denounced. In this time before the feminist revolution, I was politically ignorant and had never thought about injustices to women based on class differences. When one of the WAVE typists in my BuComm unit suddenly lashed out at me with, 'You treat me like the ground under your feet!' I thought she was angry because I seemed to ignore her existence. It didn't occur to me until years later that she probably thought I'd ignored her existence because I was an upper-class snob.

The majority of WAVE officers were college-educated or had teaching degrees. They had more privileges, more freedom, and more power than enlisted women; their relations with male officers were more friendly and informal. WAVE officers were sometimes tempted to take advantage of a system that took their superiority for granted. The typist in BuComm had probably already suffered from this licensed sense of superiority, and my own attitude was the last straw.

Many of my recollections of being a WAVE in World War II are embellished by hindsight. I had then both a sense of superiority without foundation and a craven fear of my superiors, whether they were men or women. It was good judgement on someone's part not to assign me to top priority work that required total loyalty to the war effort. One of my lesbian friends now is an ex-WAVE who had a top-secret job in the intelligence structure essential to the ultimate dropping of Little Boy.[1] I am thankful that my own work entailed nothing more deadly than revising a cookbook for enlisted men on aircraft-carriers.

---

[1] The atomic bomb dropped on Hiroshima.

PAULI MURRAY

(1910–85)

Pauli Murray, the direct descendent of both slaves and slave-owners, grew up in Durham, North Carolina. She took her undergraduate degree at Hunter College, but was refused admission to the University of North Carolina law school on the grounds of race as she would later be refused admission to Harvard on the grounds of gender. She completed her law studies at Howard during the war, when she and a group of women students organized a sit-in demonstration protesting the refusal of a local cafeteria to serve African-Americans. Murray had a long and distinguished career as a lawyer, a poet, activist, and priest in the Episcopalian church, and was one of the founders of NOW. Her autobiography is entitled *Song from a Weary Throat: An American Pilgramage*.

The fact that an accident of gender exempted me from military service and left me free to pursue my career without interruption made me feel an extra obligation to carry on the integration battle. Many other Howard University women were feeling a similar responsibility, which was heightened by the dramatic leave taking of sixty-five Howard men, who marched off campus in a body to report for military duty. We women reasoned that it was our job to help make the country for which our black brothers were fighting a freer place in which to live when they returned from wartime service. * * *

The Direct Action subcommittee attracted some of the leading students on campus, for it was important that those undertaking unorthodox activities maintain academic excellence. Also we proceeded cautiously, aware that a misstep would compromise our goal. Instead of rushing precipitously into 'hostile' territory, a group of students surveyed public eating places in the neighboring, mostly Negro community on Northwest U Street that still catered to the 'White Trade Only.' One of the most notorious of these lily-white establishments was the Little Palace Cafeteria, located at the busy intersection of Fourteenth and U streets, N.W., and run by a Mr. Chaconas. Because of its strategic location, the Little Palace had long been a source of mortification for unsuspecting Negroes, who entered

it assuming that at least they would be served in the heart of the Negro
section of the city. * * *

Finally on April 17,[1] a rainy Saturday afternoon, we assembled on
campus and began to leave the Howard University grounds in groups
of four, about five minutes apart, to make the ten-minute walk to the
Little Palace Cafeteria. The demonstration was limited to a carefully
selected group of volunteers – less than twenty students – who felt
confident they could maintain self-restraint under pressure. As each
group arrived, three entered the cafeteria while the fourth remained
outside as an 'observer.' Inside, we took our trays to the steam table
and as soon as we were refused service carried our empty trays to a
vacant seat at one of the tables, took out magazines, books of poetry
or textbooks, notebooks and pencils, and assumed an attitude of
concentrated study. Strict silence was maintained. Minutes later the
next group arrived and repeated the process. Outside, the observers
began to form a picket line with colorful signs reading 'Our Boys, our
Bonds, our Brothers are Fighting for YOU! Why Can't We Eat
Together?'; 'There's No Segregation Law in D.C. What's Your Story,
Little Palace?' Two pickets carried posters (prepared for the War
Manpower Commission by the Office of War Information) depicting
two workers – one black and the other white – working together as
riveters on a steel plate. The inscription on the poster read 'UNITED
WE WIN!'

My heart thumped furiously as I sat at a table awaiting developments.
The management was stunned at first, then after trying unsuccessfully
to persuade us to leave, called the police. Almost immediately a half-
dozen of uniformed officers appeared. When they approached us we
said simply, 'We're waiting for service,' and since we did not appear
to be violating any law, they made no move to arrest us.

After forty-five minutes had passed and twelve Negro students were
occupying most of the tables of the small cafeteria, Chaconas gave up
and closed his restaurant eight hours earlier than his normal closing
time. Those of us who were inside joined the picket line and kept it
going for the rest of the afternoon. Chaconas told reporter Harry
McAlpin, who covered the demonstration for the *Chicago Defender*:
'I'll lose money, but I'd rather close up than practice democracy this
way. The time is not ripe.' When Juanita Morrow, a journalism
student, interviewed Chaconas several days later, he admitted that

---

[1] 1943.

he had lost about $180 that Saturday afternoon and evening, a considerable sum for a small business.

Actually, the incident did not arouse the furor we had feared but revealed the possibilities for change. When told why the place was closed and being picketed, a white customer named Raymond Starnes, who came from Charlotte, North Carolina, said, 'I eat here regularly, and I don't care who eats here. All I want is to eat. I want the place to stay open. After all, we are all human.' Another white bystander, asked what he thought of the students' action, replied, 'I think it's reasonable. Negroes are fighting to win this war for democracy just like whites. If it came to a vote, it would get my vote.'

When Chaconas opened his place on Monday morning, our picket line was there to greet him, and it continued all day. Within forty-eight hours he capitulated and began to serve Negro customers. We were jubilant. Our conquest of a small 'greasy spoon' eating place was a relatively minor skirmish in the long battle to end segregation in the nation's capital – a battle that was ended by a Supreme Court decision ten years later – but it loomed large in our eyes. We had proved that intelligent, imaginative action could bring positive results and, fortunately, we had won our first victory without an embarrassing incident. (One other small restaurant in the area was desegregated that spring before final examinations and summer vacations interrupted our campaign.)

Significantly, the prominent role of women in the leadership and planning of our protest was a by-product of the wartime thinning of the ranks of male students. Twelve of the nineteen Howard University demonstrators at the Little Palace on April 17 were female. (The twentieth demonstrator was Natalie Moorman, a red-haired, six-foot-tall woman from Arlington, Virginia and a legendary figure in the struggle to desegregate the Washington area. Armed with an umbrella and a commanding voice, she regularly rode the bus from the District to its Arlington suburb and challenged bus drivers to try to enforce segregation under Virginia law once the bus reached the midpoint of the Fourteenth Street Bridge.)

Many of those young women who had joined together to defy tradition would continue to make breakthroughs in their respective fields after their college days. Ruth Powell went into mental health and became a chief of service at the Bronx Psychiatric Center in New York City. Marianne Musgrave chose the academic route and became a professor of English at Miami University in Oxford, Ohio. The youngest member of that little band of demonstrators, Patricia Roberts, carried the impact of her civil rights experiences from Howard University to the cabinet level of the federal government. Of the three pioneers whose arrest sparked the student protest, only Juanita Morrow followed nonviolent direct action as a way of life. With her pacifist husband, Wallace Nelson, she was an active leader of CORE sit-ins and other civil disobedience campaigns for many years.

CHARLOTTE FRANKEN HALDANE
(1894–1969)

One of the first newswomen to work in Fleet Street, Haldane was the author of many novels, biographies and plays. She joined the WSPU in her teens and handed out suffrage leaflets on Hampstead Heath. An ardent anti-Fascist, she joined the British Communist Party in the 1930s and reported from Spain, which she had earlier visited with her famous geneticist husband, J.B.S. Haldane, and from China. In 1941, she went to the Soviet Union, becoming Britain's first woman war correspondent employed by a daily newspaper, While there, her Communist sympathies were challenged by the evident inequalities she observed and she subsequently left the Party. In the following piece, she describes the scene which crystallized her change of heart.

Kuibyshev[1] was an interesting place. The town had been well laid out, with wide, broad streets, and good stone or brick and plaster buildings. The war was more than five hundred miles to the west and had made little impression on it. There was food in plenty. The inhabitants were well nourished and warmly clad. The streets were as well kept as those of Hankow or Kunming,[2] covered with mud or slime, with great pot-holes in the roadway and pavement, many of the buildings in equal need of care. There were several hotels. The principal one, the Intourist Hotel, had been commandeered by the NKVD[3] and was out of bounds to foreigners. They were accommodated in the Grand Hotel. This was an enormous caravanserai, containing no bathrooms, but a washroom, shared by both sexes, on each floor. It smelt like the earliest inhabited place on earth.

One silent afternoon I had gone from my room to the washroom on the floor above. At the head of the stairs was a little cubbyhole, in which one of the ancient women servants was dozing. As I turned the corner, I had a vista of an interminable corridor, completely silent and deserted. Along its quiet length pranced and played, with

---

[1] A city on the Volga, south-east of Moscow, to which Haldane had been evacuated.
[2] Chinese cities that Haldane had visited as a journalist in the 1930s.
[3] The Soviet secret police, predecessor to the KGB.

inimitable rodent grace, an enormous grey rat. I stood, watching with fascination the charming creature, as it sat on its haunches, preened its long whiskers, took another elegant ballerina leap, sat and preened again, its little black eyes gleaming and its long, pink tail twitching happily. Then, with that sixth sense peculiar to rats and mice, it became aware of my presence without so much as turning its head, and in a flash it had vanished. When I came down to the evening meal, I told my companions at the table – an Embassy clerk and a couple of RAF NCOs – of this vision. They made the obvious rejoinder, warning me of the dangers of the potent local vodka. As we ate our meal, my eyes happened to stray toward the ground. There, between our table and the window, promenaded another huge grey rat, going from table to table, daintily feasting on the crumbs which fell to it. I silently nudged one of my fellow-diners, pointed it out to him and vindicated my claim to sobriety. The poor Muscovites who had been evacuated to the Grand Hotel with us were accommodated in the basement, the men and women sleeping in separate dormitories. One of the girl clerks of the Narkomindel was awakened one night by a ballet of rats that was taking place on her bed, and promptly fell into hysterics. There were, however, no bugs in the Grand Hotel. One ingredient of its many blended odours made it clear that it had been fumigated against them shortly before our arrival.

Within a few days, Kuibyshev became crowded to the last corner by refugees, who sailed down the Volga on boats and barges, or arrived at the railway station on every train, in a pitiable condition, cold and half-starved. During the earlier part of the war, back at home, the CPGB[4] had carried on a tremendous propaganda of protest against the treatment of the evacuees and billetees in the so-called reception areas.[5] There was, undoubtedly, a great deal of improvisation, and in many cases the organization worked far from satisfactorily. But all the women and children were sheltered, some in luxurious, some in primitive and inadequate conditions. They all received their rations, the children continued their education at local schools. No one would claim that the arrangements worked one hundred per cent satisfactorily. But at the back of the violent accusations hurled at the evacuation system by the CP was the ceaseless inference that the existing imperfections were entirely due

---

[4] Communist Party of Great Britain.
[5] British children and mothers of infants were evacuated from the areas most likely to be bombed. It was their treatment that the Communist Party was making political capital out of.

to the social system, to the vile selfishness and indifference of the local
rich to the sufferings of the imported poor. Every fault and weakness
was underlined and magnified in the interest of political propaganda.
But to the best of my knowledge and recollection, not even the *Daily
Worker* ever claimed that a British evacuee child had died of starvation.

In Kuibyshev the local food supply disappeared almost overnight.
The first day of our arrival, the food shops were stacked with loaves
of bread and other provisions. From the second day onwards, the
queues began to form outside them. They grew longer and longer.
The supplies disappeared and were not replaced. The authorities
opened a special shop for foreigners only. The windows were piled
high with bread, cheese, butter, cold meats, sausages, provisions of
every kind, with caviare, vodka, champagne by dozens of bottles. The
manager was provided with a book, containing the names of all those
entitled to buy there. Outside the door stood a guard, a uniformed
NKVD soldier, with rifle and fixed bayonet. I went there to buy my
ration of chocolate, to take with me on the return journey. As I came
up to the door, an old Jew paused, to peer at the rich spectacle
displayed in the window. The soldier moved him on, roughly. 'Not
for you,' he said, 'only for foreigners.' I felt ashamed of being one.

I was already feeling shame and remorse. On the way to the shop,
I had encountered a crowd of women in white shawls, gathered
around a *droshky*, an open carriage, pulled by a tired old horse, with
the traditional Russian coachman on the box, huddled in his thick cape,
a drop on the end of his nose, running into his matted beard. In the
carriage sat two weeping women – one elderly, the other young, fair,
and pretty. I mingled with the crowd and let myself be jostled to the
edge of the carriage. The sobbing younger woman carried on her lap
a small cardboard box, similar to those in which large Christmas
dolls used to be sold in the London shops. It was festooned with a
wreath of wired white and red paper flowers. In it lay the doll, the
waxen corpse of a small child of about two, neatly and carefully
dressed in its best suit of blue woollies. The young woman was
carrying her child, dead of starvation, to the graveyard. It may well
be said that I could have seen far worse sights than this in China. It
just happens that I did not. I am well aware of the fact that dead babies,
especially during the war, were plentiful everywhere. I know, also,
that man's inhumanity to man, the callous indifference of the 'haves'
to the desperate need of the 'have-nots' exists in all places and at all
times. I cannot excuse my sentimental reaction to this trivial incident
on any of the above grounds. I can only explain it as due to the

extreme sickness of my over-sensitive conscience, the revolt of my sense of morality, the re-awakening of my mind and ratiocinatory faculties from a deep, drugged sleep.

Standing by the side of that dead baby, I swore a silent oath that never again would I get on any platform, anywhere, at any time, to use my oratorical or persuasive gifts to convince an audience of working-class men, women, and children, that the Soviet Union was the hope of the toilers of the world.

ELENA ALEKSANDROVNA SKRJABINA

(b. 1906)

Skrjabina, a graduate student in French literature, was living in Leningrad when the Germans attacked the Soviet Union in 1941. She and her family underwent the worst of the siege of Leningrad and were finally evacuated across the frozen Lake Ladoga, eventually winding up in Pyatigorsk in the Caucasus. When that city fell to the invading German army, they escaped once more to the Ukraine where she was conscripted into a labor battalion and ended in a forced labor camp in the Rhineland. After the end of the war, she was able to emigrate with her two sons to the United States, where she became a professor of French at the University of Iowa. Her diary recording her war-time experiences in the Soviet Union was published in English as *Siege and Survival* in 1971.

NOVEMBER 6 [1941]

Tarnovskaya[1] got up this morning at four. With the help of her son and energetic daughter-in-law, she forced herself into a cooperative, and got herself and us some butter. Absolutely unbelievable! We are torn by the wish to eat it all at once and the realization that we must stretch it out somehow.

Since the 20th of October, Dima[2] has been 'working' fictitiously in a workshop, thanks to George Tarnovski. Although that workshop is still being organized, Dima is already considered a worker and receives 250 grams of bread a day instead of the 125 gram ration. This is very important for Dima. He always did have a big appetite, and when the rationing started, he weakened quickly. His apathy has me in despair. He has lost interest in everything. He won't read or talk. It is hard to believe, but he is even indifferent to the bombings. The only thing that can bring him out of it is food. He is hungry all day and rattles around through the cupboard, looking for food. When he

---

[1] Lubov Tarnovskaya, a woman who was sharing the flat along with her family.
[2] Skrjabina's elder son, then aged fifteen.

can't find anything, he chews on coffee grounds or those abominable oil cakes which were once fed only to the cattle.

All of Leningrad eats oil cake now. They pay whatever is asked for it: shoes, stockings, pieces of material. You take any valuable article to the market-place, and you get this substance in exchange. It is so coarse that you can't bite into it. You can't even cut it up with an axe. You have to shave it like a piece of wood to get something like sawdust. And from this you bake pancakes. They are extremely unappetizing. And after you eat them – heartburn. The bread, too, is barely edible. There is a minimal percent of flour in it. Mostly it consists of oil cake, celluloid, and some other unknown substance. As a result of these ingredients, the bread is dry and heavy. Nevertheless, people are ready to cut each other's throats for it. In the morning, on the way home from the bakery, you must hide it carefully. There have been many instances in which the bread has been stolen right on the streets.

NOVEMBER 10

We are virtually being buried under incendiary bombs. Earlier, all the little boys in our apartment house would stand guard on the roof – Dima's friend Sergei, Dima, the son of the actress on the third floor – a bright and healthy boy – and many others – all between 12 and 16 years of age. Now nearly all of them are ill. Someone must fight the effects of the bombs and women have proved to be the most durable. * * *

NOVEMBER 12

I dropped in on an acquaintance and she treated me to the latest culinary creation: jelly made of leather straps. The recipe is as follows: boil pig's hide straps and then prepare something on the order of jellied meat. This mess is beyond description – yellow and repugnant. As hungry as I was, I couldn't swallow even one spoonful. I choked. My friends are surprised at my disgust. They eat it all the time. They say it is sold in great quantities in the market-place. However, I don't go there anymore. I have nothing left to trade. Anything I might have to offer wouldn't interest anyone.

The markets are overloaded with beautiful things: quality materials, materials for suits and coats, costly dresses, furs. These are the only things that will buy bread and vegetable oil.

Not rumors, but reliable sources, i.e., news from militia sectors, tell us that a lot of sausage has appeared at the market place – jellied meat and such – made of human flesh. To think that such a horrible possibility could be imagined! People have reached their limits and are capable of everything. My husband has already warned me not to let Yura[3] wander far from home even with nana for children are the first to disappear.

NOVEMBER 29

My former maid, Marusa, appeared unexpectedly, unexplainedly. She brought a loaf of bread and a voluminous sack of cereal. Marusa is unrecognizable. She is not the same barefoot, unkempt girl I knew. She wore a squirrel jacket, an attractive silk dress, and an expensive scarf. Added to all this, a blooming appearance ... just as if she had come from a vacation. She is not at all a citizen of a hungry, embattled city. I asked why. It turns out the reason is very simple. She works in a food warehouse. The director of the warehouse is in love with her. Whenever the workers are searched before they leave, Marusa is searched just for the sake of appearance. She carries out several kilos of butter, sacks of cereal, rice, and canned goods – all hidden under her fur jacket. Sometimes, she says, she has even managed to take out several chickens. She takes everything home, and in the evenings the director comes to work and to relax. At first Marusa lived in a dormitory. Then her brigade leader made her aware of the advantages of joint living and invited Marusa to live with her. Now this woman makes use of Marusa's rich harvest to feed her own relatives and friends. Obviously she is a very clever person. She has completely taken charge of foolish and good-hearted Marusa and under the guise of a kindly person exchanges Marusa's food products for various things. Thus Marusa's wardrobe has improved. She is delighted over these trades and little interests herself with where her precious booty goes. Marusa told me all this naively, adding that now she will try to see to it that my children did not go hungry.

---

[3] Her second son, then five years old.

Writing this, I have to think about what is happening in our unfortunate, besieged city. Thousands of people die daily, but some people have the richest comforts even under these conditions. True, during Marusa's visit I did not consider these things. Moreover, I begged her not to forget us and offered anything which might interest her.

DECEMBER 17

The alarms and air raids have stopped. They say it is because of the cold. However the mood does not improve. Starvation and death grow with each new day. Last night Ludmilla returned home quite upset. It was already dark when she started home from work. She was in a hurry. Suddenly a woman threw herself at Ludmilla and hung on her hand. At first Ludmilla was totally bewildered, but the woman explained thickly that she was extremely weak and could go no further. She asked for help. Ludmilla said she herself had barely enough strength to get home. But the woman persisted, hanging on like a leech. Ludmilla tried desperately to free herself but somehow couldn't. The woman, grasping Ludmilla's hand, dragged her in the direction opposite our apartment. Finally, Ludmilla tore herself away, tripping over snowbanks. She started to run. When I opened the door for her, she was a ghastly sight – pale, her eyes full of terror, barely able to catch her breath. Telling about what happened, she repeated over and over, 'She will die. I know it. She will die today.' I could guess the two conflicting emotions which fought within her: joy that she had escaped, that she was alive, and the horrifying thoughts about the woman she had had to leave to fate and to a certain death on this freezing December night.

FEBRUARY 4 [1942]

Last night, late, there was a knock at the front door. A man in a sheepskin coat with various military decorations in the buttonholes asked for me. He came for some documents necessary for evacuation. While I looked for the invaluable papers, he followed me with a flashlight. Slowly I turned my attention to his full, well-tended face ... literally a man from another world who accidentally came across our planet. But he is also surviving the siege of Leningrad. For the hundredth time you reflect on how different can be the situation of people who have power or advantages from that of ordinary people who have nothing but their bread ration cards. Our visitor took our papers and left. He told us that tomorrow we must evacuate.

FEBRUARY 5

A day of insane flurry has ended. The final packing took place in complete darkness. I don't know what I took, what I have forgotten. We are so tired, we can barely move. My mother, emaciated and with frightening signs of death on her face, also bustled about all day, packing this and that as if she were going to the country. My husband drove to the hospital to get Dima. I had hoped to see the boy a little improved at least, but I was gravely mistaken. Several days ago, Dima came down with dystrophy, a severe stomach ailment which now rages in our city, but despite Dima's grave condition, the head doctor at the hospital nevertheless advised me to take him with us since there is little hope for improvement in Leningrad. With the aid of a chauffeur, my husband carried Dima into our apartment.

And so tomorrow we are leaving. Our party – my seventy-four-year-old, terribly weak mother; our sixty-five-year-old nana, feet swollen, covered with boils, strength undermined by the harsh winter; gravely ill Dima who cannot walk by himself; little Yura, covered with sores, and me. Me – just barely able-bodied. I am already beginning to swell. I have especially weakened in these last few days.

The future frightens me. Where will we go and what will happen to us? My aunt, who is also supposed to evacuate with her daughter and grandchildren after her husband's burial, sighs heavily when she looks at me. I know that she doubts the success of this venture. But we will see. There is nothing we can do. There is no other way out.

Friends came to say good-bye today. Will I ever see them again? It is terrible to look at Irina, Yura's godmother, who was so convinced that no one would go hungry. She is all swollen. Her once beautiful face has turned into a transparent mask. Hunger changes the appearance of all. Everyone now is blue-black, bloodless, swollen. If someone had tried makeup to appear to be dying of hunger, he could not come up with such faces. Besides Irina, my other friend, Jennie, horrifies me. Jennie, who only a few months ago was radiant and beautiful. Nothing of her former beauty remains. She always ate very little, but now she eyes every little piece hungrily. Another friend, also named Irina, and her husband Igor, barely got here. Not long ago they were healthy, lively sportsmen; now they are old. Luckily, I had some oats, which I won't take with me. From these oats I made a last treat for my guests. How greedily all eyes were glued to that large pot full of steaming liquid. I remembered how almost exactly one year ago, on February 13, on my birthday, all these people had gathered at my home for the traditional supper. How many delicious things there were to eat ... and so many wines. And after supper – dancing and gaiety until morning. And all that was only a year ago. Ours is a gathering of ghosts.

Skrjabina's mother survived the crossing of Lake Ladoga but died shortly thereafter. Skrjabina lost contact with Dima for a time but they were almost miraculously reunited. All three survived to emigrate to the United States. Her husband, believing her dead in the labor camp, married Irina after the war.

ETTY HILLESUM

(1914–1943)

Hillesum was twenty-seven years old when the Nazis began to round up Dutch Jews for deportation and extermination; her intense and personal religious faith led her to volunteer to be interned at Westerbork, a staging area for transport to Auschwitz. Working for the Jewish Council, Hillesum reported what she saw in her letters and in a diary that records the stages of her spiritual growth. These were not published until 1982 and appeared in English in 1983 as *An Interrupted Life*. These extraordinary documents became an international best-seller.

30 SEPTEMBER [1942]

Of course, it is our complete destruction they want! But let us bear it with grace.

There is no hidden poet in me, just a little piece of God that might grow into poetry.

And a camp needs a poet, one who experiences life there, even there, as a bard and is able to sing about it.

At night, as I lay in the camp on my plank bed, surrounded by women and girls gently snoring, dreaming aloud, quietly sobbing and tossing and turning, women and girls who often told me during the day, 'We don't want to think, we don't want to feel, otherwise we are sure to go out of our minds,' I was sometimes filled with an infinite tenderness, and lay awake for hours letting all the many, too many impressions of a much too long day wash over me, and I prayed, 'Let me be the thinking heart of these barracks.' And that is what I want to be again. The thinking heart of a whole concentration camp. I lie here so patiently and now so calmly again, that I feel quite a bit better already. I feel my strength returning to me; I have stopped making plans and worrying about risks. Happen what may, it is bound to be for the good.

3 OCTOBER, SATURDAY EVENING, 9 O'CLOCK.

One ought to pray, day and night, for the thousands. One ought not to be without prayer for even a single minute.

4 OCTOBER [1942], SUNDAY EVENING

* * * 'God, you have entrusted me with so many precious gifts, let me guard them well and use them properly.' All this talking with friends is bad for me right now. I am worn to a frazzle. I lack the strength it takes to leave it all behind, to strike a balance between my inner and my outer worlds. That is my main task. They are both equally strong in me. I so love being with people. It is as if my own intensity draws what is best and deepest right out of them; they open up before me, every human being a new story, told to me by life itself. And my eyes simply read on joyfully. Life has confided so many stories to me, I shall have to retell them to people who cannot read the book of life itself.

Alone for once in the middle of the night, God and I have been left together, and I feel all the richer and at peace for that.

8 OCTOBER, THURSDAY AFTERNOON

I am still sick. I can do nothing about it. I shall have to wait a little longer to gather up all their tears and fears. Though I can really do it here just as well, here in bed. Perhaps that is why I feel so giddy and hot. I don't want to become a chronicler of horrors. Or of sensations. This morning I said to Jopie:[1] 'It still all comes down to the same thing: life is beautiful. And I believe in God. And I want to be there right in the thick of what people call "horror" and still be able to say: life is beautiful.' And how here I lie in some corner, dizzy and feverish and unable to do a thing. When I woke up just now I was parched, reached for my glass of water, and, grateful for that one sip, thought to myself, 'If I could only be there to give some of those parched thousands just one sip of water.' And all the time I kept telling myself, 'Don't worry, things aren't all that bad.' Whenever yet another poor woman broke

---

[1] Jopie Vleeschouwer, Etty's close friend in Westerbork. In a letter appended to *An Interrupted Life*, Jopie records her last sight of Etty as she was shipped off to Auschwitz.

down at one of our registration tables, or a hungry child started crying, I would go over to them and stand beside them protectively, arms folded across my chest, force a smile for those huddled, shattered scraps of humanity and tell myself, 'Things aren't all that bad.' And all I did was just stand there, for what else could one do? Sometimes I might just sit down beside someone, put an arm round a shoulder, say very little and just look into their eyes. Nothing was alien to me, not one single expression of human sorrow. Everything seemed so familiar, as if I knew it all and had gone through it all before. People said to me, 'You must have nerves of steel to stand up to it.' I don't think I have nerves of steel, far from it, but I can certainly stand up to things. I am not afraid to look suffering straight in the eyes. And at the end of each day, there was always the feeling: I love people so much. Never any bitterness about what was done to them, but always love for those who knew how to bear so much although nothing had prepared them for such burdens.

* * *

FROM A LETTER DATED 24 AUGUST 1943

There was a moment when I felt in all seriousness that, after this night, it would be a sin ever to laugh again. But then I reminded myself that some of those who had gone away had been laughing, even if only a handful of them this time ... There will be some who will laugh now and then in Poland, too, though not many from this transport, I think.

When I think of the faces of that squad of armed, green-uniformed guards – my God, those faces! I looked at them, each in turn, from behind the safety of a window, and I have never been so frightened of anything in my life as I was of those faces. I sank to my knees with the words that preside over human life: and God made man after His likeness. That passage spent a difficult morning with me.

I have told you often enough that no words and images are adequate to describe nights like these. But still I must try to convey something of it to you. One always has the feeling here of being the ears and eyes of a piece of Jewish history, but there is also the need sometimes to be a still, small voice. We must keep one another in touch with everything that happens in the various outposts of this world, each one contributing his own little piece of stone to the great mosaic that will take shape once the war is over.

After a night in the hospital barracks, I took an early morning walk past the punishment barracks, and prisoners were being moved out. The deportees, mainly men, stood with their packs behind the barbed wire. So many of them looked tough and ready for anything. An old acquaintance – I didn't recognize him straight-away, a shaven head often changes people completely – called out to me with a smile, 'If they don't manage to do me in, I'll be back.'

But the babies, those tiny piercing screams of the babies, dragged from their cots in the middle of the night ... I have to put it all down quickly, in a muddle because if I leave it until later I probably won't be able to go on believing that it really happened. It is like a vision, and drifts further and further away. The babies were easily the worst.

And there was that paralysed young girl, who didn't want to take her dinner plate along and found it so hard to die. Or the terrified young boy: he had thought he was safe, that was his mistake, and when he realised he was going to have to go anyway, he panicked and ran off. His fellow Jews had to hunt him down – if they didn't find him, scores of others would be put on the transport in his place. He was caught soon enough, hiding in a tent, but 'notwithstanding' ... 'notwithstanding,' all those others had to go on transport anyway, as a deterrent, they said. And so, many good friends were dragged away by that boy. Fifty victims for one moment of insanity. Or rather: he didn't drag them away – our commandant did, someone of whom it is sometimes said that he is a gentleman. Even so, will the boy be able to live with himself, once it dawns on him exactly what he's been the cause of? And how will the other Jews on board the train react to him? That boy is going to have a very hard time. The episode might have been overlooked, perhaps, if there hadn't been so much unnerving activity over our heads that night. The commandant must have been affected by that too. '*Donnerwetter*, some flying tonight!' I heard a guard say as he looked up at the stars.

People still harbour such childish hopes that the transport won't get through. Many of us were able from here to watch the bombardment of a nearby town, probably Emden. So why shouldn't it be possible for the railway line to be hit too, and for the train to be stopped from leaving? It's never been known to happen yet, but people keep hoping it will with each new transport and with never-flagging hope ...

The evening before that night, I walked through the camp. People were grouped together between the barracks, under a grey, cloudy sky. 'Look, that's just how people behave after a disaster, standing about on street corners discussing what's happened,' my companion said to me. 'But that's what makes it so impossible to understand,' I burst out. 'This time, it's *before* the disaster!'

Whenever misfortune strikes, people have a natural instinct to lend a helping hand and to save what can be saved. Tonight, I shall be 'helping' to dress babies and to calm mothers and that is all I can hope to do. I could almost curse myself for that. For we all know that we are yielding up our sick and defenceless brothers and sisters to hunger, heat, cold, exposure and destruction, and yet we dress them and escort them to the bare cattle trucks – and if they can't walk we carry them on stretchers. What is going on, what mysteries are these, in what sort of fatal mechanism have we become enmeshed? The answer cannot simply be that we are all cowards. We're not that bad. We stand before a much deeper question ...

In the afternoon I did a round of the hospital barracks one more time, going from bed to bed. Which beds would be empty the next day? The transport lists are never published until the very last moment, but some of us know well in advance that our names will be down. A young girl called me. She was sitting bolt upright in her bed, eyes wide open. This girl has thin wrists and a peaky little face. She is partly paralysed and has just been learning to walk again, between two nurses, one step at a time. 'Have you heard? I have to go.' We look at each other for a long moment. It is as if her face has disappeared, she is all eyes. Then she says in a level, grey little voice, 'Such a pity, isn't it? That everything you have learned in life goes for nothing.' And, 'How hard it is to die.' Suddenly the unnatural rigidity of her expression gives way and she sobs, 'Oh, and the worst of it all is having to leave Holland!' and, 'Oh, why wasn't I allowed to die before ...' Later, during the night, I saw her again for the last time.

* * *

If I were to say that I was in hell that night, what would I really be telling you? I caught myself saying it aloud in the night, aloud to myself and quite soberly, 'So that's what hell is like.' You really can't tell who is going and who isn't this time. Almost everyone is up, the sick help each other to get dressed. There are some who have no clothes at all, whose luggage has been lost or hasn't arrived yet. Ladies from the 'Welfare' walk about doling out clothes, which may fit or not, it doesn't matter as long as you've covered yourself with something. Some old women look a ridiculous sight. Small bottles of milk are being prepared to take along with the babies, whose pitiful screams punctuate all the frantic activity in the barracks. A young mother says to me almost apologetically, 'My baby doesn't usually cry, it's almost as if he can tell what's happening.' She picks up the child, a lovely baby about eight months old, from a makeshift crib and smiles at it. 'If you don't behave yourself, mummy won't take you along with her!' She tells me about some friends, 'When those men in green came to fetch them in Amsterdam, their children cried terribly. Then their father said, "If you don't behave yourselves, you won't be allowed to go in that green car, this green gentleman won't take you." And that helped – the children calmed down.' She winks at me bravely, a trim, dark little woman with a lively, olive-skinned face, dressed in long grey trousers and a green woollen sweater. 'I may be smiling, but I feel pretty awful.' The little woman with the wet washing is on the point of hysterics. 'Can't you hide my child for me? Go on, please, won't you hide him, he's got a high fever, how can I possibly take him along?' She points to a little bundle of misery with blonde curls and a burning, bright-red little face. The child tosses about in his rough little cot. The nurse wants the mother to put on an extra woollen sweater, tries to pull it on over her dress. She refuses, 'I'm not going to take anything along, what use would it be ... my child.' And she sobs, 'They take the sick children away and you never get them back.'

Then a woman comes up to her, a stout working-class woman with a kindly snub-nosed face, draws the desperate mother down with her on to the edge of one of the iron bunk beds and talks to her almost crooningly, 'There now, you're just an ordinary Jew, aren't you, so you'll just have to go, won't you ...?'

A few beds further down I suddenly catch sight of the ash-grey, freckled face of a colleague. She is squatting beside the bed of a dying woman who has just swallowed some poison and who happens to be her mother.

* * *

I pass the bed of the paralysed girl. The others have helped to dress her. I never saw such great big eyes in such a little face. 'I can't take it all in,' she whispers to me. A few steps away stands my little hunchbacked Russian woman, I told you about her before. She stands there as if spun in a web of sorrow. Later she said sadly to me, 'She doesn't even have a plate. I wanted to give her mine but she wouldn't take it, she said, "I'll be dead in ten days' time anyway, and then those horrible Germans will get it."'

She stands there in front of me, a green silk kimono wrapped around her small, misshapen figure. She has the very wise, bright eyes of a child. She looks at me for a long time in silence, searchingly, and then says, 'I would like, oh, I really would like, to be able to swim away in my tears.' And, 'I long so desperately for my dear mother.' (Her mother died a few months ago from cancer, in the washroom near the WC. At least she was left alone for a moment, to die in peace.) She asks me with her strange accent in the voice of a child that begs for forgiveness, 'Surely God will be able to understand my doubts in a world like this, won't He?' Then she turns away from me, in an almost loving gesture of infinite sadness, and throughout the night I see the misshapen, green, silk-clad figure moving between the beds, doing small services for those about to depart. She herself doesn't have to go, not this time anyway.

I'm sitting here squeezing tomato juice for the babies. A young woman sits beside me. She appears ready and eager to leave, and is beautifully turned out. It is something like a cry of liberation when she exclaims, arms flung wide, 'I'm embarking on a wonderful journey, I might find my husband.' A woman opposite cuts her short bitterly. 'I'm going as well, but I certainly don't think it's wonderful.' ***A bit of her history in her own words: 'My time wasn't far off when they threw me into prison. And the taunts and the insults! I made the mistake of saying that I couldn't stand so they made me stand for hours, but I managed it without making a sound.' She looks defiant. 'My husband was in the prison as well. I won't tell you what they did to him! But my God, he was tough! They sent him through last month. I was in my third day of labour and couldn't go with him. But how brave he was!' She is almost radiant.

'Perhaps I shall find him again.' She laughs defiantly. 'They may drag us through the dirt, but we'll come through all right in the end!' She looks at the crying babies all round and says, 'I'll have good work to do on the train, I still have lots of milk.'

* * *

The tide of helpers gradually recedes; people go back to their sleeping quarters. So many exhausted, pale and suffering faces. One more piece of our camp has been amputated. Next week yet another piece will follow. This is what has been happening now for over a year, week in, week out. We are left with just a few thousand. A hundred thousand Dutch members of our race are toiling away under an unknown sky or lie rotting in some unknown soil. We know nothing of their fate. It is only a short while, perhaps, before we find out, each one of us in his own time, for we are all marked down to share that fate, of that I have not a moment's doubt. But I must go now and lie down and sleep for a little while. I am a bit tired and dizzy. Then later I have to go to the laundry to track down the face cloth that got lost. But first I must sleep. As for the future, I am firmly resolved to return to you after my wanderings. In the meantime, my love once again, you dear people.

Two weeks later, Etty Hillesum was transported, with the rest of her family, to Auschwitz. She threw a postcard from the train which was found and sent on by farmers. It said, 'We have left the camp singing.' She died in Auschwitz on 30 November 1943.

CHARLOTTE DELBO

(1913–85)

An important French intellectual, poet, novelist and dramatist, Delbo survived Auschwitz. She was active in the Resistance, together with her husband, the Communist leader George Dudach. They were both arrested in 1942 and Dudach was executed. Delbo was sent to Auschwitz in 1943. Almost immediately upon her liberation from the camp, Delbo began work on *Auschwitz et après*, from which the following is taken, but did not publish it until twenty years later.

We were deep down in that ditch since early morning. The three of us. The commando[1] was working further on. From time to time the kapos[2] prodded us, just to see where we were at digging that ditch again. We were able to talk, had been talking since early morning.

To talk was to plan going home, because to believe we would return was a way of forcing luck's hand. Those who had stopped believing they were going back were dead. One had to believe it, against all odds, incredible as it might seem, one had to lend to this return certainty, reality and color, to prepare it by conjuring up each and every detail.

Occasionally, one of the women voicing a common thought interjected: 'How do you envision getting out?' There we were. The question sank in silence.

To shake off silence and the anguish it covered, another would venture: 'Perhaps one day we'll no longer wake up for roll call. We'll sleep a long time. When we wake it'll be broad daylight, and the camp will be still. Those who step out first from the barracks will notice that the guard post is empty. All the SS will have fled. A couple of hours later, the Russian reconnaissance units will be here.'

Another silence answered this anticipation.

---

[1] The work party.
[2] Inmates who acted as guards.

She added, 'First, we will have heard the cannons' report. Far off at first, then drawing closer. The battle of Cracow. With Cracow taken it'll be the end. You'll see, the SS will flee.'

The more detailed her description, the less we believed it. By tacit agreement, we'd drop the subject and pick up again our impossible plans with that particular logic of all crazy talk.

We were talking since early morning, glad to be away from the rest of the commando, away from the kapos' shouts. We didn't have to bear the truncheon's blows punctuating these shouts. The ditch was getting deeper with every passing hour. Our heads no longer protruded over the top. As we reached the marl, we stood with our feet in water. The mud we cast over our heads was white. It wasn't cold – one of the first mild days. The sun warmed our shoulders. We were at peace.

A kapo came along shouting. She signalled to my companions to get out, and marched them off. The ditch was deep enough, not sufficient work for three. My friends knew well the fear that each and every one of us feels when we're separated from the rest, when we're left alone. To hearten me, they said: 'Come on, hurry up. You'll join us.'

Here I am, at the bottom of the ditch, alone, and so disheartened that I wonder whether I'll reach the end of the day. How many hours are left before the blow of the whistle which marks the end of work, the moment we line up to go back to camp, in ranks of five, arm in arm, talking, talking to distraction.

Here I am all alone. I can't think of anything any longer because all my thoughts collide with the anguish which dwells in all of us: How will we get out of here? When will we get out? I'd like to think of nothing. But if this lasts, no one will get out. Those who are still alive say to themselves each day that it's a miracle they held out for eight whole weeks. No one can see further than a week ahead.

I'm alone and frightened. I try to keep digging. The work isn't moving. I attack a last bump at the bottom, evening it out. Perhaps the kapo will decide it's enough. I feel my bruised back, its curve paralyzed, my shoulders torn by the shovel, my arms unable to cast spadefuls of muddy marl over the top. I'm here, all alone. I feel like lying down in the mud to wait. To wait for the kapo to find me dead. It's not so easy to die. It takes a long time, hitting someone with a shovel, or a bludgeon, before he dies.

I continue digging a little longer, scooping up two or three spadefuls of earth. It's too hard. As soon as you're alone, you think: What good

does it do? What for? Why not give up ... Better now, on the spot. Surrounded by the others, one is able to hold out.

I'm all alone, alone with my haste to join my companions, and my temptation to give up. Why? Why must I keep on digging this ditch?

'Enough! That's it for now!' A voice shouts from above. '*Komm schnell*!' I pull myself out, leaning on the shovel. My arms are weary, the back of my neck aches. The kapo is running. She runs across the road by the side of the marsh. There's the fill. Women like ants. Some carry sand to those who pound it flat, levelling the terrain. A huge, flat space, stretching under the sun. Hundreds of women are standing, like a frieze of shadows profiled against the light.

I follow the kapo, who hands me a pounder and a blow. She directs me towards a team of workers. I look for my friends. Lulu calls me: 'Come next to me, there's a spot,' and she makes room for me in the line of women who are pounding the ground, holding the pounder with both hands as they raise it and let it fall. 'Come here to pestle the rice!' How does Viva find the strength to joke like this? I can't move my lips, even to venture a smile. Lulu is worried: 'What's the matter with you? Are you ill?'

'No, I'm not ill. I can't take it anymore. I'm all in today.'

'That's nothing. You'll get over it.'

'No, Lulu, I won't. I'm telling you I can't take it anymore.'

She didn't answer anything. It's the first time she's heard me speak like this. A practical woman, she lifts my tool. 'Your pounder is real heavy. Take mine. It's lighter and you're more tired than I am because of the ditch.'

We exchange tools. I start pounding the sand, like the others. I look at all these women going through the same gestures, with their arms weaker and weaker as they lift the heavy mass. Armed with their bludgeons, the kapos move from one to the other. I am overwhelmed with despair. 'How will we ever get out of here?'

Lulu looks at me smiling. Her hand grazes mine, to comfort me. And I repeat, letting her know it's useless: 'I'm telling you I can't take it any more today. This time it's true.'

Lulu has a good look around us, and seeing there's no kapo nearby she takes hold of my wrist, saying: 'Get behind me, so they won't see you. You'll be able to have a good cry.' She speaks in a whispering, timid voice. Probably this is just what I needed since I obey her gentle shove. Dropping my tool upon the ground, but still leaning on its long handle, I cry my eyes out. I thought I did not want to cry, but my tears welled up, and they're running down my cheeks. I let them flow, and when one of them touches my lips, I taste the salt and go on weeping.

Lulu continues to work and stay on the lookout at the same time. Occasionally she turns back, and with her sleeve, softly wipes my face. I keep on crying. I'm not thinking of anything. I just go on crying.

Now I no longer know why I am crying, when Lulu suddenly pulls me: 'That's enough now! Back to work. Here she comes!' She says it so kindly that I'm not ashamed of having cried. It's as though I had wept against my mother's breast.

SYLVIA SALVESEN

(b. 1890)

A close friend of Maud, Queen of Norway, and connected by marriage to the Scottish aristocracy, Salvesen began to plan her Resistance work even before her country was actually invaded. Her activities caused her to be arrested and imprisoned twice in Norway before she was finally sent to Ravensbrück in July, 1943, where she remained for nearly two years. She used the fact that she was a doctor's wife (her husband was physician to the king of Norway) to achieve a post in the camp hospital, where she was frequently able to intervene to save the lives of women prisoners. After the war, she was a leading witness at the war crimes of the Ravensbrück staff. In the following excerpt, published in English in 1958 as *Forgive, But Do Not Forget*, she recalls her testimony. Following her release from Ravensbrück, Salvesen spent her energies seeking help and rehabilitation for the political prisoners among whom she had lived in the camp.

After the war, Salvesen was called to testify at the war-crimes trial in Hamburg of those responsible for the atrocities at Ravensbrück.

At long last the great moment had arrived and I entered the witness-box as the first to testify. It was one of the most dramatic experiences of my life.

On the left were the members of the Court with the Judge Advocate in his grey wig, and exactly opposite me the Prosecutor, Major Stewart, and his assistants. On the right were the accused, sixteen in number. If looks could kill, I should have fallen down dead on the spot. Never have so many furious glances been directed toward me at one time. Dr. Adolf Winkelmann and Matron Marshall caught my eye among the rest, almost as if their deeper hatred made their gaze the first to reach me; then I heard Major Stewart's calm voice and turned immediately to face him. After I had answered a few questions about my arrest and imprisonment in Norway, he said, 'Will the witness try to give a picture of Ravensbrück camp, her first impressions of it, the daily life there, and her experiences?'

This was the question I had been dreading, for I feared I would not be able to make my reply vivid enough.

I began by saying, 'If I were the world's greatest orator, the world's best poet or painter, I could not bring Ravensbrück before you, but I hope that God will enable me to find words to give you some idea of it.

'Painters of all nations have tried to represent the horrors of Hell, and my own first impression of Ravensbrück carried my mind back to a picture by a Norwegian artist that I had seen as a child.

'When, on the arrival of our Norwegian party, we were marched inside the camp walls – thirty dirty, downcast women – we saw for the first time human beings whom we could not distinguish as being men or women. They were emaciated, dirty, clad in rags, bare-legged, and wearing wooden shoes, so that with their close-cropped heads they looked entirely sexless. Yet it was not this that made me think of Hell – it was their dead eyes. If I am now to describe the camp to you, you must think of me as merely a window through which you are looking. I want only to show you what my dead and living comrades suffered, and why so many of the survivors are nervous wrecks whose minds have been affected as well as their bodies.'

For the remainder of the day my examination-in-chief continued and I took the members of the Court with me on a mental tour of that terrible camp as I described its filth, its stench, and its horrors.

It seemed but a short while before I heard the voice of the President of the Court saying, 'The Court will now adjourn until nine o'clock tomorrow morning.'

For two more days the questioning went on, examination, cross-examination, and re-examination, and finally I was questioned by the Judge Advocate and the Court.

I cannot give an account of all the questions that the members of the Court put to me, for that would take too long, but the last thing the Judge Advocate asked me was this: 'Might it not be possible that the terrible conditions in Ravensbrück were due, at any rate partly, to the enormous transports that arrived during the last few months?'

'Yes,' I answered, 'but it was a crime to give orders of this kind, and a crime to obey. Yet the greatest crimes in Ravensbrück were not those committed against our bodies, but against our minds and against our souls. In this ocean of wickedness and brutality the power to believe and to hope was drowned. This was the reason why the prisoners in Ravensbrück had dead eyes, and that we now hear from all countries that so many of our comrades have, after their return home, slipped into the darkness of mental illness. And many of us, when we sit quietly, thinking that we are not observed, have what has been called the "concentration camp look."'

For the next few days, one by one, like so many avenging angels, the remainder of the prosecution witnesses went in and out of the witness-box each with her horrifying tale to tell. The details of their evidence now filled the papers of almost every country, and the world was shaken. When before in all history had crimes so terrible and so stupendous been perpetrated? As one of the witnesses said, 'The aim at Ravensbrück was to make everything as physically and spiritually as hard as possible for us and the ultimate objective was the total extermination of us all.'

At length the last prosecution witness had been called, and the sixteen began their defence.

The German barristers were now faced with a more difficult task than any of their profession had ever encountered. They had to defend people who had lost every right to be called human beings, and who had behaved worse than animals. They were responsible for the suffering, torture, illness, and death of thousands of innocent women, and were accused of having misused them as guinea-pigs for operations, treated them as slaves, driven them to death exhausted by suffering, privation, and starvation. Those who could no longer be used as slaves were killed by lethal injections or were shot, and when this was not quick enough, they were sent in their thousands to the gas-chamber.

The curtain went down on the first scene in the settlement of the German account.

MATRON ELIZABETH MARSHALL

'Appearances are deceptive.' Nothing could be more true than this proverb when applied to Elizabeth Marshall, Matron and ruler of Ravensbrück hospital, the nerve centre of the whole camp. Together with Dr. Percival Treite, the doctor in charge, and the other commanding officers, Matron Marshall was responsible for the conditions in the camp.

With her rounded figure and her attractive face, her plump well-kept hands, her neat uniform and a mask of amiability, the first impression she gave was that of a little elderly good-natured nurse.

To look at her with the thought of Florence Nightingale in one's mind, and then to see her as she was in reality, was a terrible shock. To see her shouting out orders, brutally pushing sick prisoners aside – perhaps even hitting them – or sending them off in transport to new suffering, starvation, often death, with a hard face and an expression of disgust – to see this only once would make a life-long impression on anyone's mind. To live with it day in, day out, for a year and a half was almost unendurable.

It was only by degrees that all her abominations came to light, for, to begin with, she always tried to win over a new prisoner who was given work in the hospital, in order to find out if the latter could be used to further her own ends and evil intentions.

Her object was to exploit the enemies of Germany to their last breath and without mercy to the advantage of the 'mighty Fatherland.' She did this so cleverly that she would keep a woman prisoner going exactly as long as she could be useful, and not a second longer. This was her aim, and unfortunately she achieved it only too often.

As a rule Matron Marshall herself supervised the selection of those prisoners who were only 'partly serviceable,' and was herself responsible for giving out the 'red cards' which later became so notorious and so dreaded. Sooner or later they always led to sick transport, which for many was the ticket to the end of the journey – the gas-chamber.

Matron stole the prisoners' parcels and gave them to the members of the SS, the German Hospital staff, and to other officials and personal friends, distributing only a fraction of the contents of their own parcels to a certain number of the sick as a sign of great favour.

She refused to distribute the dried milk, of which she had plenty, to the newly born babies and was, therefore, directly responsible for the death of hundreds of them. She told Sister Gerda[1] to put them out of the way by means of lethal injections, and when the latter managed to evade these orders, she saw to it that the children disappeared in some other way more quickly than conditions warranted. In February 1945, about a hundred and twenty children were born, of whom eighty died before the month was out, and probably the rest before the mothers were given their freedom.

Matron used to employ her free time, including her free evenings, in making out lists of the 'tubercular' patients and the so-called 'mental cases' who, once they were on her list, were as good as sent

---

[1] A German nurse who did what she could to help the prisoners.

to the gas-chamber. Many in this latter category were only temporarily mentally deranged because of shock, starvation, illness, or solitary confinement with torture. Nursing, kindness, and freedom would have brought them back to life. They were, however, a burden on the Third Reich, and Matron helped to dispose of them.

Was there a glimmer of humanity left in this woman? Yes, I surprised her once with Nikolas in her arms, the first child born in the camp, and in addition, a Russian, one of Germany's most deadly enemies. She was actually prattling to the baby, who was too small to understand anything but the friendly tone of her voice. Nikolas smiled and Matron smiled back at him.

Another factor which made her more understandable to us, if not more sympathetic, was her all-embracing fanaticism. To her, Germany was everything, and Hitler was the Führer who was to make Germany ruler of the world.

How could she find peace in her mind? Only by learning to know herself and acknowledging her faults. Was that within the realm of possibility? When I saw her again among the accused in Hamburg, I thought it was not. If looks could have killed, she would have killed not only me, but everyone involved, even those accused with her. She seemed to radiate hatred, but as the days went on, her expression changed. As she sat there listening to the recital of all the dreadful things that had happened in Ravensbrück, told so clearly, so calmly and convincingly, some sort of impression seemed at last to have been made.

She seemed to have shrunk in her seat as she gave me a last terror-stricken glance. Did she understand, or had she begun to suspect, what I meant when I wished her and Germany peace when we finally went from Ravensbrück leaving her weeping behind us?

Had she begun to suspect that the Germany she had worshipped, and which was sinking in dust and ashes before her eyes, could only rise again if its sons and daughters, understanding the faults they had committed, would acknowledge that they had become a band of criminals and not a Herrenvolk,[2] and try to do penance and bring a new spirit into their country? Then – and only then – could Germany regain peace.

Would the violent shock which it certainly must have been for her to be condemned to death pull off her mask? Would she see herself as she really was? None of us who were witnesses in the Hamburg

---

[2] Master race.

trial thought that she would be condemned to death – we thought her age would save her. We were entirely neutral towards her and had no definite wishes in the question of life or death for her. We only wished to tell the truth about her as about all the others. It was the Court who had to decide. But perhaps the death sentence was the greatest mercy for her, the last chance she had of finding her way out of the darkness.

* * *

THE CURTAIN FALLS

The Ravensbrück trial in Hamburg had come to an end. The Court had pronounced its sentence. Of the sixteen accused, one of them, the devil doctor Adolf Winkelmann, was found dead in his cell the day before sentence was pronounced. He had died of heart failure. The remaining fifteen were all found guilty, eleven of them being sentenced to death by hanging. Among them were Dr. Percival Treite and Matron Marshall. Of the remaining four, two received fifteen and two ten years' hard labour. They had been found guilty of causing the deaths of thousands of women in one of the worst of all the camps, Ravensbrück – women who had died from malnutrition, ill-treatment, torture, disease, and dirt.

The curtain went down for the last time on this sinister drama. Now the world knew the truth about Ravensbrück. Did Germany, did the world, learn anything from what they had heard? Have you and I learnt anything? Or have these hundreds and thousands of women, these millions of prisoners in Germany, endured inhuman captivity, or suffered an ignominious death, in vain? That is the question that the witnesses in the Ravensbrück trial put to the world and to themselves.

We witnesses came from England, France, Holland, Belgium, Poland, Czechoslovakia, Austria, Denmark, and Norway; we came, not through motives of revenge, not to gloat over our enemies and persecutors, but that Europe – and indeed the world – should be built in future on surer foundations.

We who had lived through this hell feel a great responsibility to do our best to ensure that such things should never happen again.

Let us forgive – but not forget.

FRAUEN: PERSONAL NARRATIVES

Over a period of almost ten years, Alison Owings visited Germany to collect the testimonies of women who had been alive and in Germany during the Nazi years. She went initially, she tells us, with 'the naive sisterly shaded hope ... that the German women would provide a collective sense of reflection and remorse, and perhaps persuade me that they had not supported Adolph Hitler after all.' Not surprisingly, the hope proved vain, but she emerged with a collection of extraordinary oral histories, of which the following, with Frau Anna Fest, a concentration camp guard at Ravensbrück and elsewhere, is among the most remarkable.

A JOB IN ITS OWN CATEGORY

In the fall of 1944, the Nazis called for Germany to attain 'totaler Kriegseinsatz' [mobilization for total war]. Frau Fest said each company was ordered to release a certain percentage of its employees for the mobilization. She, whose stiffened hand[1] relegated her to 'the ones they could use the least,' was among those released. She said [her employer] sent her to the local employment office, which in turn sent her to the employment office in the town of Allendorf.

There she was assigned her total mobilization job. She was told, she said, that she had been 'drafted to watch over foreign work forces.' She said her impression was that she would oversee their work in a factory and be helpful in whatever way she could be. She was, she added, 'so dumb.'

'Then with ten or twelve other women who'd also been taken from work, we were sent to what we'd been told was instruction at a manufacturing plant. We were sent, however, to Ravensbrück.'

There the women would receive two weeks of 'instruction,' and some searing memories. Survivors of Ravensbrück concentration camp for women considered it hell. Anna Fest, then twenty-four

---

[1] She had been injured in a bombing raid on the laboratory in which she was working.

years old, said her group of young women was unaware of the destination and had 'incredible fun' on the train ride there. 'We were being foolish, like young things sort of are, no?' Then they asked a male passenger, a civilian from the area, where they should get off. 'He said, "Well, don't you know where you're going" and he told us, and it was, of course, an insane shock.'

Yet, she said, even when she saw the sign, Ravensbrück Concentration Camp, she misunderstood. 'I thought it was a manufacturing plant. And we thought we'd be trained to learn the manufacturing procedures and then instruct the foreign workers. There was absolutely no talk of that ...' She stopped. 'We arrived at the holding room, sort of at the camp gate, and we saw how they were being brought in and out and guards stood there and already we saw a kick and sometimes a box on the ear too, and we began to grumble. One of the guards said, "Go ahead, you can grumble. I don't have anything against it. But if you want to be on the inside too, that's your business. I'd advise you to keep your mouths shut."

'It was such a shock to me. Even today it practically makes me crazy. When I think about it I could burst out weeping in front of you. Something so *fürchterlich* [horrendous]. They were human beings and should be treated like human beings.'

The second year we met, she related a similar incident that 'incredibly horrified' her. She had been eating with her group at a table overlooking the gate area when a group of prisoners arrived from Poland. Ravensbrück's male SS guards 'received' them. One guard 'got among them and began beating a woman. I jumped up. A guard who sat next to me pushed me back down and she said, "Obviously, you are tired of living. Stay seated if you can and look away. You have no idea how many of your kind who have rebelled are already prisoners themselves." Of course, I didn't say another thing.'

* * *

Frau Fest also indicated she knew the worst of what went on inside, even if she did not see it. Having been to Ravensbrück myself, I said I was told 'the ashes' were dumped into the nearby lake. Frau Fest responded that she and another woman had taken out a paddleboat on the lake one afternoon, that she must have noticed something, chided herself how could she have, and concluded if they did it, they must have dumped the ashes at night. Neither of us had mentioned where 'the ashes' came from.

During the two-week training period, Frau Fest and her young colleagues were inducted into the SS. They were issued SS uniforms. When the two weeks were up, the group was given a temporary leave. 'I was so happy when I came back home. Then my mother saw I wore an SS uniform. She said, "Child, that is my death." It was true. She got so insanely upset and was a little unstable in terms of nerves. She got stomach cancer during that time. She always swallowed all upsetting things.'

Frau Fest soon learned that she was not to be assigned to Ravensbrück after all but to one of fourteen 'work camps' specializing in munitions, near Allendorf. The camps were under the jurisdiction of Buchenwald.

* * *

Frau Fest said her relative good fortune at being sent to Allendorf rather than having to stay at Ravensbrück, was compounded by the kind of women she was to guard. From her first mention of them and every time thereafter, her voice and her face reflected awe. The women were Hungarian Jews.

'I had the luck to get a small detachment of [about ten] women who were very intelligent. I was alone with them. And outside the central camp area, we essentially could do what we wanted, no one looking over us.'

She said her day spanned what was considered a 'completely normal working day.' She got up about 5 a.m. and usually was back in her barracks by 6 p.m.

Every day was about the same. 'In the morning, I had to be at the gate. They came out and then I had to receive them, so to speak. To sign that so many women went with me to the plant.' (Her prisoners' work shift started at eight, she said.) 'The same thing happened in the evening, when we returned.' She said she was never allowed in the inner camp where the women slept and ate. During the work hours, she said, she stayed in the factory with her group. 'I looked to see what they were doing individually and talked with them. They all spoke German. Only intelligent women could be used for this work. I sometimes asked questions, how are you doing that and so forth,' and, she whispered, 'sometimes I was able to help them a little. Although that was really not allowed.'

She said the prisoners had a fifteen-minute breakfast break and at most a half-hour lunch break. In the evening she took them to the gate of their barracks and returned to hers, to which she was 'basically confined.' Some evenings she took a walk with other guards, and, infrequently, went to the nearby village for a movie. But usually she stayed in her bunk, writing or reading. It was less trouble, she said.

'If we wanted to go out, we had to have a certificate of passage and if we wanted to go home, a certificate of leave. If I could get the time, I'd go home to Sonnenfeld. And because I was one of the few who lived there, I did some shopping for the camp. I remember, for example, buying things for Christmas, all possible kinds of baking ingredients and setting some of it aside for my mother and mother-in-law so they could bake for Christmas, too. And I bought pencils and so on for myself, and then the prisoners baked and made Christmas tree ornaments.'

* * *

'It's very possible,' she added, 'that the women, the group I knew, collectively highly intelligent women, also maybe had a more political and worldly view than I did. I didn't *have* any such thing then. Where would I have got it from? I'd only learned what was fair and unfair, but *no* more than that.'

Her assessment that she was handicapped by her background came up again in regard to anti-Nazi Germans. 'As a simple person one didn't have the overview.' * * *

Frau Fest also implied that her own modest background made her feel worse for having to guard women she felt were her superiors in terms of education and social class. She sighed deeply. The situation was 'very, very difficult' for her, she said. 'Let's say we have, as I did, a group of people. And it included a woman doctor. And it included women theologians. And it included women scientists and women who were accustomed to managing a large home, and wives of professors and so on, who told us what they had at home and *how* they used to live. I could speak with them because I was alone with them. That was very depressing for us, that now you are somehow supposed to supervise the women. That was an extreme degradation.

'You didn't even think how it all evolved. You just tried to make the best you could of the day. I always thought, you can't make things unnecessarily bad for the women. They have it bad enough. Then they cried and kept hoping some kind of mail would come and no mail *came*. And when you as a woman are alone and don't know

where the other family members are and when new women came and
were asked right away, have you seen her or him and have you any
idea, that oppressed you very much, without question. I was always
very happy when I could go home and talk about it all with my
mother and cry myself out. It was quite a burden on my nerves.'

[As the war drew to a close, Frau Fest found herself part of a contingent
guarding a forced march of prisoners toward the east, to Czechoslovakia.
She claims to have put her life in jeopardy along the way by protesting the
indiscriminate killing of prisoners by an unidentified man who was himself
finally killed in an air raid. After the war, Frau Fest was arrested by the Allied
authorities and interrogated by 'former German Jews.']

She said she was taken to a small hut. Inside were the two officers
and a couple of German Shepherd dogs. One officer screamed
questions and accusations at her. If she did not answer 'as he wished,
he kicked me in the back and the other hit me' with his fist. The dogs
insured she did not get away.
[She maintained that the women guards had never been armed, even though
several others had broken down and confessed to carrying pistols. 'I had
no pistol. I couldn't say, just so they'd leave me in peace, yes, we had pistols.
The same thing would happen to the next person to testify.']
     What she referred to as 'the bad part,' however, was that during
the proceedings, the door of the hut was left open so that German men
standing outside waiting to be questioned had to see and hear it all.
'That must have been terrible for them. When I went outside, several
of them stood there with tears running down their cheeks. What
could they have done? They could do nothing.'

[A fellow prisoner was the infamous Ilse Koch, who had lampshades made
of the skins of Jews. Frau Fest remarked that Koch would have little to do
with the other prisoners, though they had tried to befriend her. When asked
why, she replied:]
'Well, somehow she was ultimately, in the long run, also a woman
... And she made you feel bad when she always slunk around and
never was with others. We thought it's terrible enough for us to be
locked up and when a person is completely isolated, it's really terrible.
Actually, well, from what one heard about her, there was also a little
...' Frau Fest finally came up with the word she wanted. It was
'disdain. She could not be a good person,' she added. 'But there were

many others who weren't good, and one must sort of accept them as they were, in a sense. In another sense, they made one feel bad, so one thought one should really try to make life easier.'

[Frau Fest was interned at Dachau, then tried and sentenced to prison. She did two years. Years later, she was informed that she had been unjustly imprisoned, was declared a 'prisoner of war,' and received 300 Deutschmarks compensation. At her final interview with Owings, she reflected on the entire experience.]

* * *

'You know,' she said, 'when I think about it in hindsight, during that whole time, one really had a pretty thick "board in front of one's face." There was so much that one simply did not see. Even today, when our daughter asks, "Mutti, what was it really like then? Did you both have any relations with Jewish people?" That we did have, but it never occurred to us as such. For example, I had a colleague at work, at Behringwerke, who was half Jewish, and at the time she was kind of set upon. There were many who avoided her. And I always said, "What's that all about? Why are they doing that?" I picked her up in the mornings and we always went to work together, we sat together at lunch, and generally talked among ourselves.'

* * *

Asked if she had ever heard the comment about Jews having been at fault themselves, Frau Fest said never, but added, 'It was said some Jewish business people cheated others. But we have a saying. The worst is the "white Jew."'

The 'white Jew' is a Christian.

JUDITH MAGYAR ISAACSON

(1925–)

Judith Magyar was nineteen when she was sent, along with her mother and aunt, to Auschwitz, and then to Hessisch Lichtenau in Germany where they worked in a munitions factory. (See Anna Fest's account of being a guard in a similar facility.) All three survived their incarceration. After the war, Magyar married an American and emigrated to the United States, where she became a lecturer in mathematics and Dean of Students at Bates College. Although she had sworn in Auschwitz that she would live to record her experiences in a book, she turned her back on writing after the war and studied mathematics as a way of repressing the past. Her *Seed of Sarah: Memoirs of a Survivor* was published in 1990. She felt impelled to write it following an evening at which a young student asked her if she had been raped in the camps.

In the following excerpt, the three women have just been transferred from Auschwitz to Hessisch Lichtenau.

Every day, before we left for the factory, and again on coming back to the Lager, we lined up for *Zähl Appell*.[1] At Auschwitz, *Zähl Appell* was a senseless, Kafkaesque torture, interminable hours of agonized huddling; here they simply counted our heads, from one to one thousand.

As I stood at *Zähl Appell* on that sunny afternoon, I dreamed of Paris and the Sorbonne; I'd study there, I hoped, by fall. I stood barefoot, in a drab shapeless dress, but my dreaming head was capped by an azure kerchief, winged and magical.

I was enormously proud of that bit of sky-blue cloth, having outwitted the whole Lager system for it: I pilfered it at the weapons factory out of a bin of wiping rags, I sneaked it back to the Lager hidden under my blouse, I hemmed it with a needle I begged off a comrade and washed it in ersatz coffee I stole at the risk of my life. Lathered in hot coffee, rinsed in cold water, and pressed by my palm, my

---

[1] Head count.

kerchief emerged, radiant. True, it was nothing but a swatch of torn mattress cover, but I had gambled my life for it and won.

I stood at *Zähl Appell* on that fateful afternoon, with my bald head capped in azure – as if Maeterlinck's bluebird of happiness had perched on my shorn crown.

To my left – close enough to touch – the electric barbed wire fence; to my right, rows upon rows of unpainted barracks. A soft breeze brought the scent of grass – there had been no grass at Auschwitz – and with it, that line from Ady: 'Aki él, az mind, mind örüljön – all who live, rejoice, rejoice.'

* * *

Suddenly, I realized that the Kommandant had departed from his usual script as he turned to Manci: 'Suchen Sie mir ein sauberes Mädchen – Find me a clean girl.'

Would he use us for his harem? I agonized. The Kommandant's face was impassive; I watched Manci's for clues. The kapo[2] blushed and a nervous twitch fluttered one eyelid. Her sisters and friends stood in the front row, ready to grab the best jobs, but Manci's glance avoided them. Clearly the kapo was searching for a victim. Whom will she choose? – I wondered, relieved to be standing in the back. I stretched my neck in all directions: hundreds and hundreds of young faces, each framed by a drab kerchief. Poor Manci, what an awesome task ...

'Hurry!' barked the Kommandant.

Marci's eyes swept the heads. 'You!' she pointed me out. 'You in the blue kerchief.'

I have no memory of the next few moments; I must have become mentally paralyzed. Did the Kommandant call me from the ranks? Did I give my mother a desperate parting glance? I must have come to my senses just as the gate opened to let me out – me and the SS Kommandant. Desperately I craved the anonymity of the crowd, the protection of the fives, the guards, the hounds. The irony of it! – I thought.

The Kommandant strode ahead in his stiff breeches and his pounding boots. Instinctively I followed, my head cast down, my eyes on the gravel road. I had a flash of recognition, as if I had followed a past master in such dumb obedience. Do women inherit memories of rape?

---

[2] Prisoner who was also a guard. Judith had rejected the post earlier.

I recalled the myth of the Sabine women and the tale of Hunor and Magor and their abducted mates, the legendary ancestors of Huns and Magyars. 'My plight is not unique,' I told myself. 'I'm caught in an ancient rite of sex and war.'

As I followed the Kommandant through the village, I wondered what the inhabitants of Lichtenau thought of us: a slave girl stamped with a huge red cross following her armed master. Did the burghers of Lichtenau feel pity for me? It was a civilized little town, neat and peaceful as Kaposvár[3] had been. Women nodded to each other 'Grüss Gott'[4] as they met on the sidewalks. But they averted their eyes from me.

From time to time, the Kommandant glanced back as if checking on his shadow. I walked some ten paces behind him, keeping it constant. Only once did I lag for a moment – by a mountain ash brilliant in the setting sun. If only I could turn into a tree ... I feared rape, and wondered what intercourse might mean in physical terms. The girls' gimnazium[5] had censored our reading, and my sex education derived from a handful of post-Victorian novels.

I now tried to recall a favorite scene from Hemingway's *For Whom the Bell Tolls*: the hero and the heroine making love in a sleeping bag. But another scene kept interfering: the rape scene at the barber shop.

I had read Thomas Mann's *Joseph and His Brothers*, and I began to fantasize about winning the Kommandant's trust. Even as a child I was intrigued by the tales of triumphant slaves: Joseph as Pharaoh's confidant; the Greeks introducing arts and religion to the Romans. But male slaves were no models! What if I should become pregnant? 'D'you know, Jutka,' my mother had hinted a thousand times, 'you were born *exactly* nine months to the date of my wedding?' A boast and a warning at the same time. My vanquisher's breeches puffed out at each stride: nine months from today I might give birth to his bastard.

Closing my eyes, I saw us scuffle on a couch. Should I beg him to kill me? How do I say it in German? 'Bitte, töten, Bitte, töten mich.' I mustn't panic. There must be a way out.

Of course, there always was and always will be a way out for captured women to avert death: by becoming concubines. I ruminated about the lot of all the women captured in all the wars, in every

---

[3] Her home town in Hungary.
[4] Literally, 'God's greeting,' but the common way of saying hello in southern Germany and Austria.
[5] High school.

inhabited spot on this planet. The Sabine and the Magor mothers were famous models, but similar dramas must have unfolded millions of times. I could hear Mr. Kóváry's lecture: 'The enemy raped and plundered, they slaughtered the men and took all the women and children hostage.' Of course it was always the enemy who committed those detestable acts. Never one's own nation. Never one's own tribe.

What became of all those abducted women? Why hadn't I identified with them before? The majority must have been enslaved or murdered. But some, like the Sabine and Magor women, became trusted mates. For women, submission was the safest tactic. The only tactic?

I tried to protect myself into the role of a concubine: sexy, docile. Vainly, I conjured up some simple scenes: baring my breasts, helping the Kommandant with his bath. What do a man's genitals look like?

The Kommandant's shadow was blending into dusk, and I railed at the sun for abandoning me to my fate. No more dreaming and fantasizing! Not some mythical figure but I, Jutka Magyar, would be raped tonight.

I became alert, wrought up, like before an exam. I must have a plan. I knew I had one advantage, I spoke German well. My grandfather, a devoted teacher, had instructed me until the day he died. I had been thirteen, but already familiar with the classics. For an instant, I could hear my grandfather's elderly voice reciting my favorite poem, Schiller's *Die Bürgschaft*.

'What do you think of this, O'papa?' I wanted to ask him. 'Here I am in Germany at last, but not to study literature. Would you have believed this? What should I do? What should I do?' If grandfather were here, he'd speak for me. And the Kommandant would listen; people always listened to O'papa.

My other grandfather came to mind, the baker, Vágó. 'Don't be afraid to speak to any man,' he had told us in the ghetto. 'They all had a mother, same as you and me.'

Quickly I thought of a possible scenario. I could pretend I had venereal disease. 'Syphilis,' I'll call it, the name must be the same in German. We had studied some of the symptoms, because the disease had killed Ady, the foremost Hungarian poet. But Dr. Biczó had discussed it psychologically, not medically. Could syphilis be detected on the genitals? Would the Kommandant examine me? I projected the scene in horror.

With trembling fingers, I uncovered my dizzy head. The azure-blue kerchief floated limp in my hand. Why had I stolen that bit of ill-fated cloth? Why did I wash and press and sew it? Only to embellish my naive head. What silly vanity. I touched the moist, stiff bristles. Perhaps my boyish look would move him to pity. But dare I count on such a meager strategy?

We had reached the opposite end of the village and I still had not found a viable plan. Should I plead for his pity? The Kommandant was an officer, and naively, I expected him to be an educated man. He might also be sentimental. Germans often were. I recalled the heroes of grandmother Klein's German romances: fierce and daring, but instantly moved to pity by the plight of women. 'Lemonades,' my grandfather had dubbed her books, and he banished them from the living room. Those heroes of hers were surely exaggerated, but wasn't an SS Kommandant an exaggerated character also? Just this past week, I managed to defy one of them at gunpoint. Do I dare take the risk again? I must – unless I find another way out.

I recalled my studies in German, in psychology. I made up one opening sentence, then another. The mental effort reminded me of my preparations for the baccalaureate exams only the summer before. I tried to think of the best words, the most-apt German expressions. I wished I had a dictionary. My first sentence must have the power to reach his soul, if he had one. But that was my only hope, the chance I was gambling on.

It was dark when the Kommandant turned off the road. He swung open the gate, strode up the path, and bade me follow. My heart pounded, as it had never pounded before, not before any exam, not before any danger. What shall I say the moment I cross the threshold?

By supreme willpower, I restrained my racing heart. Like an actress stepping on the stage, I stepped into the lighted house.

As it turned out, Jutka was wanted as a housecleaner for the Kommandant's mistress, a very desirable position because she was bathed and fed. Regrettably, she was merely being used as a stalking horse by the kapo – when it became clear that there was no danger in the job, Jutka was replaced by the kapo's best friend.

AGNES NEWTON KEITH

(b. 1901)

The American wife of a British agriculturalist working in Borneo, Keith was imprisoned with her two-year-old son, George, after the Japanese occupied the island. *Three Came Home*, her account of the years she spent in a Japanese prison camp, was published in 1946, the year after her release. Keith had previously published a book about Borneo, *Land Beneath the Wind*, which had been popular in its Japanese translation and which earned her the regard and occasional protection of the American-educated Colonel Suga, Commandant of Internees in Borneo. Keith returned to Borneo after the war and continued her literary career.

In the women's camp in Kuching we joined women and children from other parts of Borneo, to form an aggregate population of 242 persons. Although in one camp, we lived in three community groups: 120 Dutch Roman Catholic nuns, 20 English Roman Catholic nuns, 73 women, and 29 children. Some months later we were joined by 12 more British and Dutch women, 20 Sisters, and 6 children. Malay was the common language in camp between Dutch and English people.

The best thing that happened to me in captivity happened here in Kuching: I was thrown into close contact with a community of Roman Catholic nuns. Before this I really knew nothing about them, except through the three on Berhala Island, Mother Rose, Sister Clitus, and Sister Frances Mary. They were white-robed, soft-spoken, touched by divinity, apart from us – but they scarcely seemed human.

Now in Kuching I met nuns as women, and sisters, and mothers, hard workers and friends. Here I met them as people who sang, and laughed and made jokes and had fun. As people who prayed and fasted as a privilege and joy, not as a duty. As women who had chosen a way of life, not had it thrust on them, and who loved it. As women who never, never, refused to give help. As women who were sorry for *us*, tried to help *us*, because *they* had the Way and the Life; while we, poor fleshly creatures of this world and now cut off from this world, had nothing.

We secular women living with our own sex had already tested ourselves, and found ourselves wanting. We could not get on without men, their stimulation, comfort, companionship. I say companionship, because very soon, with poor food, hard work, and nervous strain, that was all we had the sexual strength to long for, or to offer.

But the Sisters were different, they were complete. They were wedded to Christ and the Church, and for the first time in my life in Kuching, I saw that this was so. Then for the first time it became credible to me that they were Holy Brides. They formed in general a background of prayer and peace, for the rest of our world which had gone mad.

The thing that struck me first of all was the Sisters were happy; next, resourceful; third, they were holy; and finally they, like ourselves, could sometimes be hysterical.

The English Sisters were from convents at Sandakan, Jesselton, and Kuching, twenty of them to begin with, and forty when some months later the Japanese interned the nursing Sisters who had been working in the Kuching hospital for the Japanese.

The English Sisters wore white robes with white veils. When they were cooking or working they tucked these veils behind their ears like little dust caps, rolled up their sleeves, and folded up their skirts to keep them out of the dirt; then the Sisters looked like white napkins folded into fancy shapes.

The Dutch Sisters were working missionaries and lived in three groups in camp and came from different parts of Dutch Borneo. They wore grey robes, and black and white pin-striped ones like pillow ticking. Another small group of about ten Dutch Sisters were the Slot Sisters, the Holiest of the Holy: they were contemplatives, and only prayed and thought. In peacetime their only contact with the world was through a slot in the gate. They were of the order of Poor Clares, possessing nothing, wishing nothing, and prison camp was the ideal place for them. They wore heavy brownish robes like sacking.

All these costumes, except those of the Poor Clares, were the tropical-climate workday costumes. On special feast days the Sisters brought out their rusty, black, home habits, dusted them off, put them on, and looked at each other with satisfaction – the same satisfaction that we showed when we got dressed up and went to meet our husbands.

As our clothes wore out we made shorts out of trousers, play dresses out of skirts, short dresses out of long ones, and finally left large open spaces, becoming gradually more and more visible ourselves. But as the Sisters' habits wore out they had to remain invisible, so as the material of the habit disappeared it was replaced by a hand-sewn patchwork of pieces – sometimes not all white.

Finally when they had no gowns left for sickness, or emergency use, or bed, they were forced to acquire some of the colored clothes from the secular women, and I think they thoroughly enjoyed the excuse to use color. I held a lottery once for a royal blue dinner dress, and it was won by a Dutch Sister who made it into a handsome gardening frock which she wore while distributing manure. She told me she enjoyed wearing it immensely because it was such a nice color.

The first thing I did when I got to Kuching was to sell my three sheets for five dollars each to the Sisters for habits.

The smart thing for each mother to do was to get herself adopted by a Sister, as the sisters were unfailingly kind-hearted and hard workers. The Sister was then referred to as 'your' Sister, and came around on feast days with extras of food for your child, helped you to do sewing, helped you to plant a garden, helped you to work, and helped you to worry.

My Sister was Sister Claudia, a Dutch Sister, ten years older than I, with snapping black eyes which held both peace and challenge, and beautiful chiselled features. Sister Claudia was always ready to give me practical help, but the best thing she did for me was to exist as a lovely and lovable person.

* * *

The Sisters were great on singing and fun. Usually I loved the feast days: the singing of high, sweet reedy voices, the deeper-toned murmur of prayer; the clatter of dishes and party food (where they got it, God only knew, but they got it!), the laughter and dancing and mellowness that spread to the people around. Usually I loved the feast days.

But some days, as life grew grimmer, I found myself wishing that they'd quit singing, with nothing to sing for, from my point of view.

They prayed for peace, believed it would come; set dates, and hours and deadlines for it – and when it didn't come they said, 'Thy will be done,' and prayed again. They reconciled themselves, either by strong faith or by delusion. They were happy, either because they didn't know any better, or because what we knew better, and what kept us from being happy, was wrong. Anyway, they were happy, when the rest of us were beating vainly against the bars of our prison.

* * *

There was something that kept us going in Kuching, beyond just rice and greens. Each one of us was beginning to know that it is not enough to exist, that one must have a reason for existing. 'Man liveth not by bread alone, but by every word that proceedeth out of the mouth of God,' was never so true as in prison camp. And the less bread there was, the more we needed the Word.

The word that proceeded out of the mouth of God for me was the warning not to be consumed by hate. Hate is a wasteful emotion; for my own sake I didn't wish to hate the Japanese, or the people about me.

Every night when I lay down beside George I was filled with love for him. Every night we said the Lord's Prayer together. I was not praying for an answer, or to praise the Lord, but to ease myself. I was looking for rest and peace, and a way to make life bearable, when it was not bearable.

With George beside me I could know that love holds together in time of danger, love soothes and strengthens, love builds up, where hate destroys. I could pray then to love and to God, the two inseparable.

I went to bed at dusk most nights, and lay awake several hours before sleeping. I got up several times during the night to smoke cigarettes, because of hunger. I went out to the latrines several times each night as a result of improper diet. My ribs and shoulder still pained me and kept me awake.[1] I had time at night to think.

I thought of all the young men of all races, who were dying all over the world in battle, who had at some time lain like George at their mothers' side. When those boys died, what did they die for? How often must they have asked themselves this question. I could not believe their answer was 'For hate.' Hate is neither worth living nor dying for.

We in prison were now the mistreated ones. Yet it would be only a matter of time, and the turn of the tide, before we would be the abusers, and our captors the abused, because we had in ourselves the same instincts for brutality. It was war that we must hate, and not each other.

It was the practice of the Japanese to make us unwilling witnesses to their abuse of our fellow prisoners. These exhibitions were public,

---

[1] Keith had been severely beaten after she reported a Japanese guard for attempting to rape her. The beatings were designed to get her to confess to making a false accusation. Had she signed the confession, she would very likely have been executed for conspiracy.

and the victim was detained in public view long after punishment. A dog may hide away when in pain, but not so a prisoner.

During these episodes I have never seen a victim fail in fortitude or lose the dignity of courage. At such times the thought came to me of Christ, who suffered persecution bravely on the Cross. It was not Christ who was shamed, but the persecutors. Watching these men and boys who were so brave I saw that the only shame for them would be if they should ever change places with their persecutors. * * *

On the road down which we carried firewood we usually passed British soldiers at work. They were almost naked, without shoes or trousers, half-starved, and scarcely able to carry the loads under which they struggled. Our handsome guard could never pass by one of these soldiers without kicking him on his naked body with his own well-booted foot. * * *

This Japanese lad had another victor's gesture. When displeased, annoyed, fed up with life, he would call a British soldier out of his group, and command him to stick out his tongue. He would then snap the man's jaw onto his tongue, with a swift uppercut.

Unwillingly, I witnessed this boy's progress throughout two years of war. I made up my mind that I would sooner see my own son die of starvation, in camp, than live to grow up and be like that. I learned then that I hated the spirit of brutality in man more bitterly than I hated anything that the Japanese could do to me.

* * *

On September 11, 1945, the camps which held Keith and her husband were finally liberated by the Australian army. Her captors were themselves imprisoned to be tried for war crimes. Colonel Suga, whose family had perished at Hiroshima, committed suicide before he could be executed. In time, the Keiths travelled to Victoria, British Columbia, where Keith had the opportunity to reflect on her experiences.

From out of war, from out of death, we three came home to the North American continent. Here in spring we watched the yellow and the purple crocuses appear, the purple polyanthus and violets, the pussy willows, plum blossoms, and forsythia. The trees that were dead swelled with life, and the plants that had withered turned green. The rain smelled of new life, and new earth; death and decay seemed far removed. Once more we were warmed with the sweetness and virtue of life in its seasons. * * *

After I had been home for some time, living in peace on this continent, with rest, good food, and vitamin pills, the continued pains in my chest, side, and arm, and inability to use one hand normally, sent me to a doctor. His examination of me, and X-rays, revealed the scars of two broken ribs, evidence of an injury to my shoulder socket, and an injured tendon in my left arm, the results of Nekata's questioning in Kuching.[2] In due time these improved, and now for the first time in three years I can lie on my side and breathe without pain.

The doctor was the first person to whom I had ever told the story of how I received from Lieutenant Nekata six eggs for wounded honor and broken bones. I had had three reasons for keeping silence in the past. At first in camp I dared not speak, from fear for myself and my husband; and then I wanted to forget; and then after peace came I did not want the victors to take revenge upon the vanquished for brutality, which is the guilt of war, more than of the individual. I knew what it was to be helpless in the hands of the enemy. Those reasons are now invalid and the villains of the story are dead.

In talking to the doctor, I broke through the aura of horror and ignominy with which I had come to surround the affair. I saw the occurrence for what it was, just one more incident in war.

I told the story to Harry then, but I wasn't sure how he would take it. Once anticipates some emotion from a man when telling him that his wife has been attacked, kicked, and beaten. Subconsciously, I think I expected a little melodrama.

There was none. He knew, even while I was telling him, what I was going to say. I saw in his face, as he listened, distress for me, and regret, but no surprise. I saw an acceptance of brutality and a resignation to suffering which those who do not know captivity will find it hard to understand. He took it all for granted; he could feel no private resentment that this had happened to his wife.

I saw that we had come far from our old concepts of honor and disgrace. In war, we women must fight with all of ourselves, whether we are fighting against Japanese soldiers or atomic bombs.

Keith planned to join her husband, already in Borneo, the following Spring.

---

[2] Nekata was the commandant of the camp who sought to force Keith to retract her accusation of rape. The incident ended with Nekata giving her a present of food coupled with the demand that she tell no one of what had happened to her.

LUCIE AUBRAC (LUCIE BERNARD)

(b. 1912)

With her husband, Raymond Samuel, Aubrac was an active member of a Resistance group, Libération Sud, in Lyon, where the notorious Klaus Barbie was head of the Gestapo. When she was six months pregnant with her second child, Aubrac engineered a daring raid on a transport conveying her husband back to prison, thus saving him from certain death. The account of that action comes from her memoir *Ils partiront dans l'ivresse*, which were the code words used in the London broadcast alerting them to their imminent rescue. Although the book takes the form of a diary, it was written forty years after the events described.

In order to ensure that Raymond must be transported back and forth from prison, Aubrac concocted an elaborate story in which she played the role of Raymond's fiancée, Mademoiselle de Barbentane, seduced and pregnant, and demanding a 'marriage in extremis,' a deathbed marriage, to salvage her honor and that of her bourgeois parents. This outrageous story, and presents of silk scarves and Cognac, secured the cooperation of a German officer.

THURSDAY, OCTOBER 21, 1943

I leave my house early. The sun is rising in a blue sky and the marigolds are heavy with dew. Behind me I hear the muffled thump of a falling apple. I feel like this is good-bye to the little house that I am abandoning forever. Something is going to happen that will change my life. In July 1914, when my father went off to war, leaving his vineyard, his wife, and his little girls, was he in the same frame of mind? Mobilization suddenly forces people to break with their whole past and environment. Perhaps that's how it is when one joins a religious order. I remember the sense of renunciation I felt at the ceremony when my cousin took the veil. I was fourteen then.

As I close the door, I wonder whether the house has a memory. Does it remember the two of us, our happiness? And the relaxed times our welcome provided all those *résistants*, old friends and more recent ones. And our address! How many people had it? 'You're going to Lyon, so stop at Lucie Bernard's and Raymond Samuel's; they belong to one of our movements. They'll help you and there's always room at their place.' Every Christmas I decorate a tree. Three Christmases since the summer of 1940, with small gifts and simple cards, which I give to anyone who happens to be there then. You should have seen the surprise of these rough men, committed to underground combat – their emotion and their gratitude. A little warmth, a breath of normal life in the midst of all the dangers and anonymity. I always managed to have a few provisions around so I could improvise a meal. All the reserves I had built up as if it would be a normal winter for me are being left behind today, in the basement. Maria,[1] who returns tomorrow from her summer in the Indre department, will find them.

The real house of a real family, like one in peacetime, is no more. A house that gave people in hiding the memory of stability and the urge to regain it. A real house where, since the spring of 1941, our comrades had watched our happy little boy[2] be born and grow up. He was the only child in our world of lonely people. He was there like a promise of the return to happiness and security.

* * *

I meet my comrades at the garage. Two of them are in the process of replacing the right front door of our Citroën. They have removed the window, which didn't slide down completely inside the door; that would have made it difficult to steady the submachine gun aimed at the German driver. I can't help giving more advice: 'Daniel, we drive side by side; you get your weapon out, you steady it, you aim, and you shoot right on target and fast. You did practice, you timed it?'

'Don't worry, Catherine,[3] I know my Sten gun by heart. I've tried it out in the same conditions. After sixteen rounds it shows some wear, the silencer takes away some strength, but it's a good machine. The first three shots will be bull's-eyes. Don't worry – it's as good as done!'

I stand there, feeling a little heavy. I'm in my sixth month. The smell of the oil and the gasoline turns my stomach. I stay there, unable to leave. These boys are so ready for tonight. They realize they are

---

[1] The housekeeper.
[2] Jean-Pierre; he was two-and-a-half years old at this time.
[3] Lucie's underground name.

engaged in a difficult and even dangerous task. Several of them have wives and children. They know they are going to liberate a man who was one of the leaders of the secret army. I told them, long ago, that he is my husband. They know the strength of my love, my determination, my will to prevail. More than anything else, they are grateful for my assuming, despite my pregnancy, the same risks they faced over the past months, and being there tonight with them, fighting with them, fighting just like all the others in the group. Our feeling of unity, or esteem, is total – that's why desertion is impossible. I leave them quite simply: 'See you tonight, you guys, each one at his place, after five-thirty.' At the garage door I turn around for a last wave. Under the blue light, filtered by the glass roof with its blue-painted panes, five men watch me leave. My last memory: Alphonse slams shut the windowless door of the Citroën while José and Février slowly wipe their hands on a greasy rag.

I'm hungry. In the center of town I buy, without ration coupons, a cookie described as a macaroon. I nibble on it as I walk – it tastes like a mixture of sand and bran. It's a fine autumn day. On the sidewalk, wooden soles clatter rhythmically; their thickness makes the women's silhouettes – already heightened by the built-up curly hairdos on top of their heads – even taller. There are lines outside all the stores. Each day the quest for food in exchange for coupons starts all over again. How removed I feel from these everyday problems! Today my own quest has quite another object. Among the women waiting in these lines may be the mother or the sister of one of the boys at whose side I will be fighting tonight. I can imagine tomorrow's conversation in these lines: 'The Resistance attacked a German truck full of prisoners just outside of Montluc.'

I imagine shoulders straightening, glances becoming livelier, unexpressed jubilation: the invincible Gestapo bit the dust. I wonder to myself how many dead Germans we will have to our credit. At Mrs. Gros's on the Place des Jacobins I change clothes. Then I have a cup of bouillon and a sausage with some cabbage at the restaurant next door. For the last time I go off to play the part of the young girl seduced. I walk up the Avenue Berthelot from the Gallieni bridge. I'm amazed that I'm not nervous. Action is the best tranquillizer.

Raymond is already standing in the lieutenant's office when I enter. The officer has taken precautions to avoid my being seen by the soldiers escorting the prisoner. I bet he sends me away first. It's the usual ceremony: he welcomes me with the utmost courtesy, pretends not to see Raymond, addresses him with contempt, hands me a paper with the date and place of birth of François Vallet,[4] looks at us while we examine the contract, which Raymond accepts at once, and says to me: 'This is all, right? Don't come back without an appointment. Let me know, through my friend at the Carlton, and wait until he says you are to come.'

I can clearly see he is scared. Is there gossip among his subordinates? Maybe his boss has detected something? I don't know. In any case, he is nervous. He opens the door of his office, looks out into the corridor, and says: 'Go now. Good-bye, miss,' this time without kissing my hand.

I was barely able to talk to Raymond. He risked only a quick wink when I looked at him while the other peeked into the corridor. So he did understand.

Halfway down the stairs my legs fail! All of a sudden I hear someone running behind me. It flashes through my mind that Raymond understood nothing, that he is trying to escape on his own from that office. Then a big devil of a young soldier, his arms overflowing with dossiers, rushes past me, taking the steps two at a time to cross the courtyard and disappear in the building at the back. Whew!

On my way out I go directly to the town hall of the arrondissement; I enter the office of vital statistics and deposit a form requesting the posting of the banns. Maybe the lieutenant had me shadowed? Maybe he is watching my coming and going to see what I do? As I leave the town hall, Maurice, my guardian angel, precedes me, then lets me pass him just before the trolley station. I enter the Marquise de Sévigné tearoom and order a hot chocolate. It's a concoction of cocoa husks sweetened with saccharine. It's hot and has the vague aroma of chocolate. I feel like ordering another but resist the temptation. With this baby beginning its sixth month, my bladder gives me problems. I must not drink too much liquid. That would be the height of irony, to be obsessed by a terrible need to pee later on when we go into action. Now it's time to take off my nice suit, to wash off my makeup. I have some difficulty climbing the six flights to Mrs. Gros's apartment; she is not at home. I leave her a note to say good-bye. This room, which was Ermelin's hideout before becoming the official residence of Miss de Barbentane, retains few traces of our presence. It will have been a dressing room. Tonight our successive molting, Raymond's and mine, will bear fruit: we're going to be metamorphosed ...

---

[4] Raymond's false identity; the Germans had not succeeded in uncovering his real name.

How well I know these streets, the embankments, the trolleys, the bridges of Lyon. At five-twenty I step off the trolley on the rue Jean-Macé. At five-thirty I'm seated in the rear of the Citroën, behind the driver. Let's hope the gates of the school of health open quickly and we don't attract attention by staying parked for a long time. At five minutes to six the last act begins: as a curtain raiser, two German soldiers come out to direct the very sparse traffic on the avenue Berthelot. Christophe starts the car. The gate opens, here comes the pickup truck, appearing from a street perpendicular to the avenue. It follows the avenue and accelerates. We follow. None of us speak. Daniel holds the submachine gun on his knees. I am holding the pistol tightly in my hand. We turn sharp left, now we're on the boulevard des Hirondelles.

I say to Christophe, 'Our turn.'

He accelerates. We pull up next to the driver's cab. Daniel shoots – no noise of any detonation can be heard.

Then something amazing happens: the German van just slows down and stops without a jolt at the curb. 'You missed them,' Christophe says. But as we climb out through the left-hand doors to take cover behind our car, we see the German driver slump over the wheel while his neighbor slides on top of him. The guards in the back, surprised by this unexpected stop, jump down with weapons in hand. Our men have already taken up position behind their car; the quicker of the two guards somersaults and disappears into the railroad gully. Within two minutes we have emptied our clips, and so have the Germans. But they are dead. By the glow of our headlights, in the midst of the fighting, I see Raymond jump out with another man linked to him. I scream: 'Watch out – the one in the raincoat is Raymond.'

'Shit!' says Lyonnet, turning his Sten gun away. 'I've hit him.'

Maurice calls out to Raymond, cuts his handcuffs with the special pliers, and they take off in the third Citroën toward the planned refuge. Meanwhile, our buddies transfer the remaining prisoners to our van.

At six the tobacco factory workers are let out. The headlights of the German truck are still on, and by their light, from behind my Citroën, I see a lot of workers dive for cover in the road. All except for one with a bicycle, which he holds by the handlebar so it is up on its back wheel, apparently trying to shield his face with the front wheel. A bag of potatoes falls off his baggage rack. He hesitates, goes back, picks it up – a ludicrous episode in the play we are performing.

I yell: 'Let's get out of here now, fast.'

In the car, next to me, Chevalier is bleeding. He is conscious and coherent, but he took a bullet in the mouth. We have to get him to our doctor, who was alerted beforehand.

I thought the show was over, but it's not time to lower the curtain yet. The doctor has Chevalier sit astride a chair, with his head and arms leaning on the chair back. He unbuttons the collar of his shirt.

'You're lucky,' the doctor says. 'Look. The bullet went out the back. Since you can move, it means nothing vital has been touched. I've got to evacuate all that blood forming a big hematoma, then we can disinfect. Christophe, hold the basin.'

The doctor begins to press and the blood flows.

'Daniel, take over for me,' says Christophe, white as a sheet and he goes to vomit in the toilet. A minute later, Daniel is in the same condition.

'It's your turn,' the doctor says, handing the basin to me.

Once the wound is thoroughly cleaned and bandaged, the doctor says to Chevalier, who hasn't flinched: 'I'm giving you a tetanus shot, just to be on the safe side.'

Our buddy, who has been absolutely mute, with his mouth open, ever since leaving the boulevard des Hirondelles, finds his voice again: 'Oh no! I don't like shots.'

How dearly I love my three terrorists! They risk their lives, are ready to accept any dare, but are terrified at the sight of blood or a needle. We all laugh about it.

* * *

Lucie joins Raymond, who has been only superficially wounded. After four months, they are reunited.

Just as I have imagined it, he has slowly filled one of his pipes and smokes as he walks up and down. He can't chew with his wound, so I eat everything on the tray that Mrs. Nicholas has left in the room. I'm sleepy, but I want to listen to what he is saying. After all, he has four months of silence to recover. He talks on and on, smoking and drinking the rum in the little bottle. I'm sleepy and doze off to the sound of his voice.

I open one eye when I feel the soft touch of his lips on my stomach and a lukewarm moisture. Is he crying? No. His wounds are bleeding from all the talking; the dressing on his cheek is all red, completely soaked with blood. We don't wake our hosts. I fall asleep next to a

man who looks a lot like an Easter egg, with a towel tied around
his head.

After the rescue, Lucie and Raymond went into hiding. They were finally
flown out to London in another dangerous and daring action by the British
Secret Service only days before Lucie gave birth to her daughter, Catherine,
in a London hospital in the middle of an air raid.

In 1983, Klaus Barbie was extradited to France, where he stood trial for
war crimes. His trial was a major test of the Holocaust denial theory, but
he was finally found guilty and sentenced to life imprisonment. The trial
prompted Aubrac to publish her memoir, *Ils partiront dans l'ivresse* (They
will leave in the exhilaration of victory) in 1984. In 1987, the Aubracs won
a libel suit against Barbie's lawyer, who, as part of his defense of Barbie, had
cast doubt on their participation in the Resistance.

RITA J. KUHN

(b. 1927)

The daughter of a German Jewish father and a Lutheran mother who had converted to Judaism, Rita Kuhn lived in Berlin through both the Nazi regime and the war itself. She and her immediate family owed their survival to her mother's 'Aryan' status and to her devotion which prevented their deportation and presumable death. After the war, Kuhn emigrated to the United States, where she pursued her education, earning a master's degree in classical literature and a PhD in comparative literature. She lives in California, where she is completing work on her memoirs. The following excerpt is taken from that work in progress.

A week had passed since my arrest[1] and neither my father nor I were called back to work which filled us with unease. We knew of the labor shortage and that every worker was needed to intensify the war effort to compensate for the loss of Stalingrad and Leningrad. It was an ominous sign.

Then, on March 5th, a Friday, my mother went, as usual, to pick up our ration cards at a school nearby. She left early that day, but contrary to our expectations, she returned soon after and, as she entered the door, the expression in her face held us locked in fear. Her lips were tightly shut like a sealed tomb; her eyes avoided looking at us directly and when she finally spoke her voice sounded hollow, as though it had become the vessel of some higher order. 'They wouldn't give them to me. You have to go get them yourselves,' she told us, her eyes still averted.

'That's it,' my father said in response to the news, his voice remarkably clear and steady. 'Put on some extra layers of clothes.' There was no need for further explanation. We followed his advice with a fearful knowledge deep within us.

We set out for the school. Once inside, my mother directed us to a room with several SS men in it, some standing, some seated behind tables with papers piled before them which they examined with stony

---

[1] Kuhn had recently been rounded up by the SS and unexpectedly released.

faces. They were automatons, set in motion by an invisible master-mind, performing their function with cold and impenetrable regularity. Our papers were checked; the SS officer sitting behind the desk snapped an order to another one standing near us: 'Take them away.'

My mother made ready to join us as we followed the officer but he brushed her aside with a brusque 'No! Not you!' Her face changed color, looking ashen and rigid with fear; her arms dropped helplessly to her side and the look in her eyes, full of non-comprehension and wounded with sorrow, followed me into the room which became our prison and follow me all the days of my life. The key turned in the lock with a finality which brooked no dissension, no reversal. Without a word, we sat down on the classroom chairs, connected by a knowledge swallowed in silence.

Time stopped. We waited for more people to arrive and did not want to think beyond that. And again we waited. I wanted something to break this anxious quietude, this nameless uncertainty.

Suddenly a woman's voice startled us with its piercing, desperate screams. 'Let me see my children. You can't take my children from me ... I want to go with my children.' We listened and could not identify the voice until my father turned to Hans[2] and me and said, loud enough for the others in the room to hear, 'Das is doch unsere Mama' – that is surely our Mama. There was a stir in the room, for my mother was known to many from helping in my grandmother's store. Her voice, usually low and gentle, never raised, even in anger, was stretched beyond recognition by a terror so great it rose above any concern for herself as she faced fully armed SS men.

Finally, the door swung wide open and a group of SS men entered and ordered us to follow them.

A truck was waiting for us in the middle of the street and the loading proceeded noiselessly and in broad daylight. There was no lack of witnesses. I looked at my mother, turned to stone from grief at her children being taken from her. Just then the truck turned a corner and left a void where my mother used to be.

We stopped before an unfamiliar building for the unloading. Once inside, the SS were separating men, women, and children. An orderly with a yellow star took me up a flight of stairs to a room and said curtly, 'Stay here,' pointing to a straw mattress on the floor. A foul smell

---

[2] Her brother.

emanated from it. The room was medium-sized, lit by a bare bulb which gave out a feeble light. I wanted to run but I knew I couldn't. I sat down on the straw sack and surveyed the room. I made out the shapes of three women lying on their mattresses opposite mine. One of them was huddled in a corner to my left, and the other two near a window to my right. My arrival had made little impression on them; no one moved and there was no exchange of greetings. How could one welcome anyone to such a place? Their silence and immobility only added to the gloom and sense of abandonment of this place, in sharp contrast to my own state of agitation and need for human contact. I seemed to be no longer in the world of the living and was curious to know how long they had been here, forgotten by the outside world.

Hope had died here. Time held no dimension for these women whose bodies seemed locked in the same position as on the day they were thrown in here. The image of a sack of potatoes, carelessly tossed into some corner and left to rot, came to mind.

Language too had died here. The lack of air, warmth, and energy in these languid bodies was not conducive to conversation so that, more than ever, I thought of my father and brother and wondered if they were still in the building with me. Stifled by the silence and the gloom and the musty odor, I asked one of the women how long she had been penned up here. She welcomed this overture to talk and told me of an incredible incident that had taken place outside our prison. From the day people were imprisoned, there had been a protest by the gentile wives of the Jewish husbands held here in Rosenstrasse 2–4, demanding the release of their family members. A few desperate women shouted in a chorus: 'Give us back our men. Give us back our men.' It had gone on all week. She herself could hear the cries through the only window in our room. There were short intervals when the SS succeeded in dispersing them, but a few hours later, the women would continue in increasing numbers. As a result of this protest, many prisoners were released, but others were sent to camps in the East. The logic of their fate escaped her 'because of the crazy nature of the Nürnberg laws.'

'And one day, in the middle of this protest,' she continued, 'the SS officer in charge of this place came into our room and, standing erect and proud, his hand pointing to the window, he told them, "Do you hear that? They are your relatives. They want you to go home. We are proud of them. Das ist deutsche Treue (that is German loyalty)."'

I must have given her a look of disbelief because she went on to tell me of another incident.

'But that wasn't all,' she continued. She had heard it from a woman who had since been released and who had witnessed this scene when she arrived at Rosenstrasse. A verbal exchange had taken place between that same SS officer and two men, the husband and son of a Jewish woman interned here. The two men were advised by the officer that the woman would be safe if the men agreed to take her home and have her reside with them. The men refused, whereupon the officer yelled at them in language usually reserved for Jews: 'Ihr Scheweinehunde! You don't deserve to be Germans! Raus mit euch! (Get out of here).' And with that he threw them out of the door in an ill-concealed fit of rage.

She finished the story with a 'Tja' and I knew we were thinking along similar lines in pondering this enigma of a man who could momentarily place his avowed values of family loyalty, long honored by Germanic tribes, ahead of his prescribed duty of sending Jews to their deaths. Such inconsistency, such incongruity between morality and depravity, can be more frightening than the blank hatred most SS officers expressed toward Jews. The element of unpredictability and incongruity elicited more fear than the behavior we usually expected from such men, And then, leaning forward slightly for fear of being overheard, she whispered audibly enough, 'I don't like to think of SS men as being human, but this man, so proud of the German tradition of fealty to family that he extends it even to Jews, is too human for my liking.'

Nighttime brought another kind of terror with the sound of sirens announcing the approach of allied bombers. In response to my customary jumping out of bed to rush to shelter in the basement, I heard a woman's voice reminding me that there was no such shelter for those interned here. I lay down again on my mattress and when the first bombs fell near us, I covered my head with the vile-smelling horse blanket to lessen the noise of explosions all around us. I could no longer make a distinction between my body's shaking and that of the building. The window rattled as if it would burst and I saw the two silent women move away from it.

When the 'all clear' signal finally sounded, I was bathed in sweat despite the freezing temperature in the room.

Some time in the afternoon, an orderly came to ask me to follow him downstairs. Two lines of children were waiting, one for boys, among them Hans, the other for girls, which I joined. Somewhere to my left I heard the measured tread of boots approaching and a calm voice telling us to listen quietly to his instructions. He paced his words with deliberate smoothness. He informed us that we were allowed to go home and should wait for our release papers. He told Hans and me that our father would be released later. I wanted to believe him because the alternative was too unthinkable.

I had no tears left when we were reunited with our mother, even tears of joy because joy had long ago fled from our life. My father came later the same day.

The next day, a Sunday, Herta Goedicke related her version of the protest on Rosenstrasse to which she had gone to get word about her mother whom she was able to take home from there. She was witness to the demonstration and to how the women faced the machine guns of the SS to demand the release of their husbands. One woman told her that at one point they had had enough and had yelled: 'Ihr Mörder (you murderers).' They dared not shoot. 'Can you imagine,' she asked us, 'these women broke down the walls of silence.'

We looked at one another and then my father looked at my mother and said, calm and proud, 'And so did you, Mama. And so did you.'

GERTRUDE STEIN

(1874–1946)

Although Jewish, Stein and Toklas remained in France throughout the German occupation, counting on their age, their celebrity, and the intervention of a friend very close to Marshall Pétain to protect them. In *Wars I Have Seen* (1945) Stein considers the meaning of the wars that marked her lifetime and provides a description of her and Alice's life during the war. In the first of these selections, she explains their decision not to flee the occupying forces; in the second, the ironic detachment with which she has recorded the years of fear and privation slips as she expresses her joy when American soldiers finally arrive in their remote village.

We had recently quite a number of difficult moments. America had come into the war, our consul and vice-consul in Lyon with whom we had gotten very friendly because they had taken a summer home right near us and kept a white goat called Genevieve, and there we first found out that you could have goat's milk that did not taste of goat, had been interned first at Lourdes and then taken to Germany and now I went to Belley to say good-bye as we were moving. My lawyer said everything was nicely arranged and we thanked each other and said what a pleasure it had all been, and then he said and now I have something rather serious to tell you. I was in Vichy yesterday, and I saw Maurice Sivain, Sivain had been sous-prefet[1] at Belley and had been most kind and helpful in extending our privileges and our occupation of our house, and Maurice Sivain said to me, tell these ladies that they must leave at once for Switzerland, tomorrow if possible, otherwise they will be put into a concentration camp. But I said we are just moving. I know he said. I felt very funny, quite completely funny. But how can we go, as the frontier is closed, I said. That he said could be arranged, I think that could be arranged. You mean pass by fraud I said, Yes he said, it could be arranged. I felt very funny. I said I think I will go home and will you telephone Madame d'Aiguy to meet me. He said shall I walk home with you, I did feel

---

[1] A local official.

very funny, and I said no I will go home and Madame d'Aiguy will come down to see you and arrange and I went home. I came in, I felt a little less funny but I still did feel funny, and Alice Toklas and Madame d'Aiguy were there, and I said we are not moving to-morrow we are going to Switzerland. They did not understand that and I explained and then they did understand, and Madame d'Aiguy left to go and see the lawyer and arrange and Alice Toklas and I sat down to supper. We both felt funny and then I said. No, I am not going we are not going, it is better to go regularly wherever we are sent than to go irregularly where nobody can help us if we are in trouble, no I said, they are always trying to get us to leave France but here we are and here we stay. What do you think, I said, and we thought and I said we will walk down to Belley and see the lawyer and tell him no. We walked down to Belley it was night it was dark but I am always out walking at night, I like it, and I took Alice Toklas by the arm because she has not the habit of walking at night and we got to Belley, and climbed up the funny steps to the lawyer, and I said I have decided not to go. Madame d'Aiguy was still there and she said perhaps it was better so, and the lawyer said perhaps we had better go and then he said he had a house way up in the mountains and there nobody would know, and I said well perhaps later but now I said to-morrow we are going to move to Culoz, with our large comfortable new house with two good servants and a nice big park with trees, and we all went home, and we did move the next day. It took us some weeks to get over it but we finally did.

But what was so curious in the whole affair was its unreality, like things are unreal when you are a child and before you know about realism as we did in the Spanish–American war and the Russo–Japanese war just that.

* * *

What a day of days, I always did say that I would end this book with the first American that came to Culoz, and to-day oh happy day yesterday and to-day, the first of September 1944. There have been six of them in the house, two of them stayed the night and then three were there besides the first three not here at Culoz but at Belley. Oh happy day, that is all that I can say oh happy day.

This is the way it happened. We go to Belley about once a month to go shopping and the bank and things like that and yesterday Thursday was the day, so we went over in a taxi, and when we got to Belley as I got out of the taxi several people said to me, Americans are here. I had heard that so often that I had pretty well given up hope and I said oh nonsense but yes they said, and then the son of the watchmaker who had been the most steadfast and violent pro-ally even in the darkest days came up to me and said the Americans are here. Really I said yes he said well I said lead me to them, all right he said they are at the hotel so we went on just as fast as we could and when we got to the hotel they tried to stop me but we said no and went in. I saw the proprietor of the hotel and I said is it true there are Americans, yes he said come on, and I followed and there we were Alice Toklas panting behind and Basket[2] very excited and we went into a room filled with maquis[3] and the mayor of Belley and I said in a loud voice are there any Americans here and three men stood up and they were Americans God bless them and were we pleased. We held each other's hands and we patted each other and we sat down together and I told them who we were, and they knew, I always take it for granted that people will know who I am and at the same time at the last moment I kind of doubt, but they knew of course they knew, they were lieutenant Walter E. Oleson 120th Engineers and private Edward Landry and Walter Hartze and they belonged to the Thunderbirds and how we talked and how we patted each other in the good American way, and I had to know where they came from and where they were going and where they were born. In the last war we had come across our first American soldiers and it had been nice but nothing like this, after almost two years of not a word with America, there they were, all three of them. Then we went to look at their car the jeep, and I had expected it to be much smaller but it was quite big and they said did I want a ride and I said you bet I wanted a ride and we all climbed in and there I was riding in an American army car driven by an American soldier. Everybody was so excited.

Then we all said good-bye and we did hope to see them again, and then we went on with our shopping, then suddenly everybody got excited army trucks filled with soldiers were coming along but not Americans, this was the French army in American cars and they were happy and we were happy and tired and happy and then we saw two who looked like Americans in a car standing alone and I went over and said are you Americans and they said sure, and by that time I was confident and I said I was Gertrude Stein and did they want to come back with us and spend the night. They said well yes they

---

[2] Their poodle.
[3] Members of the Resistance.

thought the war could get along without them for a few hours so they came, Alice Toklas got into the car with the driver and the colonel came with me, oh a joyous moment and we all drove home and the village was wild with excitement and they all wanted to shake the colonel's hand and at last we got into the house, and were we excited. Here were the first Americans actually in the house with us, impossible to believe that only three weeks before the Germans had been in the village still and feeling themselves masters, it was wonderful. Lieutenant Colonel William O. Perry Headquarters 47th Infantry Division and private John Schmaltz, wonderful that is all I can say about it wonderful, and I said you are going to sleep in beds where German officers slept six weeks ago, wonderful my gracious perfectly wonderful.

How we talked that night, they just brought all America to us every bit of it, they came from Colorado, lovely Colorado, I do not know Colorado but that is the way I felt about it lovely Colorado and then everybody was tired out and they gave us nice American specialities and my were we happy, we were, completely and truly happy and completely and entirely worn out with emotion. The next morning while they breakfasted we talked some more and we patted each other and then kissed each other and then they went away. Just as we were sitting down to lunch, in came four more Americans this time war correspondents, our emotions were not yet exhausted nor our capacity to talk, how we talked and talked and where they were born was music to the ears Baltimore and Washington D.C. and Detroit and Chicago, it is all music to the ears so long long long away from the names of the places where they were born. Well they have asked me to go with them to Voiron to broadcast with them to America next Sunday and I am going and the war is over and this certainly this is the last war to remember.

CHRISTA WOLF

(b. 1929)

In her extraordinary meditation on her childhood in Nazi Germany, *A Model Childhood*, the prominent German novelist raises issues of guilt, innocence, and responsibility through a confrontation between her childhood self, 'Nelly,' her adult, unnamed consciousness, and her daughter Lenka.

The Kristallnacht – the name was coined later – was carried out between November 8 and November 9: 177 synagogues, 7,500 Jewish businesses within the confines of the Reich were destroyed. In the course of governmental action, all Jews were expropriated after this spontaneous outbreak of public indignation; their sons and daughters were expelled from schools and universities. No Jewish girl in Nelly's class. Years later a girl from her class will refuse to sing the carol 'Noel, Noel, Born is the King of Israel!' because of its glorification of Judaism. The music teacher, Johannes Freidank,[1] whose son was killed in Poland during the first days of the war, flies into a rage and tells his favorite class – they make an excellent choir – that Jewish girls never used to refuse to sing Christian songs. Nelly's classmate won't tolerate being compared to a Jewish girl. The music teacher, fuming with anger, challenges his pupil to report him.

She didn't do it.

A speech that Dr. Joseph Goebbels gave in 1937, a speech that Nelly, too, may have heard over the radio, contained the following sentences: 'Without fear we may point to the Jew as the motivator, the originator, and the beneficiary of this horrible catastrophe. Behold the enemy of the world, the annihilator of cultures, the parasite among nations, the son of chaos, the incarnation of evil, the ferment of decay, the formative demon of mankind's downfall.'

Somebody must have said to Nelly: The synagogue is on fire. She doesn't know who said it. Although it is Charlotte's[2] face, 'perplexed-

---

[1] His name would translate as 'Freethought.'
[2] Her mother, Charlotte Jordan.

shocked,' which appears at the cue of 'burning the synagogue.' Nobody said: Go take a look!, least of all her mother. More likely the unequivocal order: Don't you dare ...

It's unbelievable and inexplicable that she went there, but she did go, you can swear to that. How on earth did she find the little square in the old part of town? Had she known where the synagogue was for her town? And she didn't ask anybody, that much is sure.

What was it that attracted her, since it wasn't the wish to gloat over other people's misfortune?

She wanted to see it.

November 9, 1938, doesn't seem to have been a cold day. A pale sun lit the cobblestones and the grass that grew in the cracks between them. The small, lopsided houses began where the cobblestones ended. Nelly knew that the little square and its surrounding houses would have appealed to her, if it hadn't been for the still-smouldering ruin in the center. It was the first ruin Nelly had seen in her life. Maybe she'd never heard the word before, certainly not in its later context: ruined city. Ruined landscape. For the first time she saw that the walls of a stone building don't burn down evenly, that they end up in a bizarre silhouette.

One of the small houses must have had a dark doorway where Nelly could hide. She may have leaned against a wall of one of the wings of the door. She probably wore her navy-blue sweatsuit. The square was empty, and so were the windows of the small houses around it. Nelly couldn't help it: the charred building made her sad, because she wasn't supposed to feel sad. She had long ago begun to cheat herself out of her true feelings. It's a bad habit, harder than any other to reverse. It stays with you and can only be caught and be forced to retreat, step by step. Gone, forever gone, is the beautiful free association between emotions and events. That, too, if you think of it, is a reason for sadness.

To Nelly's great amazement and alarm, people were coming out of the door of the burned-down synagogue. This meant that the lower floor, where the Jews most probably had some kind of altar – as is customary in other churches – wasn't completely burned out or destroyed and buried by falling debris. It's sometimes possible, then, to enter still-smouldering ruins – All of this was entirely new to Nelly.

If it weren't for these people – an inner image whose authenticity is undeniable – you wouldn't be able to claim with such certainty that Nelly, a child with imagination, was near the synagogue on that afternoon. But the human figures who were running fast, yet without haste, from the door of the synagogue to the small frame house straight across – these were the men whom Nelly had never seen, either in pictures or in real life. She didn't know what a rabbi was, either. The sun had jobs to do. It shone on the objects those men were holding in their hands (were 'rescuing,' Nelly thought intuitively). A kind of chalice must have been among them – is it possible? Gold!

The Jews, legless in Nelly's memory because of their long caftans, went into their destroyed synagogue at the risk of their lives and rescued their holy, golden treasures. The Jews, old men with gray beards, lived in the miserable little houses on Synagogue Square. Their wives and children were perhaps sitting behind the tiny windows, crying (Blood, blood, blooood, blood must be flowing as thick as can be ...) The Jews are different from us. They're weird. Jews must be feared, even if one can't hate them. If the Jews were strong now, they'd do away with us all.

It wouldn't have taken Nelly much to have succumbed to an improper emotion: compassion. But the healthy German common sense built a barrier against it: fear. (Perhaps there should be at least an intimation of the difficulties in matters of 'compassion,' also regarding compassion toward one's own person, the difficulties experienced by a person who was forced as a child to turn compassion for the weak and the losers into hate and fear. This only to point out the later consequences of previous events, which are often wrongly summarized merely by the correct but not exhaustive account: 177 burning synagogues in 1938 make for ruined cities beyond number in 1945.)

Nelly was too embarrassed to stay where she was standing. Charlotte had taught her tact: mostly things one didn't do. One didn't stare at the mouth of the hungry while he was eating. One didn't talk to the hairless about his bald pate. One didn't tell Aunt Liesbeth that she didn't know how to bake. One didn't stand there gloating at others' misfortunes.

Nelly counted the strange, bearded Jews among the unfortunates.

* * *

The faces of the witnesses at the Auschwitz trial in 1963 in the historic town hall in Frankfurt am Main. In the factory-owned concentration camp – Monowitz – I.G. Farben calculated an average life expectancy of prisoners working for them to be from four to six months. The SS had promised them that all weak prisoners could be disposed of. The SS and I.G. Farben together worked out their economy interrelation, Farben participated in the perfection of the penal system. An expert appraisal recommended this particular location for the construction of a mill, because 'soil conditions, water, and limestone, as well as the availability of labor – for instance, Poles, and prisoners from the Auschwitz concentration camp – were favorable for the setting up of a mill.'

And in the evenings, the questions of young people, students in their sparsely furnished apartments in Frankfurt, who became passionately involved in the course of the trial: they seemed to be looking for some horrible secret at the bottom of your souls, or consciences. You were unprepared for their demand that you yield your secret. You were used to assuming that horrible secrets did exist, among older people who were unable or unwilling to reveal them. As though you could be relieved of the duty to lay a hand upon your own childhood. While the landscape of your childhood moved, as though by itself, into the shadow of the Auschwitz ovens.

But the secret we're looking for is the blatant lack of any secret. Which is why perhaps it can't be revealed.

In the fall of 1943, Nelly was crouching on the fields of the estate, digging up potatoes, together with a row of Ukrainian women. Her feeling toward these strangers wasn't pity, but rather a shyness, the strong notion that they were different, a notion which was not based on any secret, but on Julia Strauch's[3] history lessons: her being different made her more valuable. Nelly wasn't allowed to put her potatoes into the same basket as one of the foreign workers. Did she think about the soup which was being dished out for the Ukrainians from a separate pot? Would it have occurred to her to get up and walk the thirty steps across the separating abyss, over to the foreigners, who were sitting along the same edge of the field, and hand one of them her own bowl, which had pieces of meat swimming in the soup?

---

[3] One of 'Nelly's' teachers, a dedicated Nazi.

The horrible secret: not that one didn't dare, but that the thought didn't occur to one. All attempts to explain stop at this fact. The usual thoughtlessness of the well-fed with respect to the hungry doesn't explain it. Fear? Certainly, if there had been such a temptation. But the temptation to do the natural thing no longer occurred to her. Nelly – innocent, so far as she knew, even exemplary – was sitting there, chewing her meat.

It wasn't Nelly, at any rate, who complained to Julia when the overseer of the estate, a one-legged veteran, scolded the German Girls for doing sloppy work, in front of the Ukrainian women. It would have been up to her to inform Julia, because she was the leader of the work group. But she felt ashamed of the sloppiness, in front of the Ukrainians, whose eyes didn't give away whether or not they had understood what was going on. Instead it was her friend Hella who informed Julia by telephone, and the overseer was made to apologize the next morning. Nelly felt ashamed, that was all.

CRISTAL BANGHARD-JÖST

(b. 1949)

In 1975, members of a woman's peace organisation, Women for Peace, in Heilbronn, [West] Germany began to collect personal histories from women who had lived through the Nazi regime and the war in the hope that such stories would discourage German participation in the cold war. (A missile base was under construction in the area.) The group collected some thirty memoirs though it was, by its own account, 'unable to find participants who had been active in a Nazi organisation – BDM: Bund Deutscher Mädchen (League of German Girls), NS-Frauenschaft Partei (Nazi Women's Union), or NSDAP-National Sozialistische Arbeiter Partei (the Nazi Party).' Nor did they find any Jewish women or survivors of sexual abuse. The following selection, 'In the Stocks,' was written by Cristal Banghard-Jöst, born in 1949, and expresses some of the questions to which the post-war generation of German women sought answers.

For weeks after reading the account of your ordeal in Jacobi's book [see excerpt that follows], dear sister, you took possession of me. I could only see things from your perspective, from the perspective of the stocks. But I could not comprehend why the townspeople of forty years ago – so full of destructive lust – spat in your face and threw stones, and why the hate of thousands who gathered in the marketplace was directed against you and not against the brutal Nazi stalwarts of Heilbronn. I could also not understand why your tormentors employed the rituals of a witchcraft trial in the middle of the twentieth century. Did they believe you had celebrated a Witch's Sabbath with the Pole – or were they afraid you could destroy their mad order of life? You so bravely defied the inhuman laws of the Nazis by showing affection for a ragged, undernourished 'sub-human.'

I wanted to search for you to find out if you are still alive or if they let you die so as not to have to bother with you anymore. From you, your friends or your family, I could learn about what cruel behavior people are capable of when oppressed by a political system. We could learn from your story, because at that time Europe had gone out of control. Today the world is in the process of learning about it.

To track you down, I asked dedicated historians of local Heilbronn history who have published works on the Nazi period about your case. I wanted to know who betrayed you, but most of all I wanted to know your name, so that I could ask at the city registry if you are still alive. The local historians couldn't answer my questions. They had heard anecdotes about you, but during the war years when Party members went on witch-hunts in Heilbronn, they were all in concentration camps, prisons or at the front. One professor, however, was able to support my research by giving me advice, searching for eyewitnesses and directing me to the archives where the local newspaper, the Heilbronner *Tagblatt*, was kept almost in its entirety. But during the war there were almost no reports in the local section about particularly brutal activities by the Brown Shirts, such as the torture of political dissenters in the basements of the Gestapo or excesses against the Jews. The local editors presented their readers with stories about honest and upright public officials with whom they could identify. So nothing is written of your humiliation nor about the rampaging Nazis who needed props from the torture chamber to maintain their power.

From time to time there are reports of draconian sentences against women who broke the Nazi law forbidding contact with war prisoners. The prison terms were often very long, apparently applied legally by judges who have never had to account for their acts. But since your punishment was most probably not initiated by a court but by the Party, former functionaries must have known your name and the background of the spectacle. They must have carefully prepared the show during their meetings. I therefore wrote politely for information to all the Nazi leaders I knew about, but I received not a single response. They were shielded from me in their lovely homes and splendid gardens by their wives or secretaries or daughters. They likely had good reason to be silent.

I became impatient, I wasn't making progress. I encouraged friends and acquaintances to find some trace of you; I was after them constantly. I spoke to at least a hundred pleasant-looking older people on the bus, in stores and in the townhall square. Most of them were very reserved, many turned quickly away from me, some insulted me. Quite a few knew of you, but nothing specific. Surprisingly, though, they all said you took your own life. In some versions you drank pesticide or hydrochloric acid; in others you hanged yourself on a big fir tree or turned on the gas valves. As best I can piece your story together, your Polish boyfriend was shot by uniformed men on the Kopfer [a brook not far from the city]. Here are some extracts about you from conversations taken down for me by friends in the Workshop of Women for Peace:

> I lived on Schillerstrasse and was just a child. We went to the marketplace because we wanted to see the show. The entire square and the Kaiserstrasse were full. The woman was led through the entire city on foot, by two men. People spat at her and called her whore and other obscenities. I had the feeling that no one was against what went on and that the people were pleased. (Frau F.)

> The people were very excited. I was also there, but when I saw her face I knew that she was a common whore who carried on with everyone. No harm done. It isn't worth making a big thing out of it. (Frau G.)

> People came from surrounding villages to see the show. Maybe she was out of line; you don't do that when your husband and brother are in the field. (Frau R.)

> In 1941 I was an apprentice in a shop on Main Street and I witnessed the whole affair. The woman was led through the crowd on an oxcart. There was a man in front of the cart beating on a tub. The woman was about thirty-five or forty years old and had long black hair. Such events keep coming to mind during one's whole life. (Frau Z.)

I am astonished that most of the women watching were not morally outraged by the type of punishment you received. They didn't see the humilation of their own sex in your degradation, nor that they had been reduced to nothing more than the 'property' of the male of the Nordic master race, at his free disposal, to be punished when they dared to break his taboos. All attempts at women's emancipation ended in the stocks.

I first became aware of just how great the intimidation of women was, in April 1984, after an article appeared with an appeal from the Workshop of Women for Peace to all readers who knew about your case and others like yours to get in touch with me. It is odd, dear sister, that since that time I've lost sight of you as I learn of the horrible fates of other women at the time.

At least twenty people, for the most part women, contacted me in response to the appeal. From four callers I learned that many more women had their hair shorn, though with less ceremony and audience than you. My informers lived near the abused women during the war and knew their names. Two of the women were certain that their earlier acquaintances had died in the meantime. The two others had lost track of their old neighbors in the '60s. Pity for the victims and decades of suppressed anger against the tormentors moved these women to call me. They encouraged me to bring the crimes against your sisters into the light of day.

One woman told me of a forty-year-old woman in an outlying area who had her hair shorn because she slipped some food to a Russian. The woman was very poor herself and acted purely out of pity. Another caller recounted that a farmer's wife, forced to manage the farm during the war with a prisoner of war because her husband was at the front, was beaten by Party members until she admitted to having an affair with the foreign laborer. Her hair was cut off in her own house. The laborer disappeared without a trace.

A further case was told as follows: a young, single, very beautiful woman was considered standoffish by her peers, who envied her because of her long dark hair and her proud carriage. She was supposed to have been rather reserved toward men. An awkward, unattractive man – most likely longing for her body – testified at the local Brown House [the local Nazi Party headquarters] that he had caught her with a Frenchman. As a result, that evening on her way home she was attacked by a horde of uniformed men and seriously beaten.

And finally I heard about a young secretary who met a war prisoner working as a translator in her office and had a child by him. This woman had her hair shorn and was mistreated by the Nazis toward the end of her pregnancy.

I didn't receive any concrete information from the majority of the callers, who were probably members of the victims' families. They all wanted to remain anonymous and requested or demanded aggressively that I not publish anything about these incidents. This was a typical call:

Why are you writing about it after almost forty years? You can't publish that. The whole countryside is talking about it. The woman has had serious heart trouble for the past five days (since the article appeared in the newspaper *Heilbronner Stimme*). She's afraid her grandchildren could find out.

What woman? Why shouldn't the grandchildren find out? Did I really cause her to become sick by writing about the crimes committed against her? Do I have the right to continue my research when I might cause such suffering? I leave out all the names in my account and cross out every concrete reference in order not to hurt you all again. But why are you so well-protected? Can it be that your families are ashamed because of you? That in forty years they've learned nothing? Listen to the response that one of our Workshop members got to her inquiry about your victimization:

Questioner: I'm calling for the Workshop of Women for Peace –

Respondent (interrupting): 'Well, I've had enough of you. I read the article about you in the *Heilbronner Stimme*. You know, all the people who are for the foreigners today, who even want to give them the right to vote – they're ruining Germany. Back then I had a completely different idea of what Germany could become. But today they let in all the refugees and the Turks too. Things are so bad today that a German apprentice has to compete with a Turk for a place on the workbench. If that's how they want it they should just open all the borders and they'll bring in the hashish and dominate our lives. But you shouldn't call that Germany anymore. Also, I'd really like to know where you got my name. Who gave it to you? That really bothers me. You know, I was against Hitler, I have it in writing. I was fourteen years old when he came to power. I didn't elect him, but I had to suffer because he was elected. I raised my son alone back then. I was alone. Today I never speak about those days. Nothing comes out of me. I've been through enough. Consider me dead, you'll learn nothing from me. Good-bye!'

Although the Workshop caller had made no reference to foreign workers, this respondent answered automatically, with the right-wing slogans of your former tormentors. She and other women were tortured to such an extent that they took on the ideology of those who punished you. They don't have the strength to resist, because their powers of resistance were broken long ago. It has been observed in the dictatorships of Latin America, whose torture chambers were shaped by SS officers and people from the Gestapo, that after serious beatings the flayed victims identify with their torturers, after losing their own personalities.

The terrorizing of women who dared to have a relationship with a non-German continued after the war. In 1946 a teacher was held down by a gang of men who cut off her hair because she had been seen with an American soldier. A long trail of sawdust was scattered in front of the homes of girls who had contact with Black Americans. These examples are probably only the tip of the iceberg, because the victims so often remain silent. For socio-psychological reasons it is impossible for them to publicly denounce the wrong done to them. But why are their families ashamed along with them? Are the families of the perpetrators ashamed as well? Why hasn't a district attorney prosecuted the criminals of his sex who humiliated you women so much that your later life was ruined? Why have the criminal acts of these men to this day not even damaged their social prestige? Have people's ways of thinking changed so little in the last decades?

[Uwe Jacobi, The Missing Records from Town hall, Heilbronn, 1981, p. 88. From an entry in the diary of a teacher, September 1942.]

The marketplace fills within minutes. Laughing and jeering are in the air. Mayor Gultig lends a hand as the flowers are removed from the steps of the town hall.

Toward five o'clock the crowds become frightening. A man carrying a chair over his head makes his way through the throng. 'She's sitting over there!' someone screams suddenly. The pushing and shoving become wild. Women shriek hysterically, children are almost smothered, a wolfhound chomps at the bit.

The show begins.

The thirty-nine-year-old woman, accused of having relations with a Pole, is lifted onto a truck and pushed into a chair. A few spit at the 'penitent,' biblical stones fly.

Suddenly a determined young man in overalls appears at her side. They say he works for the city. He hacks off her hair lock by lock with a giant pair of tailor's scissors. As each lock falls he presents the woman to the gaping population who roar each time.

The festival moves toward its climax. The 'barber' switches to a two-millimeter shaver, then to a one-twentieth of millimeter for the precision of his work. Her scalp turns into a billiard ball. She's shown to the people over and over. The defamed woman is expressionless, her face looks as if modeled out of clay.

Behind the author a young boy stands on his bike. 'My whole life I've always hoped to see a woman without hair,' the boy calls out. 'It's just like I imagined it.'

As the crowning glory to his act the man in overalls gives a speech to the people. 'The time must come again,' he announces with full conviction, 'in which unprincipled women are stripped and whipped in the public market place in front of the entire council!'

That's not all the barber has to say. 'German blood must be protected with all means acceptable to German sentiment.'

It is later said the defamed woman, mother of two children, hung herself.

MURIEL KITAGAWA

(1912–1974)

Kitagawa was born in Vancouver, BC, the daughter of a Japanese mill worker and a seamstress. As a Nisei (second-generation Japanese-Canadian), she felt the full weight of racism and devoted her energies to combatting discrimination against Japanese-Canadians as a journalist for *The New Canadian*, a Nisei bi-weekly newspaper. She was also active in the struggle to achieve the vote for citizens of Japanese ancestry. When people of Japanese descent were ordered interned on the Canadian West Coast during the Second World War, she avoided deportation by moving to Toronto with her husband. The house they owned in Vancouver was confiscated and sold, leaving them virtually penniless. Nevertheless, throughout this period, she continued to write in protest against the injustices committed against her people in the name of the war effort. This description of conditions at Hastings Park is taken from a letter to her brother, Wesley, in Toronto; this letter, and others from the same period were one of Joy Kogawa's sources for *Obasan* (q.v.).

Early in 1942, Kitagawa visited Hastings Park, a hastily-converted former agricultural exhibition site, where the wives and children of the men who had been moved to the interior of the province to do manual labor were being held, sometimes for months. The inmates were charged $10.00 a week for their room and board, money which was deducted from the $20.00 a week paid their husbands for their labor.

APRIL 20, 1942

Dear Wes:

I went to the Pool[1] yesterday to see Eiko who is working there as a steno. I saw Sab[2] too who is working in the baggage ... old Horseshow

---

[1] Hastings Park Manning Pool at the Pacific National Exhibition Grounds.
[2] Earlier, Eiko Henmi was dismissed as a student nurse from Vancouver General hospital; Saburo Takahashi, an engineering student, was arrested for possessing a 'map,' a hand-drawn set of directions to a friend's house. He was later released.

Building. Sab showed me his first paycheque as something he couldn't quite believe ... $11.75. He's been there for an awful long time. Eiko sleeps in a partitioned stall, she being on the staff, so to speak. This stall was the former home of a pair of stallions and boy oh boy did they leave their odour behind. The whole place is impregnated with the smell of ancient manure and maggots. Every other day it is swept with dichloride of lime or something, but you can't disguise horse smell, cow smell, sheeps and pigs and rabbits and goats. And is it dusty! The toilets are just a sheet metal trough, and up to now they did not have partitions or seats. The women kicked so they put up partitions and a terribly makeshift seat. Twelve-year old boys stay with the women too. The auto show building, where there was also the Indian exhibit, houses the new dining room and kitchens. Seats 3000. Looks awfully permanent. Brick stoves, 8 of them, shining new mugs ... very very barrack-y. As for the bunks, they were the most tragic things I saw there. Steel and wooden frames with a thin lumpy straw tick, a bolster, and three army blankets of army quality ... no sheets unless you bring your own. These are the 'homes' of the women I saw. They wouldn't let me into the men's building. There are constables at the doors ... no propagation of the species, you know ... it was in the papers. These bunks were hung with sheets and blankets and clothes of every hue and variety, a regular gypsy tent of colours, age, and cleanliness, all hung with the pathetic attempt at privacy. Here and there I saw a child's doll and teddy bear ... I saw babies lying there beside a mother who was too weary to get up ... she had just thrown herself across the bed ... I felt my throat thicken ... an old lady was crying, saying she would rather have died than have come to such a place ... she clung to Eiko and cried and cried. Eiko has taken the woes of the confinees on her thin shoulders and she took so much punishment she went to her former rooms and couldn't stop crying. Fumi[3] was so worried about her. Eiko is really sick. The place has got her down. There are ten showers for 1500 women. Hot and cold water. The men looked so terribly at loose ends, wandering around the grounds, sticking their noses through the fence watching the golfers, lying on the grass. Going through the place I felt so depressed that I wanted to cry. I'm damned well not going there. They are going

---

[3] A friend, Fumi Katsuyama.

to move the Vancouver women first now and shove them into the Pool before sending them to the ghost towns.[4]

* * *

The other day at the Pool, someone dropped his keys before a stall in the Livestock Building, and he fished for it with a long wire and brought to light rotted manure and maggots!!! He called the nurse and then they moved all the bunks from the stalls and pried up the wooden floors. It was the most stomach-turning, nauseating thing. They got fumigators and tried to wash it all away and got most of it into the drains, but maggots still breed and turn up here and there. One woman with more guts than the others told the nurse (white) about it and protested. She replied, 'Well, there's worms in the garden, aren't there?' This particular nurse was a Jap-hater of the most virulent sort. She called them 'filthy Japs' to their faces and Eiko gave her 'what-for' and Fumi had a terrible scrap with her, both girls saying: 'What do you think we are? Are we cattle? Are we pigs, you dirty so-and-so?' You know how Fumi gets. The night the first bunch of Nisei were to go to Schreiber[5] and they wouldn't, the women and children milled around in front of their cage, and one very handsome mountie came with his truncheon and started to hit them, yelling at them, 'Get the hell back in there.' Eiko's blood boiled over. She strode over to him and shouted at him: 'You put that stick down! What do you think you're doing! Do you think these women and children are so many cows that you can beat them back into their place?' Eiko was shaking mad and raked him with fighting words. She has taken it on her to fight for the poor people in there and now is on the black list and reputed to be a trouble-maker. Just like Tommy and Kunio.[6] I wish I too could go in there and fight and slash around.[7] It's people like us who are the most hurt ... people like us, who have had faith in Canada, and who have been more politically minded than the others, who have a hearty contempt for the whites.

* * *

Eiko, Fumi and I, and all of us, have gotten to be so profane that Tom and the rest of them have given up being surprised. Eiko starts out

---

[4] Detention camps in the interior of British Columbia.
[5] One of the 'ghost towns,' a detention camp.
[6] Tom Shoyama and Kunio Shimizu, prominent community activists.
[7] She had recently given birth to twins in a difficult delivery which had left her debilitated.

with 'What the hell' ... and Fumi comes out with worse. It sure relieves our pent-up feelings. Men are lucky they can swear with impunity. (Hell ... I can smell horse all of a sudden ...)

* * *

I'll write again soon.

> With love,
> Mur.

JOY KOGAWA

(b. 1935)

Like other Japanese-Canadians resident on the West Coast, Kogawa was interned with her family during the Second World War. *Obasan*, her novel about those years which appeared in 1981, was the first to deal with the treatment of Canadians of Japanese descent and is based on her own experiences and on letters and documents from the period. In the following excerpt, Naomi, the narrator, now grown, learns for the first time of the fate of the mother she last saw when she was five years old, waving goodbye to her as she left for Japan to deal with a family emergency. The war broke out before she could return to Canada and Naomi never saw her again.

There are only two letters in the grey cardboard folder. The first is a brief and emotionless statement that Grandma Kato, her niece's daughter, and my mother are the only ones in the immediate family to have survived. The second letter is an outpouring.

I remember Grandma Kato as thin and tough, not given to melodrama or overstatement of any kind. She was unbreakable. I felt she could endure all things and would survive any catastrophe. But I did not then understand what catastrophes were possible in human affairs.

Here, the ordinary Granton rain slides down wet and clean along the glass leaving a trail on the window like the Japanese writing on the thin blue-lined paper – straight down like a bead curtain of asterisks. The rain she describes is black, oily, thick, and strange.

'In the heat of the August sun,' Grandma writes, 'however much the effort to forget, there is no forgetfulness. As in a dream, I can still see the maggots crawling in the sockets of my niece's eyes. Her strong intelligent young son helped me move a bonsai tree that very morning. There is no forgetfulness.'

When Nakayama-sensei reaches the end of the page, he stops reading and folds the letter as if he has decided to read no more. Aunt Emily begins to speak quietly, telling of a final letter from the Canadian missionary, Miss Best.

How often, I am wondering, did Grandma and Mother waken in those years with the unthinkable memories alive in their minds, the visible evidence of horror written on their skin, in their blood, carved in every mirror they passed, felt in every step they took. As a child I was told only that Mother and Grandma Kato were safe in Tokyo, visiting Grandma Kato's ailing mother.

'Someday, surely, they will return,' Obasan[1] used to say.

The two letters that reached us in Vancouver before all communication ceased due to the war told us that Mother and Grandma Kato had arrived safely in Japan and were staying with Grandma Kato's sister and her husband in their home near the Tokyo Gas Company. My great-grandmother was then seventy-nine and was not expected to live to be eighty, but, happily, she had become so well that she had returned home from the hospital and was even able on occasion to leave the house.

Nakayama-sensei opens the letter and holds it, reading silently. Then looking over to Stephen,[2] he says, 'It is better to speak, is it not?'

'They're dead now,' Stephen says.

Sensei nods.

'Please read, Sensei,' I whisper.

'Yes,' Aunt Emily says. 'They should know.'

Sensei starts again at the beginning. The letter is dated simply 1949. It was sent, Sensei says, from somewhere in Nagasaki. There was no return address.

'Though it was a time of war,' Grandma writes, 'what happiness that January 1945, to hear from my niece Setsuko, in Nagasaki.' Setsuko's second child was due to be born within the month. In February, just as American air raids were intensifying, Mother went to help her cousin in Nagasaki. The baby was born three days after she arrived. Early in March, air raids and alarms were constant day and night in Tokyo. In spite of all the dangers of travel, Grandma Kato went to Nagasaki to be with my mother and to help with the care of the new baby. The last day she spent with her mother and sister in Tokyo, she said they sat on the tatami[3] and talked, remembering their childhood and the days they went chestnut picking together. They parted with laughter. The following night, Grandma Kato's

---

[1] The narrator's aunt, who raised her. *Obasan* means 'Auntie.'
[2] The narrator's brother.
[3] Matting covering the floor in a traditional Japanese house.

sister, their mother, and her sister's husband died in the B-29 bombings of March 9, 1945.

From this point on, Grandma's letter becomes increasingly chaotic, the details interspersed without chronological consistency. She and my mother, she writes, were unable to talk of all the things that happened. The horror would surely die sooner, they felt, if they refused to speak. But the silence and the constancy of the nightmare had become unbearable for Grandma and she hoped that by sharing them with her husband, she could be helped to extricate herself from the grip of the past.

'If these matters are sent away in this letter, perhaps they will depart a little from our souls,' she writes. 'For the burden of these words, forgive me.'

Mother, for her part, continued her vigil of silence. She spoke with no one about her torment. She specifically requested that Stephen and I be spared the truth.

In all my high-school days, until we heard from Sensei that her grave had been found in Tokyo, I pictured her trapped in Japan by government regulations, or by an ailing grandmother. The letters I sent to the address in Tokyo were never answered or returned. I could not know that she and Grandma Kato had gone to Nagasaki to stay with Setsuko, her husband who was a dentist, and their two children, four-year-old Tomio and the new baby, Chieko.

The baby, Grandma writes, looked so much like me that she and my mother marvelled and often caught themselves calling her Naomi. With her widow's peak, her fat cheeks and pointed chin, she had a heart-shaped face like mine. Tomio, however, was not like Stephen at all. He was a sturdy child, extremely healthy and athletic, with a strong will like his father. He was fascinated by his new baby sister, sitting and watching her for hours as she slept or nursed. He made dolls for her. He helped them to dress her. He loved to hold her in the bath, feeling her fingers holding his fingers tightly. He rocked her to sleep in his arms.

The weather was hot and humid that morning of August 9. The air-raid alerts had ended. Tomio and some neighbourhood children had gone to the irrigation ditch to play and cool off as they sometimes did.

Shortly after eleven o'clock, Grandma Kato was preparing to make lunch. The baby was strapped to her back. She was bending over a bucket of water beside a large earthenware storage bin when a child in the street was heard shouting, 'Look at the parachute!' A few seconds later, there was a sudden white flash, brighter than a bolt of lightning. She had no idea what could have exploded. It was as if the entire sky were swallowed up. A moment later she was hurled sideways by a blast. She had a sensation of floating tranquilly in a cool whiteness high above the earth. When she regained consciousness, she was slumped forward in a sitting position in the water bin. She gradually became aware of the moisture, an intolerable heat, blood, a mountain of debris and her niece's weak voice sounding at first distant, calling the names of her children. Then she could hear other sounds – the far-away shouting. Around her, a thick dust made breathing difficult. Chieko was still strapped to her back, but made no sound. She was alive but unconscious.

It took Grandma a long time to claw her way out of the wreckage. When she emerged, it was into an eerie twilight formed of heavy dust and smoke that blotted out the sun. What she saw was incomprehensible. Almost all the buildings were flattened or in flames for as far as she could see. The landmarks were gone. Tall columns of fire rose through the haze and everywhere the dying and the wounded crawled, fled, stumbled like ghosts among the ruins. Voices screamed, calling the names of children, fathers, mothers, calling for help, calling for water.

Beneath some wreckage, she saw first the broken arm, then the writhing body of her niece, her head bent back, her hair singed, both her eye sockets blown out. In a weak and delirious voice, she was calling Tomio. Grandma Kato touched her niece's leg and the skin peeled off and stuck to the palm of her hand.

It isn't clear from the letter but at some point she came across Tomio, his legs pumping steadily up and down as he stood in one spot not knowing where to go. She gathered him in her arms. He was remarkably intact, his skin unburned.

She had no idea where Mother was, but with the two children, she began making her way towards the air-raid shelter. All around her people one after another collapsed and died, crying for water. One old man no longer able to keep moving lay on the ground holding up a dead baby and crying, 'Save the children. Leave the old.' No one took the dead child from his outstretched hands. Men, women, in many cases indistinguishable by sex, hairless, half-clothed, hobbled past. Skin hung from their bodies like tattered rags. One man held his bowels in with the stump of one hand. A child whom Grandma Kato recognized lay on the ground asking for help. She stopped and told him she would return as soon as she could. A woman she knew was begging for someone to help her lift the burning beam beneath which her children were trapped. The women's children were friends of Tomio's. Grandma was loath to walk past but with the two children she could do no more and kept going. At no point does Grandma Kato mention the injuries which she herself must have sustained.

Nearing the shelter, Grandma could see through the greyness that the entrance was clogged with dead bodies. She remembered that her niece's father-in-law lived on a farm on the hillside and she began making her way back though the burning city towards the river she would have to cross. The water, red with blood, was a raft of corpses. Farther upstream, the bridge was twisted like noodles. Eventually she came to a spot where she was able to cross and, still carrying the two children, Grandma Kato made her way up the hillside.

After wandering for some time, she found a wooden water pipe dribbling a steady stream. She held Tomio's mouth to it and allowed him to drink as much as he wished though she had heard that too much water was not good. She unstrapped the still unconscious baby from her back. Exhausted, she drank from the pipe, and gathering the two children in her arms, she looked out at the burning city and lapsed into a sleep so deep she believed she was unconscious.

When she awakened, she was in the home of her niece's relatives and the baby was being fed barley water. The little boy was nowhere.

Almost immediately, Grandma set off to look for the child. Next day she returned to the area of her niece's home and every day thereafter she looked for Mother and the lost boy, checking the lists of the dead. looking over the unclaimed corpses. She discovered that her niece's husband was among the dead.

One evening when she had given up the search for the day, she sat down next to a naked woman she had seen earlier who was aimlessly chipping wood to make a pyre on which to cremate a dead baby. The woman was utterly disfigured. Her nose and one cheek were almost gone. Great wounds and pustules covered her entire face and body. She was completely bald. She sat in a cloud of flies and maggots wriggled among her wounds. As Grandma watched her, the woman gave her a vacant gaze, then let out a cry. It was my mother.

The little boy was never found. Mother was taken to a hospital and was expected to die, but she survived. During one night she vomited yellow fluid and passed a great deal of blood. For a long time – Grandma does not say how long – Mother wore bandages on her face. When they were removed, Mother felt her face with her fingers, then asked for a cloth mask. Thereafter she would not take off her mask from morning to night.

'At this moment,' Grandma writes, 'we are preparing to visit Chieko-chan in the hospital.' Chieko, four years old in 1949, waited daily for their visit, standing in the hospital corridor, tubes from her wrist attached to a bottle that was hung above her. A small, bald-headed girl. She was dying of leukemia.

'There may not be many more days,' Grandma concludes.

After this, what could have happened? Did they leave the relatives in Nagasaki? Where and how did they survive?

When Sensei finishes reading, he folds and unfolds the letter, nodding his head slowly.

I put my hands around the teapot, feeling its round warmth against my palms. My skin feels hungry for warmth, for flesh. Grandma mentions in her letter that she saw one woman cradling a hot-water bottle as if it were a baby.

Sensei places the letter back in the cardboard folder and closes it with the short red string around the tab.

'That there is brokenness.' he says quietly. 'That this world is brokenness. But within brokenness is the unbreakable name. How the whole earth groans till Love returns.'

I stand up abruptly and leave the room, going into the kitchen for some more hot water. When I return, Sensei is sitting with this face in his hands.

Stephen is staring at the floor, his body hunched forward motionless. He glances up at me then looks away swiftly. I sit on a stool beside him and try to concentrate on what is being said. I can hear Aunt Emily telling us about Mother's grave. Then Nakayama-sensei stands and begins to say the Lord's Prayer under his breath. 'And forgive us our trespasses – forgive us our trespasses – ' he repeats, sighing deeply, 'as we forgive others ...' He lifts his head, looking upwards. 'We are powerless to forgive unless we are first forgiven. It is a high calling my friends – the calling to forgive. But no person, no people is innocent. Therefore we must forgive one another.'

I am not thinking of forgiveness. The sound of Sensei's voice grows as indistinct as the hum of distant traffic. Gradually the room grows still and it is as if I am back with Uncle again, listening and listening to the silent earth and the silent sky as I have done all my life.

I close my eyes.

Mother I am listening. Assist me to hear you.

Additional Reading

Appleman-Jurman, Alicia. *Alicia: My Story*. New York: Bantam, 1990.

Bagnold, Enid. *Enid Bagnold's Autobiography*. Boston: Little, Brown, c. 1969.

Bar-on, David. *Legacy of Silence: Encounters with Children of the Third Reich*. Cambridge, MA: Harvard UP, 1989.

Barker, Pat. *Regeneration*. London: Viking, 1991.

Barker, Pat. *The Eye in the Door*. London: Viking, 1993.

Barker, Pat. *The Ghost Road*. London: Viking, 1995.

Berry, Paul & Mark Bostridge. *Vera Brittain: A Life*. London: Chatto & Windus, 1995.

Bielenberg, Christabel. *The Past Is Myself*. London: Chatto & Windus, 1968.

Brittain, Vera. *Account Rendered*. London: Virago, 1982.

Bryher. *Beowulf: A Novel*. New York: Pantheon, 1956.

Cadogan, Mary & Craig, Patricia. *Women and Children First: The Fiction of Two World Wars*. London: Gollancz, 1978.

Cooper, Helen M., Adrienne Auslander Munich & Susan Merrill Squier, eds. *Arms and the Woman: War, Gender, and Literary Representation*. Chapel Hill: U of North Carolina P, 1989.

Cross, Tim, ed. *Lost Voices of World War I*. Iowa City: U of Iowa P, 1989.

David, Kati. *A Child's War: World War II Through the Eyes of Children*. New York: Avon, 1989.

Davin, Dan, ed. *Short Stories of Two World Wars*. Oxford: Oxford UP, 1982.

Dent, Olive. *A VAD in France*. London: G. Richards, 1917.

Duras, Marguerite. *The War: A Memoir*. Trans. Barbara Bray. New York: Pantheon, 1986.

Elshtain, Jean Bethke. *Women and War*. New York: Basic, 1987.

Fisher, Dorothy Canfield. *Home Fires in France*. New York: Holt, 1918.

Fussell, Paul. *The Great War and Modern Memory*. London: Oxford UP, 1975.

Gilbert, Sandra M., and Susan Gubar. *No Man's Land: Volume 1: The War of the Words*. New Haven: Yale UP, 1987.

Gilbert, Sandra M., and Susan Gubar. *No Man's Land: Volume 2: Sexchanges*. New Haven: Yale UP, 1989.

Gilbert, Sandra M., and Susan Gubar. *No Man's Land: Volume 3: Letters From the Front*. New Haven: Yale UP, 1994.

Gissing, Vera. *Pearls of Childhood*. London: Robson Books, 1988.

Glover, Jon and Jon Silkin, eds. *The Penguin Book of First World War Prose*. New York: Viking, 1989.

Goldman, Dorothy, ed. *Women and World War 1: The Written Response*. London: Macmillan, 1993.

Higonnet, Margaret R., Jane Jenson, et al., eds. *Behind the Lines: Gender and the Two World Wars*. New Haven: Yale UP, 1987.

Inber, Vera. *Leningrad Diary*. New York: St Martin's, 1971.

Jameson, Storm. *Company Parade*. London: Cassell, 1934.

Kardorff, Ursula von. *Diary of a Nightmare*. Trans. Ewan Butler. London: Rupert Hart-Davis, 1965.

Kochina, Elena. *Blockade Diary*. Ed. and trans. Samuel C. Ramer. Ann Arbor: Ardis, 1990.

Koonz, Claudia. *Mothers in the Fatherland: Women, the Family, and Nazi Politics*. London: Jonathan Cape, 1987.

Laska, Vera, ed. *Women in the Resistance and in the Holocaust: Voices of Eyewitnesses*. Westport, CT: Greenwood, 1983.

Lefland, Ella. *Rumors of Peace*. New York: Harper, c. 1979.

Macaulay, Rose. *Noncombatants and Others*. London: Hodder & Stoughton, 1916.

Mitton, G.E. (Geraldine Edith). *The Cellar-House At Pervyse: A Tale of Uncommon Things From the Journals and Letters of the Baroness T'Serclaes and Mairi Chisholm*. London: A.C. Black, 1917.

Pierson, Ruth Roach. *'They're Still Women After All': The Second World War and Canadian Womanhood*. Toronto: McClelland & Stewart Inc., 1986.

Reilly, Catherine, ed. *Chaos of the Night: Women's Poetry & Verse of the Second World War*. London: Virago, 1984.

Reilly, Catherine, ed. *Scars Upon My Heart: Women's Poetry & Verse of the First World War*. London: Virago, 1984.

Richardson, Gus, et al., ed. *The Great War and Canadian Society – an Oral History*. Toronto: New Hogtown Press, c. 1978.

Rinehart, Mary Roberts. *The Amazing Interlude*. Toronto: McClelland & Stewart, 1918.

Rittner, Carol and John K. Roth, eds. *Different Voices: Women and the Holocaust*. New York: Paragon House, 1993.

Schreiner, Olive. *Women and Labour*. London: Virago, 1978.

Schweik, Susan. *A Gulf So Deeply Cut: American Women Poets and the Second World War*. Madison, WI: U of Wisconsin Press, 1991.

Shiber, Etta. *Paris-Underground*. New York: Scribner, 1943.

Smith, Helen Zenna (Evadne Price). *Not So Quiet*. (1930). London: Virago, 1988.

Stevens, Doris. *Jailed for Freedom: The Story of the Militant Suffragist Movement*. New York: Schocken, 1976.

Storey, Joyce. *Joyce's War 1939–1945*. London: Virago, 1992.

Summerfield, Penny. *Women Workers in the Second World War*. London: Routledge, 1989.

Sutherland, Millicent, Duchess of. *Six Weeks At the War*. Chicago: n.p., 1915.

Townsend, Colin & Eileen, eds. *War Wives*. London: Grafton Books, 1990.

Triolet, Elsa. *A Fine of Two Hundred Francs*. New York: Reynal & Hitchcock, 1947.

Tylee, Claire M. *The Great War and Women's Consciousness: Images of Militarism and Womanhood in Women's Writings, 1914–1964*. Iowa City: U of Iowa P, 1990.

Vassilitchikov, Marie. *Berlin Diaries 1940–1945*. New York: Knopf, 1987.

Vaughan, Elizabeth. *The Ordeal of Elizabeth Vaughan*. Ed. Carol M. Petillo. Athens, GA: U of Georgia P, 1985.

Wendel, Else. *Hausfrau At War (1939–1945)*. (1957). Durham, UK: Pentland Press, 1994.

Wheelwright, Julie. *Amazons and Military Maids: Women Who Dressed As Men in Pursuit of Life, Liberty, and Happiness*. London: Pandora, 1990.
Wicks, Ben. *The Day They Took the Children*. Toronto: Stoddart, 1989.
Women's Division of Sokka Gakkai, *Women Against War*. Trans. Richard L. Gage. Tokyo: Kodansha International Ltd, 1986.

Index

251